PADDLE
ROUTES
of Western Washington

PADDLE ROUTES

of Western Washington

___50 Flatwater Trips for Canoe and Kayak___

Second Edition
VERNE HUSER

THE
MOUNTAINEERS

Published by
The Mountaineers Books
1001 SW Klickitat Way, Suite 201
Seattle, WA 98134

© 2000 by Verne Huser

First edition 1990. Second edition 2000.

Published simultaneously in Great Britain by Cordee, 3a DeMontfort Street, Leicester, England, LE1 7HD

Manufactured in the United States of America

Editor: Lois Kelly
Project Editor: Christine Ummel Hosler
Mapmaker: Jerry Painter
All photographs by Verne Huser unless otherwise noted
Cover and book design: Kristy L. Welch
Layout: Kristy L. Welch

Cover photograph: Sea Kayaks/Skagit River/Estuary, Washington. © Joel W. Rogers
Frontispiece: Paddlers float through Tukwila on the Green River.

Library of Congress Cataloging-in-Publication Data

Huser, Verne.
    Paddle routes of Western Washington : 50 flatwater trips for canoe & kayak / by Verne Huser.— 2nd ed.
       p. cm.
    Includes bibliographical references (p.   ) and index.
    ISBN 0-89886-630-8 (pbk.)
    1. Canoes and canoeing—Washington (State), Western—Guidebooks.
2. Kayaking—Washington (State), Western—Guidebooks. 3. Washington (State), Western—Guidebooks. I. Title.
GV776.W2 H87 2000
797.1'22'09797—dc21   99-050878
                                                                          CIP

CONTENTS

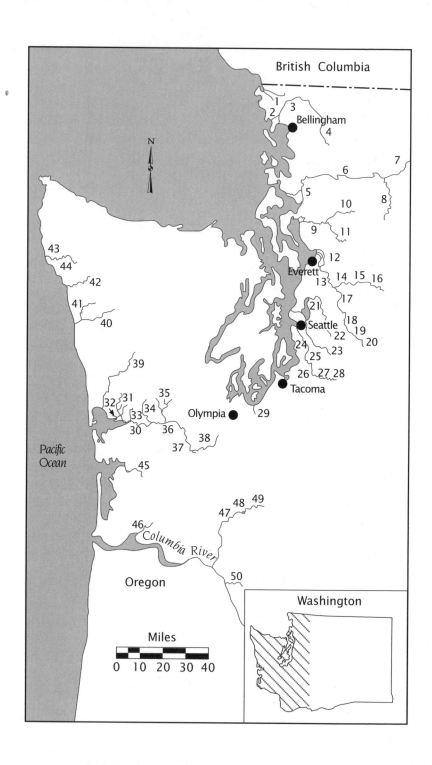

British Columbia

1
2
3
Bellingham
4

6   7

5
10   8

9   11

12
Everett
13   14 15 16

17

21   18
Seattle 19
22   20
24
25   23
26   27 28
Tacoma

N

43
44
42

41
40

39

35
31
32   34
33
30   36
37   38
Olympia   29

Pacific
Ocean

45

48 49
47
46
Columbia River

Oregon   50

Miles

0 10 20 30 40

Washington

Legend

Main river	⟨End⟩ End of route
Minor rivers and creeks	Parks
③ Mileage markers (from river's mouth)	⑤ Interstate
Highways	⑩① US highway
Roads	㉙ State highway
┼┼┼┼┼ Railroad tracks	N ◄◄► North indicator
Urban area	·--·--· Boundary line
⟨Start⟩ Start of route	⊷ Bridge

PREFACE

Twenty years ago, when I first began canoeing the rivers of western Washington, I found precious little information about them: where to launch or take out a craft, what class of water certain river segments exhibited, what I might experience on the river. This information wasn't readily available.

There were only Werner Furrer's two books (now combined into one—*Water Trails of Washington*, 1979) and Milt Keizer's *Western Steelhead Fishing Guides*, a series of map books for fishermen now available in a single volume. There were paddle clubs whose members ran trips on a number of river segments and who knew the river segments well. I could join a club (which I did) and pick the brains of those who knew the rivers (which I did), but nowhere was there a comprehensive guide to the rivers I wanted to paddle as a beginning canoeist.

Over the years a series of river guides began to appear, for the most part dealing with whitewater. Sea kayaking became extremely popular, and several books appeared for the saltwater paddler. The Mountaineers published Phil Jones's *Canoe Routes: Northwest Oregon* (1982), which included 50 river segments, most of them in the beaver state but a few in Washington. The time was ripe for the first edition of this book, which was eight years in preparation. Ten years after it first appeared, it is now time for a second edition.

This book, then, is an attempt to provide paddlers with useful information that will enable them to enjoy the rivers and associated waterways of western Washington in crafts powered not by motor but by human muscle—primarily canoes and kayaks. I have scouted all of these river segments, some of them by poling, often up the river with the tide, then back down to avoid a shuttle. This second edition incorporates a number of changes that have occurred during the past decade and includes three additional river segments, one of them 60 miles long.

Western Washington, with its heavy rainfall and numerous rivers that drain the well-watered land, remains ideal for canoeing. The rivers were highways in the early days, means of transportation and commerce. Some of them still are, but most of them have become recreational resources today.

Since various salmon species have been placed on the endangered species list, however, state and federal agencies and Native American tribes have begun to discourage the use of recreational boating on free-flowing river sections in western Washington. Tribal fishermen consider recreational boats hazardous to their fishing, and woody debris, im-properly anchored in rivers to improve salmon habitat, has become a hazard to boaters. Agencies, tribes, and boating groups have begun work-ing together to allay the concerns of all parties. As more hand-powered recreational boats appear on the rivers, more eyes are watching what's happening.

The basic cause of salmon depletion has become obvious: destruc-tion of natural salmon habitat and over-fishing. Dam building and river de-watering, extensive clear-cut logging, irresponsible agricultural prac-tices, dumping of industrial wastes and municipal sewage effluents into streams, and the development of shorelines and flood plains—all de-stroy fish habitat.

Commercial ocean harvest of salmon has reduced fish populations far more than has sport fishing in the rivers and Native American gather-ing under treaty rights. Relatively few recreational paddlers fish, but they spend a great deal of time on the rivers. They provide a powerful watch-dog service to monitor river abuses.

While many of these rivers have been altered by human activity (dams, dikes, clear-cuts, population, pollution), some of them are still pristine, certainly valuable get-aways from the noise and stress of mod-ern civilization. It never ceases to amaze me how quickly I can leave be-hind the contemporary world when I launch my canoe onto the soothing waters of a river:

- From downtown Redmond I paddle the Sammamish at rush hour alongside the Sammamish River Parkway, seeing birds and beavers as I drift placidly north, watching a mallard hen with her brood of ducklings, hearing the red-winged blackbird singing in the late afternoon;

- From Lake Sammamish, where powerboats buzz like angry hornets, I pole up Issaquah Creek, picking blackberries from the bushes that lean over the stream and watching salmon swimming upstream, warblers flitting about, kingfishers and green herons—all within half a mile of I-90;

- From a roadside fishing access south of Littlerock near Olympia, I launch into what looks like a southern swamp stream. Soon I lose the sound of logging trucks along S.R. 121 on a black-water river fringed by vegetation that mutes the sounds of civilization and masks the fumes with the fragrance of wildflowers.

My purpose in writing this book is to enable people to enjoy the rivers of western Washington safely and with a minimum of impact on these waters and their adjacent shorelines, on the fauna and flora that inhabit these areas, and on other people who use them.

Washington is blessed with many waterways—some of them badly abused, others rarely used. We can learn to care more about them if we get to know them better, and that's what this book is all about: getting to know western Washington's canoe routes and taking better care of them so that those who come after us—today, tomorrow, or throughout this new century—may know them as we have and draw both pleasure and spiritual power from them.

A NOTE ABOUT SAFETY

Safety is an important concern in all outdoor activities. No guidebook can alert you to every hazard or anticipate the limitations of every reader or paddler. Therefore, the descriptions of roads, trails, rivers, routes, and natural features in this book are not representations that a particular place or excursion will be safe for your party. When you follow any of the river routes described in this book, you assume responsibility for your own safety. Under normal conditions, such excursions require the usual attention to traffic, road and trail conditions, weather, water, terrain, the capabilities of your party, and other factors. Keeping informed on current conditions and exercising common sense are the keys to a safe, enjoyable outing.

—*The Mountaineers*

ACKNOWLEDGMENTS

I thank the following people for their advice, insight, information, and counsel in preparing this book: Paul Agrimes, Mike Bauer, Dennis Canty, Terry Danielsen, Murray Davis, Tim Davis, Roger De Spain, Al Falco, Wes Felty, Jim Greenleaf, Bob Greenwalt, Heidi and Kirk Hackler, David Harrison, Willa Huser, Lois Kelly, Gary Korb, Zella Mathews, John and Ratha Miles, James Moore, Lee and Judy Moyer, Ray and Martha Parker, Robert Michael Pyle, Bill Rafferty, Jack Remington, George Saling, Frank Schultz, Steve Starland, Michael Thomas, Ty Tice, John Vraspir, and Bob Whisnant.

Tall trees frame the Skykomish as a dory fisherman lands in the shallows.

INTRODUCTION

Canoeing has come of age in western Washington. Native American canoes have become more common as a result of the Paddle-to-Seattle program in the mid-1990s, but the modern canoe has become even more popular. The first people to thrive in this area used the canoe as a means of making their living, just as the Native Americans of the Great Plains used the horse. Few people today use canoes or horses in their livelihood: both have become primarily recreational in their application.

Western Washington was for centuries dominated by canoe routes. Aboriginal inhabitants poled or paddled the rivers and the protected saltwater routes as a way of life. Some of them ventured into the open Pacific to hunt the whale. (The Makahs recently reclaimed their tradition by killing a gray whale.) It is likely that the Yankee clipper ship was patterned after the whaling canoes of Northwest Native Americans (see Philip Drucker's *Native Americans of the Northwest Coast*). Even as European, then Asian civilizations made contact with the Native Americans of the Northwest Coast, they used the canoe routes of the people, adopting their crafts and their techniques as well.

As I began researching the rivers of western Washington to include them in this book, it became evident that it was necessary for me to know how to go upstream as well as down—as the Native Americans had. I had to learn to pole a canoe, to track or line the craft (tow the craft from shore) or simply walk it through the shallows, and thus to obviate a shuttle.

These techniques are learned by reading, talking with experts, and then practicing—as often as possible with the experts themselves. The techniques are learned by getting out on the rivers and exploring. Exploring is still possible on the rivers of western Washington, and this book is intended to provide the paddler or poler with useful information that will make that exploration easier, safer, and more meaningful.

TRIP DESCRIPTIONS

The rivers are listed in logical order from their mouths upstream and from north to south, clockwise around Puget Sound, then up the coast of the Olympic Peninsula, and finally down the coast from Grays Harbor,

Dory fishermen anchor on a shoal to test the waters of the Snoqualmie River for steelhead.

following the Columbia River upstream from its mouth. The following information is capsulized for each of the 50 trips described in this book in a standardized format for easy reference.

Location. To locate each river segment, a general location is given in relation to a nearby town or well-known feature.

Distance. The distance in miles is taken from the Washington Department of Fisheries' *Catalog of Washington Streams*, which indicates the mile-by-mile length of rivers, counting upstream from the mouth. On lakes and saltwater bodies and on the Columbia River tributaries for which the state fishery maps are not available, the mileage is estimated from USGS maps and NOAA charts. Distances will vary depending on the actual route taken by paddlers using the book.

River Time. The guesstimate of time is based on actual on-water measurements, but they are rough approximations because the segments were run at varying water levels; some of the routes were poled (generally faster than paddling); and there were occasional brief stops to take pictures, make notes, watch wildlife, explore landmarks, and record times. Numerous factors will influence paddlers' speed (time) relative to that given in this book: type of craft, size of party, level of flow, mishaps. With practice, paddlers will soon be able to judge the relative time it takes them to run a specific river compared to the times given here.

Maps/Charts. U.S. Geological Survey (USGS) maps and National Oceanographic and Atmospheric Administration (NOAA) charts (where

Submerged logs create hazards in the Quillayute River.

available) are given for each trip. The USGS maps are 7.5-minute (7.5')
series or 15-minute (15') series for the river segment, which may require
several maps for some stretches. The NOAA charts are for the coastal
areas only but may cover some river mouths (the Skagit, for example) or
even whole rivers (the Sammamish, for example).

Best Season. Most rivers in this book can be run year round. A few of
them, however, may be too low in late summer or early fall. During heavy
rains or spring runoff, many of them may be too high to run safely. As a
general rule, if the water level is up in the shrubbery, paddlers should
think seriously before launching a trip. If too many gravel bars or mud
flats are showing, the river may be too low. Water levels fluctuate season-
ally and, on reservoir-release rivers and in tidal areas, daily. Flow infor-
mation on many of the popular rivers is available by calling the NOAA
River Hotline (see **Appendix B: Recommended Resources, Weather In-
formation**). A local paddle club may also have this information.

Hazards. While the river segments covered in this book are rela-
tively mild (Class II+ at the most difficult), there are certain hazards: **sweep-
ers**, trees overhanging the riverbank that can sweep paddlers out of their
crafts; **obstacles** such as rocks, logjams, and trees in or lying completely
across the river; **cold water**, which can lead to hypothermia (loss of body
heat); **contrary tides** that run counter to the direction of intent; **wind, fog**,
and other weather conditions that can make canoeing dangerous. Spe-
cific potential hazards are listed for each segment; other hazards (such as
woody debris anchored in rivers to enhance salmon habitat) can appear
following storms, floods, other natural events, and human activity.

Shuttle. A brief description of the shuttle is given for each river seg-
ment, including the distance, the road condition, and a suggested vehicle
where appropriate (bicycle, mountain bike, four-wheel-drive vehicle, stan-
dard vehicle).

Rating. The International Scale of River Difficulty includes six classes
from easy to difficult. Class I designates moving water with a few riffles and
small waves and few or no obstructions. Class II involves easy rapids with
waves up to 3 feet, and wide, clear channels that are obvious without
scouting (studying the rapid before entering it) from the shore. Some
maneuvering may be required on Class II rivers.

Classes III to VI are increasingly difficult, but since none of the river
segments in this book are in that range of difficulty, they are not described
here. A designation of Class I- or I would indicate a very easy section of river
with little current, small waves, and few obstacles. A Class I+ designation
would suggest a section of river more difficult than Class I but not yet Class II.

In this book, each trip is rated by the following system:

Class I Still water or water moving with current less than 2 mph (benign rivers suitable for novices).

Class II River segments with current between 2 and 4 mph (some maneuvering skills required).

Class II+ River segments with a velocity of more than 4 mph or with rapids, sharp turns, or obstacles that require significant maneuvering.

Tidal Waters that involve tidal influence (saltwater stretches of bays and harbors or tidal reaches of rivers).

Some segments may be given two ratings, indicating that they are tidal but also have other characteristics worth noting. The signs + and - are used to indicate a slightly more difficult (+) rating or a slightly easier (-) rating.

Paddling—even on quiet streams with slow currents and few obstacles—entails unavoidable risks that every paddler assumes, understands, and accepts. The fact that a section of river is described in this book and is rated for difficulty does *not* mean that it necessarily will be safe for a particular paddler or at a particular water level. Because rivers are dynamic systems, conditions vary from year to year, season to season, even day to day—and certainly from paddler to paddler. Accordingly, so does the amount of preparation and knowledge required to enjoy them safely. If in doubt about their own qualifications, prospective paddlers will find many books and courses that offer the information and training needed to make these trips safely. This book offers some tips, but it is not intended to substitute for good instruction from an experienced river paddler.

These warnings are not intended to frighten qualified paddlers from taking the river trips described herein. With adequate knowledge and preparation, the great majority of paddlers enjoy safe trips down these rivers every year. But paddlers should exercise their own independent judgment and common sense.

CHOICE OF CRAFT

Flatwater boaters have several choices in crafts, but most will use canoes or kayaks. Other possibilities include inflatable crafts, either small rafts or canoes/kayaks; dories or driftboats, flat-bottomed rowboats with flared sides and heavy rocker (bow-to-stern curvature); and Sportyaks, which are small, hard-hulled dinghies.

River runners on Class I and II waters have two levels of choice: (1) whether to row or to paddle and (2) which specific craft to use for rowing or paddling.

Rowing Crafts

Rowing crafts include rafts, dories, and Sportyaks. They are generally operated with oars mounted on the craft or attached to a frame that is fixed to the craft.

Rafts. As discussed in this book, rafts are inflatable crafts, varying in design from inexpensive one- and two-person single-chamber toys made of vinyl to professional crafts with several air chambers and a cloth fabric coated with a rubberized material. The cheap rafts without a fabric base will not stand the wear and tear of river use, nor will they respond adequately to control by oar or paddle; they should not be considered for any kind of river trip above a Class I rating in this book. They are usually too insubstantial to be inflated to adequate air pressure and do not respond well to rowing. They are sometimes paddled (see below under **Paddle Crafts**).

Most of the smaller rafts are equipped with oarlocks of some kind, but many of them are unreliable. If rafts do not come with oarlocks—or if they do, but the oarlocks are inadequate—it may pay to build or buy a frame that can be fixed to the raft. Heavy-duty oarlocks made of wood or metal can then be mounted on the frame, giving the rower a better position for powering the craft and controlling its movements.

Dories. These hard-hulled, specialized rowboats have been developed for river use. They have heavy rocker, exaggerated bow-to-stern (front-to-back) convexity; flared sides; and a sharp prow (forward part of the boat's hull). They are popular among fishermen, who often equip them with a motor. Since this book deals with muscle-powered crafts, it will not discuss the use of motors. The dory is powered and maneuvered with a single set of oars.

Sportyaks. These dinghies are small, highly specialized plastic rowboats (some people call them plastic bathtubs) designed as one-person fishing boats. They fit nicely into the bed of a pickup truck, and they are lightweight and maneuverable, extremely riverworthy, and fun to row with a single pair of 5- or 6-foot oars. However, they do not move through the water with any speed and are not recommended for slow-water or salt-water trips. Sportyaks come with built-in oarlocks, but you can improve reliability by adding a metal frame to which a heavy-duty oarlock and even a suspended seat are attached.

Paddle Crafts

Paddle crafts include canoes, kayaks, and inflatable boats of two basic kinds: rafts and inflatable canoes/kayaks. They are powered and maneuvered by paddles, either single- or double-bladed.

In the world of modern boating, there are two basic differences between canoes and kayaks, since both may be decked (have an integrated top covering) and look similar: (1) canoes are paddled with a single-bladed paddle, kayaks with a double-bladed paddle; (2) canoes are paddled from a kneeling position (or from a seat suspended well above water level), kayaks from a sitting position on a low seat at or near water level. These may seem subtle distinctions, but they are important differences.

Canoes. Canoes are long, narrow, hard-hulled crafts patterned after Native American designs. Aesthetic and practical, canoes come in numerous forms, sizes, colors, and materials, from traditional wood-and-canvas to space-age fabrics. Some canoes are better for still-water use on lakes; others, for moving water in rivers.

Most people think of canoes as open crafts, but many modern canoes are decked to enable them to operate more effectively in heavy whitewater. People do run Class III and IV, even Class V rapids in open and decked canoes.

A Paddle Trail Canoe Club group stops for lunch.

River canoes should have little or no keel (a raised ridge that runs the length of the underside of the craft and tends to make the canoe track, or move in a straight line), have sides high enough to keep out the waves that might be encountered in mild rapids, and be sturdy enough to withstand some contact with obstacles (logs, rocks, the riverbank and bottom).

Canoes are made of wood and canvas (traditional), aluminum, fiberglass, and a whole family of artificial materials commonly known as plastics. A few people still make and use bark canoes, but such crafts are rare and expensive. Many wood-and-canvas canoes still exist, but relatively few are produced today. Purely wooden canoes (such as cedar strippers) are things of great beauty, but the hand-crafting that goes into them makes them too expensive or too easily damaged for everyday use; they are sturdy but require regular maintenance.

Most modern paddlers use aluminum, fiberglass, or plastic canoes. Aluminum is noisy; it conducts heat and cold; and while it holds its shape in normal use, it can be badly damaged in a traumatic situation. Fiberglass canoes are about as heavy as aluminum ones but are easier to repair; however, they do not hold their form well nor do they take the shock of serious collision as well as the modern plastics.

The plastic revolution of the past few decades has altered the canoeing industry more than any other single innovation. More plastic canoes are sold each year than were in operation a decade ago. While some of the space-age fabrics are extremely expensive, mass production has brought the price down, and many of the fabrics offer fantastic strength, lightness, and durability.

There is no perfect canoe that will do all things for all users. Probably the best overall material for canoes today is the foam-and-plastic sandwich used by several manufacturers under various trade names. In the field research for this book, an 18-foot aluminum canoe, a 16-foot plastic canoe, and a 12-foot foam-and-plastic sandwich canoe each gave good service in different ways.

A good lake canoe is not a good river canoe. The longer the canoe, in general, the faster it will move, but the more difficult it is to turn. On a river, paddlers will want to be able to turn the canoe quickly to avoid obstacles. Before buying a canoe, go on a few trips in a rented or borrowed canoe. Go with a local paddle club, both for safety and to experience the variety of paddle crafts available.

Talk to dealers. Read the literature (manufacturers' brochures, howto books, accounts in paddling magazines). Talk to other paddlers; hang out in the paddle shops. Paddlers should take their time in choosing the right canoe.

Decked canoes look a lot like kayaks and can be used very much as kayaks are used. None of the river segments in this book requires the protection of a decked canoe, but there is certainly no reason a decked canoe couldn't be used.

Kayaks. A creation of the Eskimo culture, kayaks might be considered more garment than boat: paddlers wear them rather than sit in them. Eskimos, who used them to hunt seals, walrus, and whales in the frigid ocean, learned to roll them in a life-saving technique. If the crafts tipped over in the waves, the kayakers simply rolled back to an upright position and never really got wet because each paddler was enclosed in a waterproof garment married to the craft. Used in Europe in various modifications for decades, they have also become popular as recreational crafts in North America. Kayaks are now common on Northwestern rivers.

Many early kayaks were made of wood and canvas, but a few were all wood and even fewer, aluminum. Fiberglass swept the market shortly after World War II as hundreds of paddlers began making their own crafts. It remains a popular low-cost fabric for kayaks, but most river paddlers have followed the plastic revolution.

A second revolution has been the development of flatwater touring kayaks, especially for sea kayaking. Usually fitted with a rudder controlled by the feet, such kayaks are easier to paddle than canoes, even for beginners. However, they may be difficult to handle on sharp turns and in the relatively mild whitewater of Class II rapids.

Kayaks are decked crafts, less roomy than canoes for gear and people. However, they come in one- and two-person models, with a few larger ones capable of carrying three people. Since this book generally deals with short segments that can normally be paddled in a day, there is little need to carry much gear along unless an overnight trip is planned. And even overnighters can often be done by car camping. The paddlers leapfrog down the river, canoeing or kayaking to the shuttle vehicle, where the camp gear is kept.

Folding kayaks, which have been in use for more than half a century, offer an interesting alternative. They are lightweight and fold into small packages for easy storage and transport. Most of them have sturdy frames and a rubberized fabric hull. Inflatable kayaks have improved over the past few decades and offer another alternative, especially if storage space is critical (see discussion below under **Craft Selection**).

Hard-hulled plastic sit-on-top crafts have recently begun appearing on rivers in western Washington. Designed more like surfboards or windsurfing boards and popular at coastal resorts worldwide, they are more riverworthy than air mattresses but should be considered whitewater crafts only in the hands of an experienced paddler.

Inflatables. The inflatable crafts include both rafts and inflatable canoes/kayaks (some manufacturers call them canoes, others call them kayaks, but in fact they are neither).

Paddle rafts are simply inflatable rafts that are powered and controlled by paddlers. One, two, or more paddlers (depending on the size of the craft) sit or kneel on the floor—or more frequently, sit on the side tubes of larger rafts and try to make the craft go where a common goal suggests it should.

Some paddle rafts are specially designed with a series of thwarts (cross tubes) for greater stability and to give paddlers something to brace against to help them stay in the raft. However, they are expensive. Occasionally rafts used primarily for paddle-powered trips are equipped with toe-hold straps fastened to the floor for better bracing. (**Danger:** never use foot loops big enough to allow a foot to become entrapped; in case of a capsize, the paddler could be trapped in a life-threatening situation.)

Inflatable canoes/kayaks are elongated inflatable crafts that are neither canoe nor kayak. Although they are not decked like a kayak, they are normally operated like a kayak with a double-bladed paddle. They cannot be Eskimo-rolled as a kayak can, and the paddler simply sits on the bottom of the craft, not in a seat set into the floor. Such crafts generally do not track as well as hard-hulled boats, but they are forgiving and adaptable and can be stored and transported with minimal space and hassle. They are subject to puncture, of course, but many modern fabrics are reasonably sturdy if they involve a cloth base permeated with a rubberized material.

Craft Selection

Any of the crafts mentioned above can be used on the rivers discussed in this book, but certain crafts will work better in specific situations. Weigh the options. What is needed, a small craft with little carrying capacity that one paddler can operate or a boat that will take the whole family along? Do the paddlers want to run Class II rapids or dink around the saltwater sloughs? Do the paddlers want a fast craft that can take the rapids but requires expertise to maneuver or a more stable craft that nearly anyone can manage?

Rafts, especially the larger ones, have the greatest carrying capacity, and they are both stable and forgiving. Open canoes, especially the longer ones, can carry a lot of gear and people, but they are less forgiving than a raft. The Sportyak, a one-person craft, has little carrying capacity, but one person can handle it nicely. It weighs only 38 pounds and is riverworthy enough to negotiate the worst rapids mentioned in this book.

Sportyaks and rafts, however, whether they are paddled or rowed, do not make much headway on flatwater. Paddle rafts will be better than Sportyaks for such passive waters, but canoes will be better than either because they cut through the water more efficiently. Sea kayaks may be the best bet, but the carrying capacity of kayaks is somewhat limited, and they require real skill to manage and maneuver.

Dories are remarkably maneuverable and have fantastic carrying capacity, but they are so heavy and bulky they require a trailer for transport to and from the river. Inflatables require pumps and time to inflate them; paddlers can't just throw them in the water and be off. Rowing rafts require rigging (marrying the frame to the craft) in addition to the time and effort it takes to inflate them.

Paddlers need to know what their needs are and how best to satisfy them within the characteristics of the crafts available for negotiating these relatively quiet waters: carrying capacity, lightness of weight, quickness of launch, ease of transport, hull design, stability, maneuverability, level of skill required to manage the craft, durability, and maintenance.

EQUIPMENT

Good equipment increases the enjoyment of the river experience and promotes safety. It pays to have good equipment and to keep it in good repair.

Craft-related

In addition to the craft itself, you need to consider other craft-related equipment: paddles, poles, and other devices for propelling and controlling the craft, and transportation for getting the craft to and from the river.

Propulsion and Control. Equipment for propelling and controlling a craft includes paddles for canoes, kayaks, and paddle rafts; poles for poling canoes; oars and oarlocks for dories, Sportyaks, and rowing rafts; and frames for rafts, perhaps even for Sportyaks.

Canoe paddles, which are also used on paddle rafts, come in different lengths, widths, and shapes. There are even bent-shaft paddles used by marathon and downriver canoe racers and by a growing number of recreational paddlers because they are more efficient.

The grip of a paddle, its length, the width of the blade, and the contour of the shaft are very personal considerations; but you will want a paddle that floats, is strong enough to do its job·yet light enough not to tire the paddler, and is durable, balanced, and aesthetically pleasing. A general rule for canoe-paddle length used to be "from nose to toes," but the current trend is for shorter paddles, perhaps from chin to toes. For bent-shaft paddles, it is crotch to chin for length of shaft, from the grip to the bend.

In general, stern paddles should be slightly longer than bow paddles (especially if the bow paddler is shorter than the stern paddler). Paddles should be several inches longer for paddle rafting than for canoeing because the paddler, sitting on the tube, is farther from the water. Paddlers who use a short, choppy stroke (such as Native American paddlers or marathon and downriver racers) will want a shorter, narrower paddle than those who like to use a long, slow stroke.

Kayak paddles are longer than canoe paddles and have a blade at each end, usually at right angles to each other. The double-bladed paddle enables the kayaker to keep a steady side-to-side rhythm during normal paddling. Kayak paddle blades are often curved or cupped, the concave surface serving as the power face (the side that exerts pressure against the water). For flatwater paddling, a slightly longer paddle is needed than for whitewater paddling—perhaps as long as 8 feet. The more whitewater that is encountered, the shorter the paddle should be. Paddle length is also related to the height or the arm-length of the paddler.

Green River paddlers explore the shoreline.

Wooden paddles (especially laminated ones) are traditional and beautiful, but they do not wear as well as plastic, fiberglass, or fiberglass-coated ones. Modern plastic paddles or combinations of metal and plastic are durable but garish, coming in many different colors and color combinations. Paddlers should look over the assortment at the local paddle shop and explore their options by collecting information from professional paddlers and other boaters.

For rowing, oarlocks and a pair of oars are needed. Oars are available in modern multicolored plastics, but many rowers prefer traditional wooden ones. Oars should be roughly 2/3 the length of the craft to be rowed (6-foot oars for a 9-foot boat, 10-foot oars for a 15-foot boat).

Many small inflatable rafts and all Sportyaks have built-in oarlocks, but they may not be adequate for serious rowing. One answer is a rowing frame made of wood or metal (such as those used on virtually all rowing rafts) to which oarlocks are attached. These frames are especially important on larger rafts, but keep in mind that most rafts can be paddled as well as rowed.

Frames made of wood can easily be fashioned at home. They usually rest on top of the inflated tubes and are lashed to the boat with straps attached to D-rings. Sometimes they have floor boards suspended from them to add to the raft's carrying capacity. In any case they will have an oar-mount stand on either side for attaching the oarlocks.

Metal frames made of aluminum or steel pipe tubing generally nest into the center of the raft between the thwarts (cross tubes that increase the craft's sturdiness or rigidity and provide lateral bracing against side pressure). Raft frames may have suspended floors to increase their carrying capacity. (Gear dropped into the bottom of an inflatable craft has a tendency to damage the floor when the floor fabric is crimped between gear and river rocks.) Many of the professionally built metal frames include a slot for an ice chest or cooler, which doubles as a seat for the rower. Metal frames can also be fitted with oar-mounts for attaching the oarlocks.

Transportation. A means of transporting crafts to the river is essential unless the paddlers live on the riverbank and make all their trips on one river. Pickup trucks, vans, conventional automobiles using cartop carriers, and special boat trailers are used to convey boats to and from the river. Simple and effective cartop carriers can be purchased or built.

If the car has rain gutters, metal or tough plastic stiltlike clips can be fastened onto them. Two sets of clips joined with two 2x4s create a pair of racks for carrying a canoe. (Kayaks should be hauled in form-fitting cradles.) Similar racks made of pipes instead of 2x4s are more expensive but equally effective, especially for canoes. Foam padding on the pipe racks saves wear and tear on the craft carried. Be sure to tie the crafts well—front, back, and across the top. Nothing is as disheartening as ruining a good water craft, nor as disastrous as causing an accident because of one careless mistake.

Sportyaks fit nicely into a standard pickup truck bed (or a minitruck long bed) or on a cartop carrier. Many inflatables will fit easily into a standard car trunk, but the larger inflatables may require a pickup truck bed, a van, or a trailer. Most river runners have their own techniques and methods, their own trailers or racks. Go on a few club trips and see a variety of possibilities.

Dories require a trailer, and inflatable rafts with their frames in place can be hauled to and from the river by flatbed trailer to save time. Canoe- and kayak-carrying trailers can be rented or borrowed for large-party trips.

Personal

Personal gear on a river trip should be kept to a minimum, but always take along anything and everything you might need. The old 90/10 pattern fits: 90 percent of what you take along will be used only 10 percent of the time; but if you don't have it along, you could be in trouble. Make checklists and use them; add to them and pare them down to the practical, the necessary.

Dry Bags. Waterproof bags are essential for keeping important items dry: maps, sleeping bags, food, cameras—whatever should be kept secure from the water. This is a never-ending problem on river trips and one that has been addressed successfully by a number of manufacturers in recent years.

A wide variety of dry bags, boxes, and containers can be used, not all of them the expensive commercial types. A heavy-duty plastic bag within a nylon bag is very satisfactory: the inner bag keeps everything dry, and the outer bag protects the inner bag from tears and punctures. If you spend a lot of time on the river, it may pay to purchase one of the commercial dry bags.

The old standby for many river runners is the military surplus ammo can, which comes in several sizes. Be sure the rubber seals are intact.

Clothing. Plan to take along a change of clothes if there is any possibility of getting wet—and there is always that possibility. In winter, wear pile or wool; in summer, protect eyes, head, limbs, and torso against the sun. A wet suit (which uses body-heated water to keep the paddler warm) or a dry suit (which keeps the paddler dry, thus warm) may be appropriate on cold-water rivers or during cold weather; and in the Pacific Northwest, good rain gear is essential.

Even if you are wearing sandals, shorts, and a tank top on a river trip, always have along a long-sleeved shirt, long pants, and dry socks and shoes in case of a wetting. Carry a wool shirt and a wool cap in case of hypothermia, and a down sleeping bag for winter emergencies.

Food and Drink. Ammo cans, ice chests, coolers, and thermos bottles—preferably the metal type—can hold food and drink. It may be wise to carry along some extra high-energy food for dealing with hypothermia on winter or cold-water trips. Hot coffee, tea, or chocolate is nice to have on those midwinter eagle-watching trips, and cold lemonade is great on a hot summer day. Soggy sandwiches are unpalatable: best keep them dry through proper packing and storing.

Recreational Equipment. Paddlers may include fishing gear, cameras, binoculars, Frisbees, horseshoes, soccer balls, volleyballs, and nets among their recreational gear, but the river itself provides many of the accoutrements for recreational activities. There are skipping stones, rocks for the Olympic Rock Throw or for throwing at floating sticks or bits of bark or hollow trees across the river, and beaches on which to draw pictures or write messages.

Navigational Aids. Maps and charts and compasses are important for planning trips and useful to have along in waterproof cases. Notes from a previous trip or from a friend can be useful, too, to find the take-out (the end of the river trip) or the best campsite. Guidebooks, field guides, and area descriptions will provide reference information and enhance the quality of the trip.

Safety

Washington was late in joining other western states to address boating safety on rivers. Some counties and federal agencies led the way in requiring boaters to wear personal flotation devices, and Coast Guard regulations required that they be carried in certain crafts (usually not canoes and kayaks). Now all children under 12 must wear them, all boaters must wear them in national parks, and a Snohomish County ordinance requires helmets on certain whitewater segments of the Skykomish.

The most important safety item is the personal flotation device (PFD), sometimes referred to as a life jacket. First-aid kits, repair kits, and emergency equipment are also important to have along.

Flotation. Both PFDs and extra flotation for the craft are essential for a safe river trip. The PFD is the single most important item of safety equipment. Be sure it contains adequate flotation (enough to keep the wearer afloat), that it is the right size (test it in a swimming pool to be sure), and that it is fitted and worn properly. PFDs should be worn at all times on the river, both for the paddlers' safety and for the lesson it suggests to others. PFDs can't save paddlers' lives if they're not worn.

The commonly used horse-collar jackets are not adequate for most adults and are inappropriate for children. Get a good PFD for each member of the family who plans to go on the river. Modern PFDs are comfortable (even stylish) and many come with zipper fronts and pockets for carrying items needed or useful on the river.

Extra flotation in the craft itself is unnecessary in a Sportyak, raft, or dory; essential in a kayak; and often appropriate for a canoe. Flotation can be in the form of foam blocks, sheets of ethylfoam, or air bags that can be purchased at any whitewater shop. Even inflated inner tubes will serve: anything that will displace water and help keep the craft afloat when it is full of water. (With the extra flotation in place, the craft won't be so full of water.) Extra flotation is a safety factor, a common-sense addition to the margin of safety in any craft used on the paddle routes described in this book.

Anticipation of Emergency Needs. Assuring safety lies largely in anticipation and planning, in providing the means for handling any possibility. Bow- and stern-lines on canoes, grab loops on both ends of kayaks, chicken lines around rafts, throw lines on all crafts, extra ropes (well tied to the craft, coiled and secured so they will not create a hazard in the water), and a first-aid kit are all important items worth carrying along on every river trip. So is a repair kit with everything needed to at least temporarily repair the craft and its accoutrements (such as spare parts for the air pump on an inflatable craft, a spare oarlock for any rowing rig, a craft-specific patch kit, or a spare paddle).

Bailing devices should be carried in every craft, and a sponge can come in handy for sopping up the last bit of water and cleaning up the craft. If too much water is shipped or the craft capsizes, paddlers will have to stop and dump the water or bail the craft thoroughly before continuing the trip.

Emergency Gear. Such gear includes extras of almost everything paddlers might need, from PFDs to a towel and dry clothing, matches, and a whistle. Many frequent paddlers wear a whistle on the zipper of their PFD and such emergency items as matches, knife, flashlight, and minimal first-aid kit tucked away in a waterproof container in the PFD pockets.

POWER AND CONTROL TECHNIQUES

No matter what craft is selected, paddlers need to learn how to power and maneuver it on the river. Initially, paddlers should read everything possible about handling the chosen craft. For canoeing it is hard to beat the American National Red Cross book *Canoeing*. For kayaking, try *Kayaking* by Jay Evans and Robert R. Anderson. Cecil Kuhne's *River Rafting* is a good book on rafting; William McGinnis's *Whitewater Rafting* may be too intimidating for Class I and II boaters. See **Appendix A: Further Reading** for additional suggestions.

As a general rule, keep in mind that for every action there is a counter action. That is, if the water is pushed in one direction with an oar or paddle, the craft will move in the opposite direction. If the handle of an oar is pulled toward the paddler, the water pushed by the oar blade moves away from the paddler (the oarlock serving as a fulcrum), and the boat moves in the direction of the pull.

The surface of a river is a complex of currents moving in several directions at once. Water forced against an obstacle piles up against it, then moves around that obstacle at a higher rate of speed to a lower level of the river. The water then slows down and may move back upstream to fill the hole created downstream of that obstacle. The term *reading the river* refers to learning to determine which way the currents flow by observing the surface and adjusting paddling or rowing strokes to that dynamic medium.

Although the water surface reveals much, subsurface currents also need to be considered. They are reflected on the surface but can be determined to some extent by looking beneath the surface (if the water is clear enough) to study the rocks and logs and other obstacles that give the surface its characteristic appearance. Understanding the surface appearance ultimately enables paddlers to read the river and negotiate their way through the conflicting currents. (For more detail, read my revised edition of *River Running*, which will be published in the spring of 2001; see **Appendix A: Further Reading**.)

Rowing

Rowing any craft involves using a set of oars mounted on a fulcrum known as an oarlock, which in turn is mounted on the craft to be rowed. The technique is pretty much the same for any craft, though it varies with the size and weight of boat and—to some extent—the nature of the water.

Rafts. Rowing a raft requires a sturdy frame securely attached to the inflatable boat. The oarlocks are mounted on the frame, and the rower

A *sweeper narrows the river, to the detriment of inexperienced boaters. Paddlers learn to avoid such natural obstacles.*

sits on the frame and maneuvers the craft by pulling or pushing on the grip end of the oars. The raft is positioned across the current with one oar upstream, the other downstream to move the craft across the current. The rower essentially selects the current that is going to take the raft where it should go, then rows into that current.

Additional maneuvering may be required to avoid an obstacle, to slow the craft, or to make a turn. Positioning the craft at an angle to the current and rowing either diagonally upstream or down to cross the current is called *ferrying*. The raft can be swiveled by pushing on one oar and pulling on the other, pivoting the craft quickly to reposition it for the next maneuver. The tighter the contact between raft and rowing frame and the higher the air pressure within the raft, the better the craft will respond to its oars.

Dories. Rowing a dory is very similar to rowing a raft, but the dory is more maneuverable. It may be heavier than a raft (depending on its load), but a dory can turn very quickly because its flared sides and heavy rocker result in a small area being in contact with the water relative to its large volume. Dories track better than rafts, and they require little water to float them. They are not quite as forgiving as rafts, but that is not usually a factor on Class I and II water.

Sportyaks. Rowing a Sportyak involves short, quick strokes because the oars are shorter and can be moved much more rapidly. Sportyaks are similar to dories in their maneuverability, though they are much lighter (relatively speaking) and float like corks. In waves it is important to keep the bow turned into the crest. Otherwise, the wave may swamp the boat; it will still float even when it is full of water, but why be uncomfortable? The wave might even flip the lightweight craft.

Paddling

When a craft is paddled, the paddler's lower hand serves as the fulcrum: the power exerted is applied to the water and creates a counter action—whether in a horizontal direction to make the craft move forward, sideways or obliquely, or in a vertical direction to stabilize the craft as in a brace (applying the paddle blade flat to the surface of the water with a vertical pressure, thereby bracing the craft against a capsize).

Canoes. A canoe is normally paddled with a single-bladed paddle either from a kneeling position on the bottom of the canoe or from a sitting position, utilizing the seats with which most canoes are equipped. (For greater marriage of paddler to craft, kneeling whitewater paddlers use straps across their thighs for better bracing.)

Northwest Native Americans do not talk about paddling a canoe so much as they do "pulling" a canoe, a principle (or point of view) that suggests planting the paddle in the water vertically and pulling the canoe toward that planted paddle. That is essentially what paddlers do when they paddle a canoe: place the paddle in the water—in front, behind, or to the side—and pull (or push) the canoe toward (or away from) that point.

Basic strokes for canoeing include the forward stroke (planting the paddle forward of the paddler's position in the canoe and pulling the canoe forward as the paddle moves backward in the water); the back stroke or backpaddle (planting the paddle behind the paddler's position and pulling the canoe backward as the paddle moves forward in the water); the draw stroke (planting the paddle as far to the side as possible and pulling the canoe toward the paddle as the paddle moves toward the canoe); and the pry (planting the paddle next to the gunnel, or side, of the canoe and pushing the canoe away from the paddle as the paddle moves away from the canoe).

Variations of these strokes are the J-stroke, which involves twisting the paddle into a kind of rudder to correct the canoe's variance from a straight-line route; the sweep stroke, which is a variation of either a forward or a backward stroke and a draw or pry, depending on where the stroke is started and where it ends; and the brace, which is used to maintain the balance of the canoe in rough water or in confusing currents, especially when the canoe is tipping too far to one side or the other, on the verge of capsizing.

But the high brace is more than a defensive stroke. It can be part of an efficient quick-turning stroke in which the paddlers lean far to the side—essentially a draw stroke with a severe lean of the body that ends in a brace (the reason whitewater paddlers use thigh straps).

Eddies are areas of water that move counter to the main current. They occur below (that is, downstream from) obstacles: midstream rocks or logs, or promontories projecting from the bank. An eddy is an ideal place for a turn; it helps the paddlers make the maneuver. The bow paddler in a tandem (two-person) canoe (or the lone paddler of a solo canoe) moves the bow of the canoe into the eddy with a draw stroke, while the stern paddler and the power of the current on the stern snuggle the canoe into the protective eddy. This is known as an eddy turn and is useful for landing, launching, and maneuvering back and forth across the current.

Developing proficiency will take some practice, and it works better if the paddlers have someone to teach them. Read about the techniques in a how-to book (which this isn't). Take a lesson from a proficient paddler or as part of a paddle club's regular activities. The importance of beginning a canoeing career with a paddle club or with friends who know how to handle a canoe cannot be stressed enough.

Remember, too, that the longer a canoe, the faster it moves in a straight line—but the harder it is to turn. Conversely, the shorter it is, the easier it turns. Another factor, rocker, is also involved. Rocker is the bow-to-stern convexity of the hull in the water: the greater the rocker, the easier the craft turns.

Tandem canoeing involves two people paddling a canoe together, one in the bow and one in the stern, normally paddling on opposite sides. Solo paddling obviously involves only one person paddling a canoe, usually from somewhere near the center of the craft. Tandem paddlers soon learn to coordinate their strokes for greater efficiency and stability—but here, too, some instruction can be helpful.

All the strokes can be done from a sitting position, but they are all more powerful and effective when done from a kneeling position. Kneeling also tends to lower the center of gravity in a canoe and thereby increase its stability. Many recreational paddlers alternate sitting and kneeling, going to the latter in the rapids, on quick turns, or in any potentially unstabilizing situation—such as trying to avoid a sweeper (overhanging tree).

For long-term paddling, a semi-kneeling position with the buttocks resting on the edge of the seat may be more comfortable. Paddlers with arthritic knees may be able to manage by changing position slightly every few minutes. Stretching the bad leg out is also helpful.

Kayaks. A kayak is paddled with a double-bladed paddle by one or two persons, depending on the configuration of the craft. Most experienced kayakers use a paddle with blades at roughly right angles to each other; right-handed paddlers will want the left blade up (away from the water's surface) when the right blade is in the water making a power stroke. The reverse is true for left-handed paddlers.

Kayak paddle strokes generally are shallower and at a shallower angle than canoe paddle strokes, primarily because of the double-bladed paddle. But the principle is much the same: move the water in one direction and the kayak will respond in another. Kayak paddle strokes usually alternate from side to side (again, because of the double-bladed paddle), giving the course a slight wiggle unless the wiggle is corrected by a countering rudder stroke.

Kayaks are more maneuverable than canoes, but the same facts hold true: the longer the craft, the harder it is to turn but the faster it moves in a straight line; the more rocker, the easier the craft turns; the shorter the craft, the easier it turns. Having a rudder (as most sea kayaks do) also makes the craft easier to turn on flatwater. But while the rudder is no substitute for proper paddling technique, it does help turn the longer craft on open water. All this means that for flatwater paddling, a longer kayak is more appropriate; for whitewater paddling, the shorter craft is better, generally speaking.

Since kayaks in general turn more easily than canoes (because most of them are shorter and have greater rocker), the strokes used to control and power them are more subtle—often a combination of two canoe strokes in one, as in the sweep strokes. The simplest turning pattern is using more power on one side than on the other. The stern rudder is a good solo stroke, but it is a more powerful maneuver done by the stern paddler of a tandem kayak: the paddler places one end of the paddle into the water as a rudder, holding the blade against the current to execute a turn toward the side on which the rudder is made.

Braces are vital to the kayaker because a kayak is less forgiving than a canoe. The paddler needs to be more alert to subtle changes in lateral currents, more conscious of the brace as a defensive measure. However, since the kayaker is partially enclosed in the craft and the kayak has a lower center of gravity (because the paddler is sitting so low in the water), there is a compensating stability factor—especially in touring kayaks developed for flatwater paddling.

The double-bladed paddle offers a compensatory advantage that enables the paddler to react to either side much more quickly than a canoe paddler, who might have to switch sides to execute a brace on the appropriate side.

Most of the strokes used by a canoe paddler with a single-bladed paddle can be used by a kayak paddler, although you can't pry or use a J-stroke in a kayak very effectively. Because of the nature of kayak paddling, however—the paddler's position and the double-bladed paddle—most of the strokes are used in a modified manner that will become clear only as they are applied.

As with canoeing, it is important to get some basic instruction in kayak paddling. This is best done with a club group or a commercial instructor. Many whitewater and sea kayaking equipment shops offer such instruction as a means of satisfying their customers' needs and of expanding the sport.

Rafts. Paddling rafts became a major sport in the Pacific Northwest during the 1980s, as dozens of commercial river outfitters offered paddle raft trips on most of the whitewater rivers of the region. The same crafts and techniques can be applied to the less rambunctious rivers described in this book.

The basic technique involves sitting on the side of the raft (on its inflated tube) and wielding a paddle somewhat longer than a canoe paddle (longer because the paddler is sitting slightly higher above the water than in a canoe). The basic paddle strokes are the same as in canoeing—forward, backward, draw, and pry—but they are usually applied through four orders from the captain of a paddle-raft crew:

> **forward** means for everyone to paddle forward;
>
> **backpaddle** means for everyone to paddle backward;
>
> **right turn** directs those on the right side to paddle backward and those on the left to paddle forward; and
>
> **left turn** directs those on the left side to paddle backward and those on the right to paddle forward.

It may take some practice for the crew to get coordinated. It is important to have a captain in charge so everyone works together. It is also important for the craft to be inflated to a tightness that makes it go where it is directed and for the paddlers to have a means of gripping the raft with their legs, feet, and toes so they are not thrown out of the craft by wave action or the raft's striking obstacles.

Smaller rafts may be more of a problem. Because smaller rafts are often made of cheaper materials, they can withstand less air pressure and are consequently less rigid and less maneuverable; therefore, they are not as likely to track or go where they are intended to go.

Poling

Poling is traditional among Northwestern Native Americans. As recently as 50 years ago the Nooksacks, for example, poled up and down their namesake river, often traveling as fast as 12 mph going upstream with two strong men tandem poling. Margaret Elley Felt's book about several rivers on the Olympic Peninsula, *Rivers to Reckon With*, depicts early residents engaged in poling.

The idea is to place one end of a pole (normally 10 to 14 feet long) into the river and, by pushing off the bottom, propel the craft in a given direction. It is done from a standing position in an open canoe and is far safer than it sounds. In fact, it is faster and more efficient for moving upstream than paddling, and it is an effective means of moving downstream as well. I poled the Green River from the mouth of Big Soos Creek to Fort Dent Park, a run of 23 miles in 6 hours—an average of roughly 4 mph on a relatively slow river.

Many of the rivers described in this book are ideal for poling. Rocky bottoms full of huge angular blocks can be difficult, because the pole may become entrapped between rocks and lost or bent. (Always carry along a paddle so you can retrieve a lost pole.) Gravel bottoms are often good for poling unless the gravel is so loose that it offers no real purchase for the pole. Sand and mud bottoms may offer little resistance to the push of the pole and tend to grab the pole. Clay bottoms offer a firm surface to push off from, but they too tend to grab the pole at the withdrawal stage.

In water too deep for the pole to reach bottom (such as the lakelike stretch of the Black River and the big pools in many rivers described in this book), a kayak stroke can be used, simply paddling with the pole, which offers enough resistance to the water to provide plenty of power and control.

To begin poling, simply practice standing up in an open canoe, rocking it from side to side until you are comfortable with its stability. Try this on a lake or on a river with no visible current. Then start wielding the pole against the bottom or as a kayak paddle (see above). As the pole pushes off a shallow bottom, continue the push by "climbing" the pole with the hands pushing it farther and farther behind the craft. Recover the pole with a quick pool-cue move after a final power thrust against the bottom, and set the pole for another series.

Harry Rock, National Poling Champion in the 1980s, has written an excellent series of articles for *The American Canoeist* (Vol. X, No. 1, 2, 3). Rock's book, *The Basic Essentials of Canoe Poling*, is well worth reading if you intend to take up poling (see **Appendix A: Further Reading**).

Preparation and Training

Preparation and training for running river trips can keep paddlers busy all year: reading about rivers, river-running skills, and paddle technique in the off-season (if there is one); conditioning the mind and the body with regular mental and physical exercise, which might include pool sessions (practicing paddle technique); and maintaining equipment and gear in good condition for the next river trip.

Physical conditioning is important so that paddlers don't get stiff and sore from each trip they make—or have a heart attack because they are not sufficiently well conditioned for the planned outing. Mental conditioning means that paddlers learn enough about the activity, the equipment they plan to use, and the river they plan to run so that they are intellectually ready and psychologically fit for the outing.

Of course, paddlers who run rivers every weekend throughout the year and belong to paddle clubs that have regular pool sessions already know all this; but such paddlers can always help others appreciate the need for preparation and conditioning.

SAFETY TECHNIQUES

The most important safety technique is to be prepared—for anything and everything. To take a single river trip without everything needed for any emergency is to court disaster. Rivers are not treacherous in themselves; they only seem treacherous to people who don't know them. It is the inappropriate things that people do on and in rivers—such as launching without PFDs (personal flotation devices) or without having adequate means of controlling the craft, and boating under the influence of drugs or alcohol—that give rivers a bad name as recreational resources.

Be prepared by wearing PFDs, by using extra flotation in the craft, by learning some paddle skills before launch and practicing them regularly. Get to know the river and what to expect of it before you test your luck and courage. Know your own limitations and have enough sense to stay off the river when it is too high to run safely. Plan trips carefully, and keep an eye on the weather.

Water lilies bloom in many backwater sloughs.

Once on a river, scout the potential problems: rapids, logjam, sweeper, low dam. You can normally avoid most obstacles by landing and lining (letting the craft down with a line from shore) or portaging (carrying the craft and gear around the problem). Take the safe route if there is a choice. Go in a group whenever possible, and help the group develop and practice safe techniques.

If you capsize while paddling, keep calm. You may be shocked by the water temperature and surprised by the force of the current, but do not panic. The PFDs will keep you afloat. Keep your feet on the surface, facing downstream, and scull (as you would if sitting in an inner tube). Look for obstacles—logjams, rocks, sweepers, souse holes, or keepers (strong eddies in which the current is flowing strongly upstream)—and try to avoid them.

If you should go overboard, try immediately to get back to the boat. Few people fall out of canoes without the canoe's capsizing, but they do fall out of rafts and dories. If you are in the water for any length of time, you have three things to worry about: (1) getting caught between the craft and a natural obstacle; (2) getting caught by a natural obstacle such as a sweeper, keeper, or underwater snag that would tend to hold you in place (perhaps even underwater), a condition known as entrapment; and (3) hypothermia, the loss of too much body heat to cold water.

The worst obstacle could be the craft itself. Move to the upstream end or side of the craft so it does not trap you between it and an obstacle in the river. The craft could crush you or hold you in an untenable position with the force of the current and the weight of the river in the craft. Stay with the craft (which offers additional flotation and the chance of help) only if it seems the logical thing to do. It may make more sense to swim or wade to shore, but wade only in calm water.

If you go overboard near shore in a logical place to get out of the water, go for shore and leave the craft to its other occupants or to recover later. If the water is cold, get out as soon as you can do so safely, but don't try to stand in fast-moving water; your feet can become entrapped in obstacles on the bottom. One of the best reasons to travel in a group is so there will be a support team ready to help in an emergency.

Hypothermia is the condition in which so much body heat is lost that the body ceases to function normally. Early signs are shivering, blue lips, lethargy, then loss of small muscle coordination and slurred speech. As soon as hypothermia is recognized, stop heat loss and warm the body by putting on warmer clothes or taking off wet clothes and putting on dry ones. Stop to build a fire if necessary and get high-energy foods and warm liquids into the victim (if the victim is conscious).

Remember in which direction safety lies. Is the road on this side of the river or across the river? As you float any of these rivers, be aware of their location relative to access roads and railroad tracks, have an emergency game plan in mind outlining what to do in a variety of circumstances, and know the nearest route to safety and help.

People are more important than equipment in the rescue priority. Get the people to safety before considering the craft—even though the craft may be expensive and a means of finishing the trip. (The paddlers may not finish it at all if they get caught in a logjam.) People have drowned by trying to retrieve gear after they were safely ashore.

Good paddle skills go a long way in keeping a party safe on the river, but so does common sense—sense enough not to go onto waters your party is not prepared to handle or into situations beyond the party's ability. Plan the trips. Gather information about the canoe routes. Read about them. Get the maps. Talk to people—especially those who know the river well and have run it recently.

When you are paddling on the river, keep your wits about you. Be observant. Look for problem areas. Anticipate problems. Talk to other boaters, fishermen, people along the river who might have better or more current information. Several people die on Washington rivers every year because they didn't know enough about the river to which they were entrusting their lives.

Safety equipment is of little use unless used correctly. Someone on every river trip should know enough about first aid to use a first-aid kit and to do the most basic things to provide appropriate assistance to a sick or injured person. CPR (cardiopulmonary resuscitation) is an important skill to have on any outdoor trip, especially on a river trip. CPR and first-aid training should be a primary consideration for anyone planning regular river trips.

Most accidents on river trips actually happen *off* the river: driving to and from the river, loading and unloading crafts and gear, rigging boats, building campfires (including breaking firewood), and walking on sharp or slippery rocks at the river's edge. Be aware of the potential for accidents and anticipate the problems. Watch where you step, how you lift, what you do, and how you do it—especially if you are a novice just learning the routine.

And develop a routine. There will be fewer mistakes and fewer accidents if a pattern is developed for everything that is done in the preparation for and execution of a river trip. Follow the pattern as it is perfected. There are so many things that can go wrong on a river trip that paddlers need to create a situation in which they control the circumstances as much as possible. Plan to the point of the ridiculous, and follow the plan to the letter. Control what can be controlled, and the trip will be safer and more enjoyable.

Some clothing can weigh paddlers down beyond the capacity of their PFDs to buoy them up. Boots can fill with water and pull paddlers under. For such reasons a rain suit is a lot safer than a poncho, wet-suit boots a lot more sensible than PACs (rubber-bottomed waterproof boots) or Wellies (Wellington boots, used on many northern rivers).

There are two basic safety rules. First, **never boat alone** (that is, with only one boat). Many experienced boaters occasionally engage in solo trips, but they are prepared to deal with the inherent risks and responsibilities. Second, **wear a PFD at all times on the river**. Sometimes these rules may seem unimportant on Class I and modest Class II water, but people have gotten themselves into serious trouble by not following them.

If paddlers go in a party (as they should to live by the rule of never boating alone), they may want to establish an order: for example, Bob's boat leads because he knows the river best; Sam's goes next because he's the least experienced; Alice follows as sweep because she has the first-aid kit and the most experience in general, even though she doesn't know this river as well. Formation may be broken occasionally, but as a general rule it makes sense to have some order.

Paddle clubbers, ready to launch, find safety in numbers.

A related rule is that no boat should ever get out of sight of the next boat. The lead boat shouldn't run away from the laggards, and the laggards should try to keep pace with the boats ahead. Tighten up the formation occasionally, as when approaching a riffle or a rapid. Scout rapids and troublesome areas that worry any of the boaters, and set up safety boats at critical points. All these suggestions are practiced by most paddle clubs. The use of safety throw lines (ropes stuffed in a bag that can be thrown to a person in the water or in an out-of-control craft) has become almost universal.

As mentioned earlier, one of the best ways to begin boating is to go with a paddle club. The members run safe and sane trips, and novice paddlers can learn the basics in a safe situation. Keep in mind that as paddle club officers change, addresses and phone numbers may change as well; but the Washington Water Trails Association (WWTA) can probably give you up-to-date accurate information. For the address of WWTA and various paddle clubs, see **Appendix B: Recommended Resources, Paddle Clubs in Western Washington.**

In using this book, remember that no rating system can be completely accurate or objective, that every river is different at different water levels, and that rivers can change from day to day (even hour to hour) with tidal fluctuation or reservoir release flows. Logjams, sweepers, and other obstacles can appear overnight due to natural conditions and human activity.

Some of the river segments in this book may have hazards that paddlers may feel are beyond their ability. A few of the rivers have special hazards (mentioned in the trip descriptions) that paddlers will want to portage or line—like the low dam on the Stillaguamish River (Trip 9) just downstream from the I-5 bridge or the diversion structure at RM 8.1 on the Wynoochee (Trip 34). Paddlers can usually portage or line their craft around even massive logjams.

Paddlers should always be prepared on river trips and use their best judgment. Judgment will improve as the paddlers become more familiar with the rivers' relative degree-of-difficulty ratings in this book, with different rivers at different water levels, and with their own skills, abilities, and confidence.

Use the ratings as a guide, not as an absolute. Nothing beats an examination of a potentially dangerous situation at the time and place that the condition exists.

THE NATURAL ENVIRONMENT

Nowhere except at sea or in the heart of the most pristine wilderness can the natural environment be experienced as meaningfully as on a river. It provides the very medium of travel, the fauna and flora that add immeasurably to the boater's enjoyment, and the geologic backdrop through which the boater moves.

Paddlers will observe many destructive aspects as they float these river segments—clear-cut scars; municipal and industrial pollution; dams that de-water, drown, and destroy the natural environment; commercial development and exploitation that ignore and therefore abuse the natural environment. At the same time, they will experience numerous positive elements of the natural world that may serve as inspiration and offer insights.

Aldo Leopold has said in essence that we abuse the land because we consider it a commodity that belongs to us; if we thought of it as a community to which we belong (which is closer to the truth), we might learn to use it with love and respect. No one can spend any length of time on a river without coming to better understand the natural environment and developing a higher respect for it. It behooves all paddlers to get their elected officials out on the rivers, where they can learn greater respect for the natural environment, so that their future actions may stop the abuse of it and give it greater understanding.

The Character of the Medium

Rivers. By their very nature, rivers inspire awe. They are living beings with a life of their own. They nurture life, both plant and animal. They flow toward the sea, seeking a dynamic equilibrium which they never reach. They erode the land, carving valleys and canyons, and they transport materials—organic and inorganic—creating new land in deltas and flood plains.

Rivers are bound by their bottoms and their shorelines, but those boundaries change. Flood waters scour the river bottoms and inundate pastures, farmlands, and other low-lying areas. Where humankind has been foolish enough to build in the flood plain, we hear of the treacherous rivers that have caused damage to human property or taken human life—as though humans are all that matter. (Will humans ever learn not to build in the flood plain where the river needs to go?)

Watercraft float on the surface of the rivers, displacing a small amount of water for the time they are on the river, leaving no evidence of their passing—unless the paddlers are careless and insensitive and have left their litter and human waste behind.

Rivers provide the power for paddle parties on float trips. Boaters may control their crafts, augment the downhill speed of the river or buck it for a time with pole, paddle, or oar, but ultimately it is the river that rules. Boaters must learn to go with the flow, to listen to and sense the river's messages. Unless people learn to read the river, they will never know its secrets, nor will they learn to go with the flow.

Natural woody debris in the river enhances salmon production. Houses built too close to the river do not.

Effective salmon runs need clean water, spawning gravel, woody debris, and stream-side vegetation.

Estuaries. The richest sources of life on the planet are estuaries. They are the areas where freshwater rivers meet the salty sea. The natural mixing that occurs, augmented by the twice-daily tidal stirring, creates a unique habitat used by thousands of species. Twice each day the estuary and the lower reaches of the rivers that feed it are flushed by the tide, cleansed of the waste products of life that are then recycled, even as the waters themselves are recycled in the hydrologic cycle.

Boating on estuaries and in the tidal reaches of rivers requires an understanding of the tides, their ebb and flow. A boater has to work with the tides, for they are stronger than any boater. Estuaries offer a unique opportunity to see several worlds. Think of it: at high tide you will see only the full flood of the estuary, but at low tide you get a glimpse of the muddy, sandy, or rocky bottom and of the organisms that have been covered by the swirling waters of the natural mixing bowl.

Estuaries are full of bird life: eagles, wintering snow geese and swans, summer resident ducks and shorebirds, spring and fall migrants. But so are they rich in mammals, from an occasional whale to seals and—along the shore—beavers and muskrats, deer and raccoons. They are vital feeding grounds for juvenile anadromous (freshwater-born ocean-feeding) fish.

Boaters need to be aware of the differences tides make in these productive estuaries: the swift currents that are generated, that fluctuate, that swirl in lateral loops; the mud flats left behind when the tide goes out; the fogs generated when moist air meets river and sea water at different temperatures; the difficulty of paddling or rowing against the tide. In the estuaries, more than anywhere else on the river, boaters have an opportunity to feel the pulse of the earth in its waters.

Natural History

The fauna and flora of rivers offer enough material to keep the most ardent river runner curious and mentally stimulated for a lifetime. Rivers teem with life; their bottoms serve as habitat for invertebrates, and the invertebrates feed the fish and amphibians as well as many of the birds (such as the water ouzel, which flies under water seeking its insect diet).

Fishermen try to "match the hatch" of insects on the river, fly-fishing for adult salmonoids while kingfishers and great blue herons fish for the fingerlings and fry. Bald eagles and ospreys nest along the rivers and feed on larger fish; the eagles especially congregate in midwinter to scavenge the spawned-out salmon. Spring warblers flood the rivers with their songs and nest along the banks in summer. Spotted sandpipers and killdeer frequent the river bars; ducks—mallards, mergansers, harlequins, golden-eyes—nest and feed along the river as well.

Because rivers are open, it is possible to see from the boat many woodland species of wildlife, especially birds—western tanagers, black-headed grosbeaks, flycatchers, robins, warblers. Several species of swallows feed on the insect population over the rivers, and the scavenging raven is rarely

Raccoon tracks along a western Washington riverbank

far away. Many meadow-dwelling birds can be seen and heard from the river as they conduct their courtship, including meadowlarks and Washington's state bird, the goldfinch. Birds enliven any river trip.

The natural habitat along rivers, even in developed areas, has continued to support wildlife. Few of the rivers in this book would be considered wild in any sense, but all of them—even Sammamish Slough—have beavers and muskrats. All of them have runs of anadromous fish. Many of them have deer and coyotes; a few have bear. Most of the rivers on the Olympic Peninsula have elk; many have otters, minks, skunks, raccoons, squirrels, and rabbits. All of them provide natural habitat for a great variety of birds.

The explosion of Mount St. Helens did much to make people aware of geological phenomena. In western Washington virtually every geological process known to humankind goes on, from the carving of the landscape by glaciers and rivers to the results of plate tectonics—earthquakes and volcanoes. Rivers continually carve the land, continually depositing the materials they carry down from the mountains to the lowlands. On river trips boaters can see it all happening. In fact, as boaters come to understand geological phenomena better, they will understand what makes a river do what it does in its search for dynamic equilibrium.

Canada geese enjoy riverbank grazing and grooming.

River running gets people outdoors onto the rivers where the natural world functions, following immutable natural laws. Paddlers learn to observe and to wonder about things; they learn how they all fit together and interact with one another. Paddling a river offers a course in ecology, an opportunity to see how the natural world works. (Get your political representatives out on the rivers so they too may learn.)

Conservation

Conservation has been defined in many ways, but essentially it is the antithesis of wastefulness. Anything that causes waste fails to function naturally, for there is no waste in natural systems; everything is used. Natural systems are based on recycling. So far, humans merely dabble in recycling, while using technology to create massive quantities of waste products that cannot be used by natural systems. And so far, humans have not been able to find enough places to dispose of or to store these waste products.

River users—boaters, fishermen, picnickers, campers—have an opportunity to leave the natural world in as natural a state as possible. Unless they are totally thoughtless, careless, and ignorant, passing boaters should have little impact on the waters they travel or on the adjacent lands. The swirl of water caused by paddles and oars creates little impact, and even the noise level can be controlled in muscle-powered crafts if boaters are sensitive and sensible.

All outdoor users have a moral responsibility to leave the natural world as pristine as they find it and to improve it when necessary by picking up the litter others have left. Just as only humans can prevent forest fires, only humans—all of us—can prevent the deterioration of the natural environment by treating it with love and respect.

There is no need to clear natural vegetation away to make a campsite or picnic area more comfortable. There is no need to cut living trees or scar their trunks or cut their limbs or mutilate shrubs or pick wildflowers. When these things are done, these parts of our natural world are no longer there for others to enjoy. There is no need to leave ugly fire pits, scars, and ashes on a river beach; boaters can cook on camp stoves or carry out the ashes and charcoal the fires produce. Most paddle clubs participate in annual river clean-ups, joining with other river users to maintain the waterways in as natural a state as possible.

The old admonition to take nothing but pictures, leave nothing but footprints—and not too many of them—makes a lot of sense to the

During the late summer, low water levels narrow rivers, leaving broad beaches for camping. (Note the flotation bags in the canoe.)

sensitive; and the insensitive have no business in the natural world but destruction. The environmentally aware—and that is more of us every day—frequently join together to coordinate efforts, to think globally but act locally.

A number of statewide, regional, and national conservation organizations can use your help, and they can help you as well; see **Appendix B: Recommended Resources, Conservation Organizations**.

The National Wild and Scenic Rivers System

The National Wild and Scenic Rivers System was established in 1968 by an act of Congress, which established a national policy of preserving from development and exploitation certain rivers and their adjacent environments. It also established a method for evaluating rivers and adding them to that system. Initially there were only eight rivers in the system.

At this writing, there are 155 Wild and Scenic Rivers in the nation, several of them in western Washington: the Skagit; its tributaries the Cascade and the Sauk; a Sauk tributary, the Suiattle; and two Columbia River tributaries, the White Salmon and the Klickitat.

In 1988 the President's Commission on Americans Outdoors recommended that by the year 2000 the United States set aside for protective designation 2000 rivers nationwide. While that goal was not reached, river conservation efforts continue at the grass-roots level nationwide. It is up to us to get our elected officials to give river protection a higher priority—or elect representatives who will. At present the state of Washington is represented by some of the nation's least river-sensitive politicians, some of whom rate at the very bottom of the League of Conservation Voters list of environmentally sensitive members of Congress, based on their voting records.

Several western Washington rivers have been proposed for protection, including a number on the Olympic Peninsula. So far, this has been prevented from happening by a small group of well-organized pro-exploitation lobbyists. It may be time for Washingtonians to do a little of their own thinking in the realm of preserving rivers.

A decade ago Oregon added 40 of its rivers to the national system and doubled its state system from 11 to 22 protected rivers. Washington, with more rivers, has only a small fraction of rivers protected from exploitation. A grass-roots movement has begun among paddlers and fishermen in the state to add several Washington rivers to the federal system.

More than half of the states have their own scenic rivers programs.

Red osier dogwood is a common riverside plant in western Washington.

Washington is one of those states, but it has only one river in its program, the Skykomish, and the designation is largely meaningless. It names part of the Skykomish as a state scenic river but gives it virtually no protection. Is Oregon so rich that it can offer significant protection to more than 20 state-designated rivers and more than 40 federally designated rivers? Are we so poor that we cannot?

The state legislature has taken some encouraging action in recent legislative sessions toward enlarging the State Scenic Waterways System, but if every paddler in the state gets involved, Washington can become a leader in river protection.

RIVER ETIQUETTE

River etiquette refers to manners on the river. It has nothing to do with rules or regulations, liabilities or laws; it involves common sense and sensitivity to others—on the river, on the shore, at campsites and picnic areas, at put-ins and take-outs. It includes respect for private property and public property, for wildlife and the natural environment, and for other people. In essence it involves following the golden rule: do unto others as you would have them do unto you. It is a matter of following conventions, of practicing common-sense thoughtfulness. It can be applied in many ways:

- ◆ If boaters would like to have a clean place to camp or stop for lunch, they should clean up their own campsite or lunch stop area when they leave (it will be clean for the next party, and it may encourage them to follow a pattern that will benefit all river users);
- ◆ If boaters want a quiet, peaceful river trip, they shouldn't play the boom box (in fact, they shouldn't even bring it along) or practice raucous behavior on the river;

- If boaters want the privilege of launching from or stopping at someone's private property, they should ask permission first and then keep the property clean;
- If boaters want to be treated with respect by fishermen, they should treat fishermen with respect (they shouldn't spoil fishing by paddling over fishing holes or slaloming through fishing lines);
- If boaters want a natural river, they shouldn't spoil it with litter or soap suds or apple cores or orange peelings.

Just be a decent human being. Ask permission to use private property or tribal lands; follow regulations where and when they exist; use common sense.

Beginning at the beginning, boaters should take up as little time and space as possible at the put-in. They should be well enough organized and sensitive to other boaters and other river users so that they don't intrude upon anyone else's space or time.

On the river be aware of other boaters and other river users, including fishermen in and on the water. Boaters should ask how they can least disturb fishermen by going to the left or right of them. Do not crowd other boats or intrude on groups of boaters; do not engage them in water fights or otherwise disturb their experience.

Paddlers should not intrude on other parties stopped for lunch or to camp, but they should be courteous and responsive. The other party may appreciate the insights and expertise of another river user. But thoughtful river users won't overstay their welcome.

Rope swings provide summertime play on many western Washington rivers.

At the take-out, move quickly off the ramp and out of the way of other river users. Consolidate gear, and as at the put-in, take up as little time and space as possible. Don't rush, but conversely, don't loiter.

And don't litter. Trash and garbage, bottles and cans don't belong in the river or on its banks. River users should carry out their own debris so no one else has to clean up after them. In fact, boaters can help clean up after others less careful and sensitive, thereby leaving the river a better place than before and setting an example for others.

A Native American fisherman displays his catch from the Duwamish River.

When it comes to private property, do not trespass. The waters of the state are public, but their shorelines may not be. To be safe, assume that the banks of all rivers are in private ownership. Some, of course, are public lands: public parks, Department of Natural Resources (DNR) lands, Department of Wildlife properties, and highway rights-of-way (the area under bridges is generally public land).

Ask permission to use someone's private access, picnic area, or campsite. Know that the river below mean high water mark is usually public land, but some old railroad rights-of-way may not be. Don't press the point with an irate landowner. Because of the popularity of steelhead fishing in western Washington, state agencies have acquired river access in numerous places. Such access points, if they are reliable and accessible (some aren't), are generally marked on the maps in this book. These require a conservation, fishing, or hunting license for each user. They are not free to the general public.

Native American lands are a special kind of private property. Some tribes welcome boaters, especially those in human-muscle-powered crafts, but others discourage non–Native American boaters on the reservations or require a special license or guide. Ask permission to use the rivers that flow through Native American lands, and respect the tribal decision. Be sure to go through the tribal authority; an individual tribal member might grant permission and another tribal member might take exception to the permission granted. Stick to official channels.

Public access is a big issue on some rivers: the Humptulips, for example. A favorite steelhead fishing river, it once had numerous access points on private lands, but many of them were recently closed by landowners on the Humptulips in a political power-play growing out of the county's restrictions on the mining of gravel in streambeds. Other landowners have closed their property to boaters due to litter problems. It pays to be a good neighbor on the river.

TIDES

A number of the river segments discussed in this book involve saltwater tidal areas, the lower reaches of rivers and their mouths that are impacted by twice-daily tides. Yet there is another kind of tide that boaters must consider: the rising and falling tides of reservoir-release rivers.

Any dammed river will be impacted by the flows released from its upstream dams. This is especially evident on the Skagit and the Cowlitz Rivers, but to some extent also on the Cedar, Green, Nisqually, and Wynoochee Rivers. Be sure to read any posted warnings and check the river-flow information available on NOAA's River Hotline (see **Appendix B: Recommended Resources, Weather Information**).

Pacific Ocean tides differ from Puget Sound tides, which vary from north to south and with the distance from the Strait of Juan de Fuca. The Columbia River is impacted by reservoir releases from both upstream dams and the Pacific Ocean tidal flow, which impacts the river's lower tributaries (including the Grays River/Seal Slough/Deep River complex covered in this book).

In running many of these segments, boaters need to understand a few basic facts about tides. There are two high tides and two low tides each day (most days); one of each is higher than the other. The four tides are known as higher high water, lower high water, higher low water, and lower low water. Make sense? The height of the tide is measured in feet above mean lower low water (zero). A higher high water of 6.0 following a lower low water of 2.0 means a fluctuation of 8 vertical feet.

Since the tidal (lunar) day is roughly 50 minutes longer than the solar day, the tides change by nearly an hour each day, becoming later and later until they advance to early the next day. It is important to differentiate between tides and tidal currents. Tides are indicated by the high and low vertical rising and falling of the water; tidal currents are the horizontal movements of the water as the tides fluctuate. Ebb is the seaward movement of water; flood is the inward (landward) movement.

Slack water occurs after the tides change, that is, after they reach their high or low point. That time varies with several factors and can rarely be judged exactly for a given point. Barometric pressure, wind direction, and velocity all alter actual on-site tide levels, and any constriction in the flow of the tide may slightly alter its level in a given area. It may take an hour or two in some areas before a paddler can really tell what the tide is doing.

That's why it is important to gather as much information as possible before trying tidal areas. Both tide and current tables are useful in calculating the height of the tide or its ultimate ebb. Detailed tide and tidal current tables published annually by the National Ocean Survey are available at most nautical supply stores and a few boating shops. For best information, use nautical charts in conjunction with tide and current tables to judge the specific tide levels for the desired river mouth.

The pocket-sized tide table booklets available from many fishing and boating retailers as an advertising tool or at a nominal cost are useful, but they say little about currents; nor do they give very specific information about the time it takes the tide to turn in a given area.

Most of the river segments described in this book involve only minimal tidal paddling, but saltwater reaches where currents are strong can be dangerous. The maximum danger is normally at minimal tide, that is, at the greatest ebb, when the draw-down of the tide is accentuated by the flow of the river. The currents under such circumstances—especially in shallow water and in constricted areas—can be violent. Avoid such areas at such times by consulting tide (and if possible, current) tables.

MAPS AND CHARTS

Maps (USGS) and charts (NOAA) where available are suggested for each river segment in this book, but they will do little good unless paddlers know (or learn) how to read them. Sketch maps are also provided for every river segment in the book. Each map in this book is oriented to be read traveling downstream. That is, the top of the map is downstream; the bottom is the upstream starting point. Directions such as "river left" or "river right" and references to the left or right bank also are based on a downstream-facing orientation.

River miles (RM) are measured from the mouth of the river. Thus on the Stillaguamish, the main stem is measured from where it flows into Port Susan. Since the South Fork is considered the river's main stem, the river mile measurements on the South Fork above its confluence with the North Fork continue to climb in sequence. But the North Fork mileage begins at the confluence (that is, at the mouth of the North Fork), which is its RM 0.

In some cases a river will split around an island or into a series of sloughs (the Snohomish, for example), and the different channels or sloughs will vary in length. The main channel is given the official total mileage. If, for example, the distance around an island is 2 miles by the main channel and 2.3 by the other, the accumulated distance to the head of the island from the tip will be 2 miles, not 2.3 miles.

The sketch maps, which include river miles, show only the basic details that help locate the take-out and put-in points and alternate accesses. In a few cases an adjacent map helps identify the shuttle route.

The most detailed maps are USGS topographic maps, available from some local map stores, a few paddle shops, and the U.S. Geological Survey (see **Appendix B: Recommended Resources, Map Sources**). Although 7.5' maps are more detailed, for some of the river segments in this book, only 15' maps are available. However, USGS maps may not show the rivers as well as the maps found in the *Catalog of Washington Streams and Salmon Utilization*, published by the Washington Department of Fisheries in 1975. (The road information on these maps is less reliable, however, as many of the road names and numbers have been changed.)

Local chambers of commerce and some commercial establishments produce fairly reliable area maps that may be useful in finding river accesses (Grays Harbor map of Aberdeen, Hoquiam, and Cosmopolis, for example, covers important accesses for four river segments). Milt Keizer's *Complete Handbook on Washington Steelheading* (1998) includes reasonably accurate maps showing river access points. Many parks and recreation agencies produce good maps that include river access points (for example, 11 river segments in this book can be followed on the King County Parks and Recreation map).

County maps published by the Washington Department of Transportation show rivers in reasonable detail and provide the off-river background needed to follow the shuttle routes. The commercial map of Washington State recently published by DeLorme Mapping Company is also very useful.

Charts and maps are available from Metsker Maps and Captain's Nautical in Seattle. In the realm of cyberspace, maps on CD-ROM have become available that obviate most printed maps. Many of them offer excellent detail. They can be printed out for specific river segments, protected in plastic sleeves, and used repeatedly for that stretch.

NORTH PUGET SOUND

◆

1 DAKOTA CREEK/CALIFORNIA CREEK

Location	near Blaine, northwest of Bellingham
Distance	1 to 3 miles each creek
River Time	2 to 3 hours each creek
Map	Blaine (7.5'); NOAA Chart: 18421
Best Season	all year
Hazards	tides, wind on the saltwater
Shuttle	5 miles at most on paved roads, but no shuttle needed
Rating	Class I, Tidal

Dakota Creek and California Creek both flow into Drayton Harbor just south of the U.S.-Canada border. The harbor created by Semiahmoo Spit is well protected for canoe and kayak paddling. Its mud flats offer excellent bird-watching, and the harbor provides fine views of Mount Baker and the nearby Canadian peaks. The creeks themselves allow access to amazing wildlife habitat for so urban an area. This is a quiet trip through a riverside community, a mix of majestic old homes and new condominiums that blend well into the picturesque surroundings.

Access. The easiest access, both launch site and take-out, is at Semiahmoo Park on the spit. From this put-in, paddlers can make a round trip by water, 2 miles each way, to the mouth of either creek and back (no land shuttle). The creek mouths are several hundred yards apart, but at low tide a mud flat will force a detour of more than a mile between the two.

An alternate starting (and ending) point is the left bank of California Creek at its mouth, just west of the California Creek bridge on Drayton Harbor Road. There is very limited shoulder parking here. If this access is used, it is best to arrange a shuttle for an exit pickup rather than to leave a car parked at the access. The mouth of Dakota Creek can be reached from here by paddling across the eastern edge of the harbor.

A third frequently used access that avoids the saltwater approach is a put-in on Dakota Creek under the I-5 bridge east of the Old S.R. 99 bridge. An obvious trail leads from the highway to the river.

Driving Directions. Take Exit 274 off I-5 3 miles south of the U.S.-Canada border, head toward Old S.R. 99, then turn south onto Blaine Road. Half a mile after crossing the Dakota Creek bridge, turn right onto Drayton Harbor Road (almost immediately you will cross California Creek) and

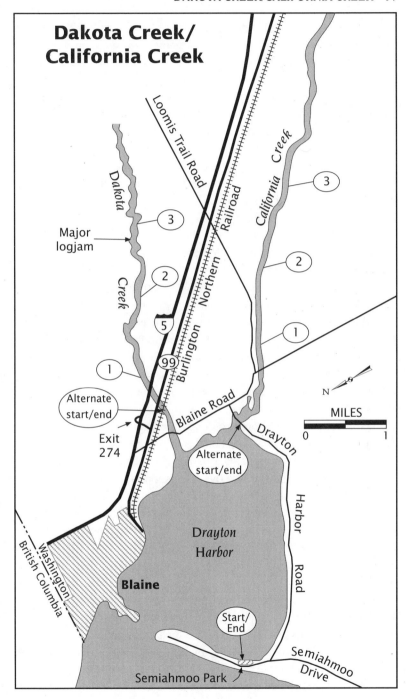

Dakota Creek/ California Creek

Loomis Trail Road

Burlington Northern Railroad

California Creek

Dakota Creek

Major logjam

Alternate start/end

Exit 274

Blaine Road

Drayton

Alternate start/end

Drayton Harbor

Harbor Road

MILES
0   1

N

Blaine

Washington
British Columbia

Start/ End

Semiahmoo Drive

Semiahmoo Park

follow it westward along the southern edge of Drayton Harbor to Semiahmoo Drive (from the left). Turn right to Semiahmoo Spit at Semiahmoo Park. Park here and launch onto the bay on the east side of the spit.

For access at the mouth of California Creek, pull off to the right on Drayton Harbor Road immediately after crossing California Creek—just after the turnoff from Blaine Road.

To find the Dakota Creek access, head southeast on Old S.R. 99 from the I-5 exit mentioned above. The access is reached by parking on the right shoulder, on the west side of the road, north of the bridge across Dakota Creek, then bushwhacking along a faint trail between the highway and the railroad tracks down to the north bank of Dakota Creek. Since it is a tough haul back up, it may make sense to plan a take-out at the mouth of California Creek, a 1-mile shuttle, round trip, or on Semiahmoo Spit, a 5-mile shuttle (see above).

Description. The navigable portions of both creeks are tidal. A good way to explore them is by paddling (or poling) upstream with the incoming tide, then following the outgoing tide back to the harbor. The eastern portion of the harbor is shallow, a mud flat exposed at low tide—forcing paddlers who would explore both rivers in one day to detour out into the harbor at low tide, not an altogether unpleasant experience because of the bird life on the mud flats and the marine life in the water (including migrating salmon during certain seasons). Bottom fish and crabs scurry along the eelgrass, and shorebirds—spotted sandpipers, dunlins, sanderlings, wandering tattlers—feed on the exposed mud flats.

Dakota Creek flows primarily with the tide, except during heavy rains, and the tidal flow is strong. The riverbed is virtually unnavigable at low tide. The lower reaches of the creek are developed. There is a shipyard near the mouth, then several bridges—Blaine Road, the Burlington Northern Railroad, Old 99, then the double spans of I-5—and finally homes set back from the creek. Within half a mile, the creek narrows, wilderness begins to encroach upon the stream, and the experience becomes more intimate.

Barnacles encrust logs and dock pilings—even living trees—and there are raccoon tracks, deer in the flesh, great blue herons, nesting Canada geese. Boreal birds abound. There are high grassy banks where geese rest in the summer sun; blackberry bushes festooned with fresh fruit in the late summer and early fall hang over the creek. Chamomile, smelling like pineapple, grows wild, ready to be picked for tea.

Dakota Creek at low tide

Forge up the creek as far as the tide or fallen trees will allow, stop for lunch on one of the grassy banks, and let the tide turn. Then return to the harbor with the pull of the tide. Explore the other creek—or call it a day.

California Creek is broader than Dakota Creek in its lower reaches. Seals occasionally follow fish into the tidal basin just above the bridge at the mouth of California Creek. Numerous waterfowl congregate here as well. Flanked by new condominiums that are soon left behind, the lower creek quickly gives way to more open country and occasional views of Mount Baker.

The creek curves, crossed by low bridges, flanked by Loomis Trail roads. Channelized in earlier days, it flows almost straight for a couple of miles. It is more open than Dakota Creek, more developed; but geese and gulls are here, as well as ducks and raptors. Deer and raccoons visit at dawn and dusk, and the great blue heron is always nearby.

Even though roads cross and parallel California Creek, paddling on its tidal waters offers an opportunity to get away from the work-a-day world. An early-morning run of either creek can be day-breaking glorious, and a late-afternoon trip may reward the paddler with a spectacular sunset.

2 LUMMI RIVER

Location	Lummi Indian Reservation northwest of Bellingham
Distance	3 miles
River Time	1 to 2 hours
Map	Lummi Bay (7.5'); NOAA Charts: 18423, 18424
Best Season	all year, best birding in winter
Hazards	low water, tides, man-made debris
Shuttle	less than 5 miles, paved and gravel roads, but no shuttle needed
Rating	Class I, Tidal

The Lummi River, marked "Red River" on some maps, is a high-water overflow channel of the Nooksack River. Channelized and diked, it may be an unappealing river at first glance, but it makes an excellent bird-watching trip—especially in the winter, when it has everything from snowy owls and both trumpeter and whistling swans to peregrine falcons and bald eagles, a dozen species of ducks, and both Canada and snow geese. It offers views of Mount Baker and the Canadian peaks and refreshing winds off the Strait of Georgia. **Note:** Permission to boat the Lummi River must be obtained from the Lummi Indian Tribal Council, 2616 Kwina Road, Bellingham, WA 98226-9298, or call 360-384-1489.

Access. Either put-in or take-out points are continuous for most of its length from adjacent roads that parallel the river: North Red River Road and South Red River Road on opposite sides of the Lummi River. It is possible to launch a lightweight boat almost anywhere along the runnable route, but the unpaved lower end of South Red River Road is badly choked with tall weeds in summer and early fall, making access difficult.

Driving Directions. To reach the Lummi River, take S.R. 540 off I-5 (Exit 260) and travel west on Slater Road to Haxton Way. Turn left (south) on Haxton to North Red River Road, and turn right—or cross the Lummi River and turn right onto South Red River Road (the two roads embrace the river). Access to the river can be made from either road.

Description. The Lummi River, named for the Lummi Indian Tribe on whose lands the river flows for all of its runnable course, offers many fine views of Mount Baker and of the Canadian peaks to the north. It flows through open country, for the most part, with its upper reaches bordered by thickets. Wintering snow geese and trumpeter and whistling swans

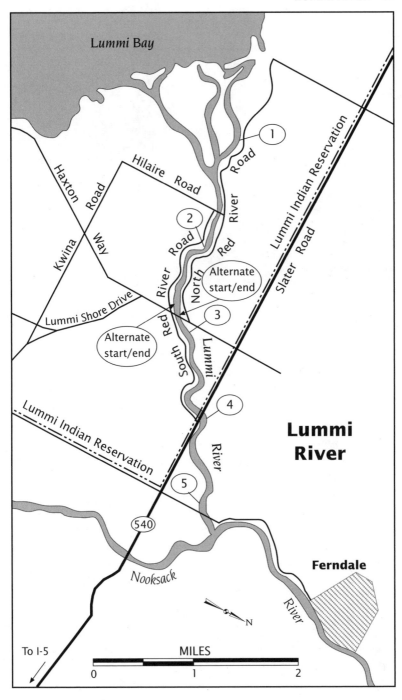

Lummi River

utilize the area, as do numerous raptorial species; it is a bird-watcher's paradise.

This can easily be a round-trip river; no shuttle is necessary if tide charts are consulted and followed. Launch near the junction of Haxton Way with either of the river-flanking roads and paddle southwestward past muskrat dens, nesting ducks, feeding pheasants, soaring raptors, and fishing great blue heron. A model-airplane flying field lies on the left bank in the first mile; don't be surprised to see and hear a variety of miniature planes.

Unfortunately, some of the riverbank has been used as a dumping ground; there are unsightly areas especially along the upper reaches of this small river. But its tidal waters are delightful, despite the fact that the river is diked. The Lummi delta attracts numerous species of bay ducks, waterfowl, and shorebirds, and great blue herons and bald eagles often vie for perching places among the pilings remaining from decaying developments along the shoreline.

Blackberries cover much of the dike, offering succulent snacks during the late summer and early fall. Winter birding is ideal, but spring migrants also stop along the Lummi. On windy days or when the tide is turning, the delta can be dangerous, but its many channels and small bays still offer relatively protected paddling.

3 NOOKSAK RIVER: EVERSON TO LYNDEN

Location	north of Bellingham
Distance	8.5 miles to Lynden, 18 miles to Ferndale
River Time	70 minutes to Lynden, 3 hours to Ferndale
Maps	Lawrence, Suma, Lynden, Bertrand Creek, Ferndale (7.5'), Lynden (15')
Best Season	all year, except at flood stage
Hazards	fast, cold water; logjams; sweepers
Shuttle	8.1 miles to Lynden, 22 miles to Ferndale on paved roads
Rating	Class II-

The Nooksack River below the confluence of its major forks is a cold, swift river that can be dangerous even to experienced paddlers. Coming off the glaciers on Mount Baker, the river is usually milky in summer and fall due to the glacial flour it carries. Often clear in midwinter, it offers the finest views of Mount Baker of any river in this book. This segment flows through farmlands, where the smells of berries, new-mown hay, silage, and manure mingle with the river smells (from spawned-out salmon in late fall to fresh mountain snowmelt in spring). This segment is part of the annual Ski to Sea Race (a multi-event race from a headwater ski slope to the mouth of the river at Bellingham Bay).

Access. From a limited-parking pullout on S.R. 544 between Everson and Strandell, there is access beneath the railroad bridge on the left (south) bank at RM 23.8. The best launch site is from a road leading to the river from S.R. 544 a few dozen yards west of the junction at the west edge of Everson, just east of the sharp (right-angle) curve on Trap Line Road.

From here downstream the river is fast, but it is broad enough to allow paddlers ample room to maneuver around and away from obstacles. While there are several possible access points in the next few miles, a public fishing access (RM 14.7) off Guide Meridian Road (S.R. 539) southwest of Lynden offers a good take-out for paddle craft, although it has no boat ramp.

For parties who want a longer run, the river is much the same to Ferndale, another 9.5 miles downstream. There is a well-developed access with a boat ramp just south of Ferndale (RM 5.8), which—from the Everson put-in—makes an 18-mile run. At this river's rate of flow, that is still an easy day's run.

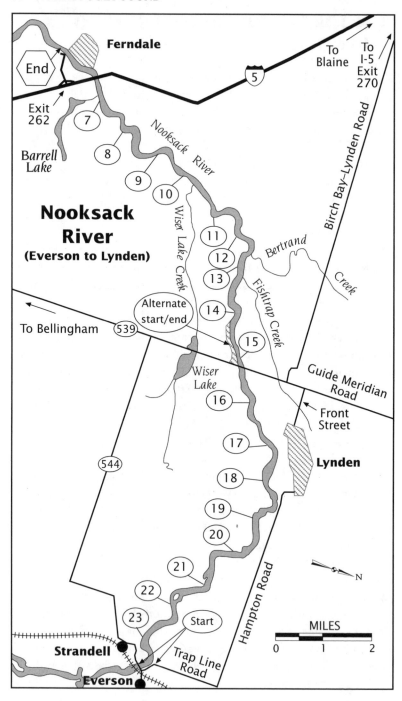

Ferndale

End

Exit 262

To Blaine

To I-5 Exit 270

Barrell Lake

7

8

Nooksack River

9

10

Nooksack River
(Everson to Lynden)

Wiser Lake Creek

11

12

13

Bertrand Creek

Fishtrap Creek

Alternate start/end

14

To Bellingham

539

15

Wiser Lake

Guide Meridian Road

16

Front Street

17

Lynden

544

18

19

20

21

22

23

Start

Hampton Road

N

Strandell

Everson

Trap Line Road

MILES
0   1   2

Driving Directions. For a take-out at Ferndale, use the Ferndale exit off I-5 (Exit 262) and head southwest. Just before reaching the Nooksack River bridge, turn left onto Hovander Road, then turn right almost immediately into the public fishing access jointly funded by the Whatcom County Parks Department and the Washington Department of Wildlife.

For the take-out on S.R. 539 southwest of Lynden, take S.R. 539 north out of Bellingham (I-5 Exit 256) to the public fishing access immediately south of the river. An alternate approach is to take the Birch Bay–Lynden Road exit east off I-5 (Exit 270) northwest of Bellingham; at S.R. 539, several miles east, turn right and drive the 1.5 miles to the public fishing access mentioned above, immediately south of the river.

For the launch site at Everson, take S.R. 539 north from this public fishing access to Front Street; turn right into Lynden and head east through town, taking Hampton Road toward Hampton, a tiny town north of Everson. At Trap Line Road, turn right and follow it south to the river at a sharp curve. Or continue onto Main Street in Everson, then right onto S.R. 544, which crosses the river.

The parking area is on the right (west) side of the southbound lane, immediately southwest of the bridge. To achieve river access, cross the northbound lane of traffic and follow a steep use-maintained trail between the road and the railroad bridge to the river. The put-in is on the left bank of the river under either of the bridges (highway or railroad), depending on how the last high water has distributed the sand, silt, and debris.

Description. The main Nooksack is cold and swift, a gray river even in summer under blue skies. Its high rating is due primarily to the fact that mishaps on the main Nooksack may have serious consequences because of the fast-flowing cold water. During winter and spring, when it has less glacial flour, it has a lovely greenish hue. The speed of the current is remarkable; at moderate water levels, paddlers can average 7 miles per hour without really trying.

The river meanders among gravel islands through agricultural land where head-high corn and berry fields (blueberries, raspberries, strawberries) line the bank, and the smell of fresh-cut hay mingles with the odor of animal waste. A dairy barn appears, a farmhouse, a wall of close-set pilings to deflect the river. Wild blackberries grow along the riverbank, and foxgloves, tansy, and Queen Anne's lace enliven the shoreline with their voluntary blossoms.

Tractor sounds mingle with bird songs and the music of the river.

Pilings along the Nooksack protect the bank from erosion.

Goldfinches (Washington's state bird), crows, song sparrows, red-winged blackbirds, red-tailed hawks, spotted sandpipers, robins, great blue herons, and several species of swallows populate the river in midsummer. Cottonwoods, willows, and alders make up the taller vegetation.

More barns and houses appear, and a few retaining walls of riprap and pilings protect the banks from erosion, especially at high water. There are logs and snags in the river (potential hazards), vast gravel bars, and good bird habitat. One canoeist finds the easy parts of the Nooksack "not scenic enough, but the birding potential is high." But so is the potential for views of Mount Baker; and the river environment, while not wilderness, offers much to enjoy, not the least of which is the fast-flowing current.

4 NOOKSACK RIVER: SOUTH FORK

Location	south of Deming (Saxon to Van Zandt vicinity)
Distance	8 to 11 miles
River Time	3 to 4 hours
Maps	Acme, Deming (7.5')
Best Season	late spring, early summer
Hazards	logjams, sweepers, high water
Shuttle	8.1 and 10.6 miles on paved roads
Rating	Class II

The Nooksack's South Fork, a perfect river for tubing or canoeing, parallels S.R. 9. The spectacular tips of the Twin Sisters can be seen from the river, and while the course of the river flows through farmlands, much of it is well wooded. There are riffles and mild rapids, temporary challenges to boaters, with few serious consequences except at high water. The South Fork is clear, the warmest of the three Nooksack forks, and offers good practice for more challenging runs elsewhere.

Access. The best put-in is at a bridge on Saxon Road about 1.5 miles southeast of Saxon at a wading and picnic spot that is a summer favorite among local residents. The launch site is from a sandy beach immediately upstream from the bridge on river right.

The best take-out is off Strand Road between Acme and Van Zandt, a public access area with a huge sand-and-gravel beach, the most popular summer recreation area in the whole valley.

An alternate take-out is the road right-of-way beneath the Potter Road bridge just west of Van Zandt. However, this is a relatively poor place to take out because the only parking is along the narrow roadside. An alternative launch or take-out site, River View Park in Acme, lies on the river's left bank immediately upstream of and adjacent to the North Fork Nooksack (S.R. 9) bridge at RM 8.7.

There is access on the right bank near the mouth of the South Fork, on a huge gravel bar at the confluence beneath the South Fork Nooksack (S.R. 9) bridge across the main Nooksack. However, this access often requires a four-wheel-drive vehicle because of the rough access road, and it may mean a long carry from the right bank of the South Fork, which can be steep and unstable at some water levels.

Driving Directions. To reach the put-in, turn east off S.R. 9 about 2 miles south of Acme, onto Saxon Road. Travel 2.1 miles (passing through Saxon) to a bridge across the South Fork, where the paving ends. There is limited roadside parking here. Park east of the bridge (the road is gravel) if possible and carry the craft down to the right bank of the river immediately upstream of the bridge.

To reach any of three possible take-outs, return to S.R. 9 and head north through Acme. The river flows beneath the highway just north of Acme and continues northward on the west side of the road for the remainder of this run. About 3 miles north of Acme (2 miles south of Van Zandt), turn left (west) on Strand Road and drive to its end, a popular local summer sunning and picnicking area with a broad beach, an ideal take-out for an 8-mile run.

The second possibility, which involves an additional 3 miles on the river, is a roadside take-out beneath the bridge just west of Van Zandt. To

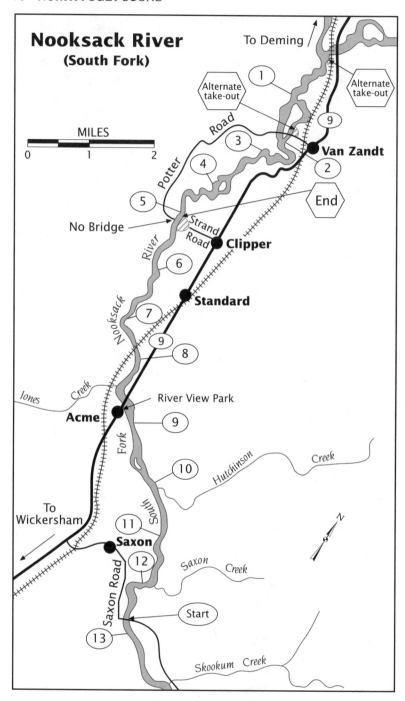

Nooksack River
(South Fork)

To Deming

Alternate take-out

Alternate take-out

MILES

0   1   2

Potter Road

1

3

4

9

● Van Zandt

2

5

End

No Bridge

Strand Road

● Clipper

6

Nooksack River

● Standard

7

9

8

Jones Creek

● Acme

River View Park

9

Fork

10

Hutchinson Creek

To Wickersham

South

11

● Saxon

12

Saxon Creek

N

Saxon Road

Start

13

Skookum Creek

reach this less-desirable access, drive north to Van Zandt, turning left (west) onto Potter Road. There is only roadside parking here, with private property on both sides; only the road right-of-way allows access.

A third possibility is to run all the way to the mouth of the South Fork, another 2 miles (total from the put-in, 13 miles). Since the main Nooksack is extremely swift here, a good Class III river, be sure to beach before reaching the confluence. Access is on river right, where there is a huge gravel bar accessible from S.R. 9 by a dirt (or mud) road that is often extremely rough. The turnoff is on the west side of S.R. 9 (between the highway and the railroad tracks) about 200 yards south of the bridge across the main Nooksack.

Description. The South Fork is shallow in summer, clear and delightful, full of tubing teenagers on a warm sunny day. The river may flow through agricultural land, but the farms are unobtrusive, shielded by forest. These same forests no doubt contribute to the extensive debris in the river. There are logjams, sweepers, and snags—occasionally trees all the way across the river—that could be problems at higher, swifter water levels. In late summer the biggest problem is low water.

The river flows over riffles, forming pools and chutes as it meanders its way slowly, occasionally swiftly, northwestward for the first 4.5 miles to the S.R. 9 bridge just north of Acme. River View Park has recently been developed on the left bank of the river just upstream from the bridge (this could easily become a river access point). The Twin Sisters peep over the eastern ridge a time or two in the next few miles.

Agricultural activities are more noticeable below Acme, but there is still plenty of forested riverbank, and the river continues to offer challenges in tight squeezes and a few sharp corners as timber debris litters the river. There is no bridge across the South Fork at Strand Road, as some maps indicate, but the access on river right at the west end of Strand Road is the best on the river.

Meandering through a couple of broad bends, the river slows perceptibly in the next few miles, forming more pools and becoming more open and more obviously agricultural. Downstream from the Potter Road bridge (a poor take-out), the railroad tracks approach the river as it continues to bend broadly and become more woodsy again until it reaches its confluence with the main Nooksack.

The South Fork is a mellow river on a warm, sunny day. Boaters might expect to see ospreys, killdeer, kingfishers, spotted sandpipers, violet-green swallows, and beaver sign. There are plenty of gravel bars and

Logjams and low water levels narrow the South Fork of the Nooksack.

sandy beaches at midsummer low water levels. At high water levels it might not be as safe a run, and under overcast skies, not as delightful.

5 SKAGIT RIVER MOUTH

Location	south of Mount Vernon
Distance	3 to 17 miles
River Time	2 to 5 hours, depending on tides
Maps	Utsalady, Conway (7.5'); NOAA Chart: 18423
Best Season	all year, especially winter
Hazards	strong tides and currents, fog
Shuttle	none needed or practical, paved roads for alternate accesses
Rating	Class II-, Tidal

The mouth of the Skagit River divides into a North Fork (actually more of a west fork) and a South Fork. Either branch can be run, but the South Fork is more accessible. It also offers better access to the Skagit Flats, where numerous migratory birds winter, including tens of thousands of snow geese. Bald eagles, trumpeter and whistling swans, and numerous ducks and geese are common winter visitors. Year-round residents include great blue herons and great horned owls, as well as shorebirds and bay ducks. The tidal flats also offer interesting marine life.

Access. The best access to the lower South Fork is from the Skagit Wildlife Recreation Area on southern Fir Island, southwest of Conway off Mann Road. A boat ramp near a major parking area offers direct access to Freshwater Slough, the most direct route to the Skagit Flats.

There is also public access at Conway on the South Fork before it splits into several sloughs and on the right bank of the river just above the branching of the main forks southwest of Mount Vernon, at RM 8.5. It is possible to launch at Edgewater Park in Mount Vernon, from the west (right) bank at RM 11.2. A public boat ramp with plenty of parking lies immediately upstream of Conway Bridge on the left bank. At Milltown on

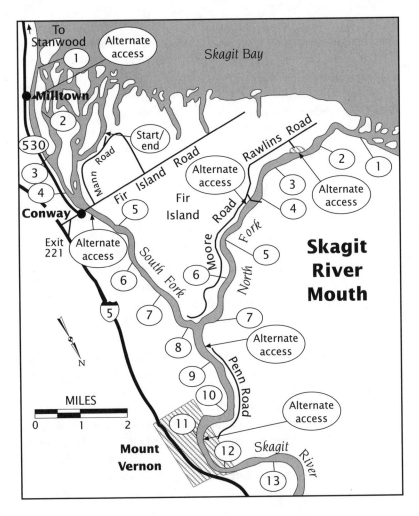

the Pioneer Highway between Conway and Stanwood, another primitive boat ramp at RM 1.4 offers additional access to the South Fork.

There is commercial access at Blake's Marina, on the south side of the North Fork at RM 2.5 off Rawlins Road, and public access on the south side of the North Fork at RM 4.2 off Moore Road.

Driving Directions. Take the Conway exit (Exit 221) off I-5 and head west through Conway and across the Skagit Bridge on Fir Island Road. Turn left almost immediately onto Mann Road, which follows the Skagit Dike south, then west to the Skagit Wildlife Recreation Area. The parking area is left of the headquarters area, and the boat ramp lies beyond (over the dike from) the parking area.

An alternate approach is to continue west on Fir Island Road to the other end of Mann Road, which T's in from the left about 2 miles west of the Skagit River Bridge. Follow the signs to the Skagit Wildlife Recreation Area mentioned above.

Description. At the Skagit Wildlife Recreation Area launch site, the river is deep and swift; a glacial green much of the year, the water is cold and surprisingly clear. It is a salmon and steelhead river and gets heavy fishing pressure, but when the fishing season is closed and the migratory birds are on the Skagit Flats, it is a boater's paradise, even in midwinter.

Paddlers should check weather reports carefully; winter storms can seriously impact Skagit Bay, the saltwater body embracing the flats.

The lower river is well wooded for the first mile or so; saltwater intrusion seems not to adversely affect the alders and cottonwoods that, with a few conifers and assorted shrubbery, form most of the riverside vegetation. Great horned owls congregate in the taller trees along the river even during daylight hours; paddlers may see as many as a dozen owls in the first mile of downriver paddling. As paddlers near the mouth of Freshwater Slough, the tall trees fade away and the highest vegetation may be the roots of stumps lying about on the flats—as often as not they serve as perches for bald eagles or great blue herons. Tall grasses also replace the tall trees for a few hundred yards, then even the grasses give way to pickleweed and other salt-tolerant species.

The pull of the tide accelerates the flow of the river current, which may move at several miles an hour. This flow enhances the downriver movement of paddle craft but, conversely, is extremely difficult to paddle against. It may be wise to carry a pole, for the bottom is shallow and sandy or gravelly in many places, offering good purchase for poling against the

The commercial boat launch area at Blake's Landing on the North Fork of the Skagit River responds to tidal fluctuations.

current, should that become necessary. It is better to check the tide charts first.

Once out on the flats, paddlers will see the thousands of snow geese they have been hearing for many minutes. The myriad birds may fly en masse, then settle down to a new feeding area, all the while making a deafening cacophony. The water may move swiftly out from under the craft. Paddlers should remain aware of the flow, lest they become stranded on the flats. There are numerous tiny channels flowing in dendritic patterns, draining the mud flats. Spending several hours stuck in the mud can be decidedly unpleasant, especially in midwinter.

There is also the possibility of becoming lost in the fog. A compass should be standard equipment for any saltwater venture by canoe. (On one trip to the Skagit Flats, paddlers were fog-bound for more than an hour. They kept their direction by compass and by the flow of water beneath the canoe. When the fog finally lifted, they were right where they'd planned to be.)

The numerous channels and branches of the Skagit Flats lend themselves to confusion. Be sure to watch the route, selecting certain stumps and promontories as guideposts. It is easy to get lost on the flats. For a first trip, it may be best to join an established group that includes people who have been out before.

When the tide turns, it takes a while for the current to begin to flow upstream with any force, but it will do so eventually, taking the paddlers back to where they started—if they selected the right route. When the river is high, the upstream current created by the tide may not be as strong as desired; but given time and paddle power, the craft will make it back.

To make a 17-mile loop around Fir Island requires reading tides carefully. For instance, paddlers could paddle northwest across the face of the flats; find a channel leading into the North Fork, and follow the North Fork upstream 7.3 miles to its confluence with the South Fork; travel down the South Fork to the right-hand channel around the east side of the island just below the bridge at Conway; then pass 1.5 miles farther downstream to the put-in—all with careful consideration of the tides.

6 SKAGIT RIVER: ROCKPORT TO NORTH-SOUTH FORK

Location	between Rockport and Mount Vernon
Distance	60 miles composed of numerous shorter segments
River Time	4 to 5 miles per hour (12 to 15 hours)
Maps	Rockport, Conway (7.5')
Best Season	all year except when river is in flood
Hazards	logjams, woody debris anchored to enhance salmon habitat, snags and sweepers, cold and fast water, big river, high water
Shuttle	approximately the same as river segment by way of North Cascades Highway (S.R. 20) or South Skagit Highway and local access roads
Rating	Class I+ to II+ depending on segment, water level, and river condition

This 60-mile-long stretch of the lower Skagit River may be well-developed by most standards and therefore considered not worth paddling; but it is such a big, fast-moving river (and, because of its width, so open) that it offers wonderful views of the North Cascades upstream. It flows through agricultural lands between logged-over hillsides, but much of the watershed remains forested with second- or third-growth timber. The river is cool and clear, slightly green in color and full of deep pools and shallow riffles, lined by gravel bars and marked by occasional islands. A favorite steelhead stream, the entire stretch has so many access points that no

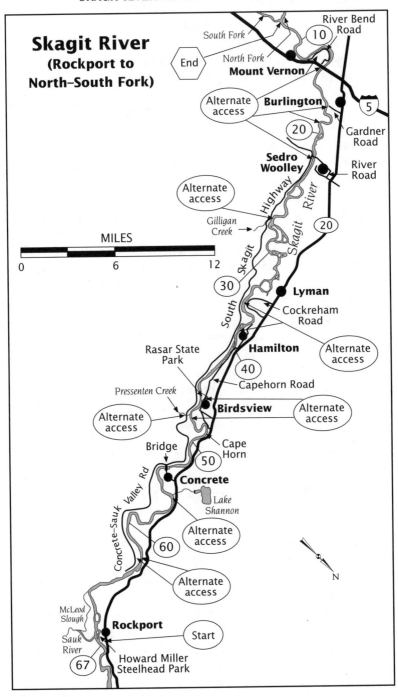

Skagit River
(Rockport to North–South Fork)

River Bend Road

South Fork

10

End

North Fork

Mount Vernon

Alternate access

Burlington

5

20

Gardner Road

Sedro Woolley

River Road

Highway

Alternate access

Skagit River

Gilligan Creek

Skagit

20

MILES

0   6   12

South

30

Lyman

Cockreham Road

Alternate access

Rasar State Park

Hamilton

40

Pressenten Creek

Capehorn Road

Alternate access

Birdsview

Alternate access

Bridge

Cape Horn

50

Concrete-Sauk Valley Rd

Concrete

Lake Shannon

Alternate access

60

Alternate access

McLeod Slough

Rockport

Start

Sauk River

67

Howard Miller Steelhead Park

N

stretch is more than 5 miles long, but you could run the whole distance in 2 or 3 days.

Access. The north side of the river roughly parallels S.R. 20, the North Cascades Highway, which serves as a main stem for numerous spur roads that lead to the river: Gardner Road at the east edge of Burlington; River Road, which leads to Riverfront RV Park in Sedro Woolley; Cockreham Road between Lyman and Hamilton; Capehorn Road in Hamilton and again in Birdsview. Rasar State Park, dedicated July 12, 1997, offers no boat ramp, but a paddler with a kayak or a lightweight canoe could readily launch here. An excellent access with limited parking lies at the mouth of the Baker River on South Everett Avenue at RM 56; four miles upstream, the John G. Young Landing off S.R. 20 just west of Sauk Store Road offers access but limited parking. Howard Miller Steelhead Park at Rockport is the ultimate access point for this segment.

By the bridge across the Skagit at Concrete, you can access both the Concrete–Sauk Valley Road upstream or the South Skagit Highway downstream, on the river's left bank. A boat ramp on the left bank of the Skagit at RM 62, immediately across from the Young Landing, was unmarked the spring of 1999; but it is an official state boat launch near the end of Skagit Ridge Road, within sight of milepost 7. (Local residents sometimes obscure or remove official signs so as to have the river access for themselves.) Other south-bank accesses lie at the mouth of Pressenten Creek (RM 46), at RM 36, between RM 26 and 27, at RM 19, and off River Bend Road at RM 13 and 14.5. If you're looking for a launch site, follow the steelheaders.

Driving Directions. For north-bank accesses, follow S.R. 20 eastward and take appropriate turnoffs to the river; for south-bank accesses, take the South Skagit Highway eastward and do the same thing. The only highway river crossing between Mount Vernon and Rockport is at Concrete.

Description. The Skagit is a big river, its upper reaches designated Wild and Scenic. At Rockport the river is normally clear except during heavy rains and at high water. Only a mile downstream the Sauk River, also Wild and Scenic in its upper reaches, enters from the left, causing a series of islands through which the Skagit braids its way downstream.

As McLeod Slough, part of the Sauk Delta, enters, the river turns sharply right to flow northwest for two and a half miles, then bends gradually left below a pair of islands and makes another sharp right at RM 59.5. In the spring of 1999 a major logjam nearly blocked the river at this point, which is visible from the South Skagit Road.

Skunk cabbage blooms in spring along the Skagit River, its bright green leaves contrasting with yellow blossoms.

At Concrete, reservoir-release water from Baker Lake and Lake Shannon on the Baker River may augment the flow. Five miles downstream the river bends sharply around Cape Horn, then straightens for a 5-mile run between Birdsview and Hamilton, the stretch that includes the new state park. The river is more gentle as it flows westward and loses gradient. Several islands split the river, and woody debris anchored near Hamilton by fisheries agencies for salmon habitat enhancement creates hazards for paddlers.

Four miles below Hamilton the river splits around a large island south of Lyman, meandering for the next 5 miles, braiding among more islands. At Gilligan Creek, which enters from the left, the river runs in a single channel for two miles before splitting around another large island near Sedro Woolley. The river has reached its tidal zone and paddlers will be bucking the tide if it's flooding, racing downstream if it's ebbing. On clear days, paddlers may catch glimpses of the San Juan Islands downstream at certain bends of the river. Development crowds in upon the river as it approaches Mount Vernon, where several take-outs offer alternative landings.

7 SKAGIT RIVER: COPPER CREEK TO ROCKPORT

Location	along North Cascades Highway (S.R. 20)
Distance	16 miles
River Time	3 to 4 hours
Maps	Marblemount (15'), Rockport (7.5')
Best Season	all year, eagle-watching in winter
Hazards	sweepers, logjams, cold and swift water, minor rapids (chutes)
Shuttle	16 miles, S.R. 20 most of the way
Rating	Class II

The Skagit River above Marblemount is clear and cold, with a greenish tint that gives it an almost pristine quality despite its reservoir-release origin. During autumn salmon migrations, especially in odd-numbered years (2001, 2003), this stretch of river is an impressive spawning stream. The streamside vegetation offers some of the finest autumn color in the North Cascades, and the fishing can be excellent, especially for sea-run cutthroat trout. It is a short stretch, with S.R. 20 along much of the route, but its roadless portions offer quiet solitude.

The segment below Marblemount is the famous eagle run, the stretch of river that has the greatest concentration of wintering bald eagles from November through February. As many as 173 eagles have been seen on a single 2-hour trip. Much of the shoreline is in private ownership, but much of the best eagle habitat is owned and protected by The Nature Conservancy in the Skagit River Bald Eagle Natural Area. Boaters are requested to launch between 10:00 A.M. and noon; to float quietly, minimizing movement and noise; and to refrain from stopping between Marblemount and Rockport.

Access. A launch site opposite the mouth of Copper Creek, within the Ross Lake National Recreation Area, offers access to the upper segment of this run. A popular boating access on Cascade River Road beneath the bridge at the edge of Marblemount provides an alternate take-out or launch site. Other accesses are possible along S.R. 20 between the put-in and the take-out.

The usual take-out is at Howard Miller Steelhead Park in Rockport, at a well-used boat ramp.

Driving Directions. To reach the take-out, drive to Rockport. Immediately

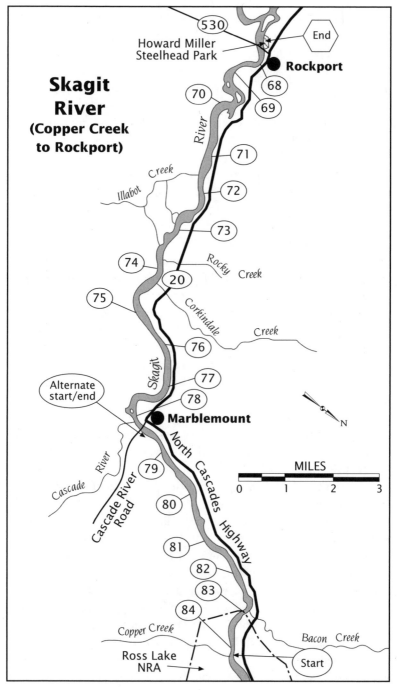

north of the S.R. 530 bridge across the Skagit, turn into Howard Miller Steelhead Park and drive west a hundred yards. The boat ramp is left of the road, on river right. To reach the put-in, drive east on S.R. 20 toward Newhalem. After crossing the bridge over Bacon Creek, which flows into the Skagit within sight of the bridge, you will enter the Ross Lake National Recreation Area. Within half a mile (between mileposts 111 and 112), on a slight bend to the left, there is a dirt road on the right. Turn right on that road and follow it to the river and the put-in, a rough ramp.

To reach the alternate access beneath the bridge in Marblemount, turn onto the Cascade River Road and cross the Skagit River bridge (visible before S.R. 20 makes its turn to the north). Immediately beyond the bridge, turn left onto a dirt road that doubles back north of the bridge and leads to the riverbank beneath the bridge on river left.

Description. The first mile of river is as peaceful and pristine as any, a favorite salmon-spawning stretch where vine maple and old man's beard offer colorful contrasts in the fall. At the end of the first mile, Bacon Creek comes in on the right, an important tributary for salmon spawning, where dozens of fish may be seen working their way upstream.

Below the Bacon Creek delta, the river swings to the left through a series of chutes, the only rapid on this stretch. The river broadens and shallows below this point, providing excellent spawning beds for the salmon, which can be seen in the clear water during the fall. An old cabin molders in the rain forest on the left bank.

The road follows the river rather closely for the remainder of this short trip, but the wooded left bank suggests a deeper wilderness than exists, and the bucolic setting conveys a peacefulness well worth experiencing. Even though the cozy little homes along the right bank represent development, it is both gentle and historical, for the most part, fitting into the natural world of the Skagit.

From the popular launch site under the bridge at the east edge of Marblemount, the river flows gently south past the mouth of the Cascade River—another element of the National Wild and Scenic Rivers System, as is this part of the Skagit. It turns west (forming a deep pool next to a modest cliff), then north, then west again in a big bend through Marblemount. It flows past the back yards of residences, through Studebaker Hole (named for the old car body once used as riprap that has lodged on the left bank), and over a little riffle as the river narrows to the left.

The road embraces the river for a mile, then drops away as the river flows beneath some high-power cables carrying electricity to Seattle from

Rafters drift the Skagit River through Marblemount.

the dams upstream. Beaver cuts appear near the power line crossing, as tiny Corkindale Creek flows in from the right (north). The left bank, privately owned, is lined with cabins and weekend homes. Rocky Creek comes in from the right at a point where many commercial river trips stop for lunch.

Immediately downstream, the major eagle concentration begins just as the river divides around an island. The usual route is to the right, but at higher water levels, the left-hand channel is possible, though it may have more logjams and sweepers than the main-flow right-hand route. In the next few miles the river splits and meanders, providing the eagles with daytime roosts and gravel bars for feeding on the spawned-out salmon that litter the shore in late fall and early winter.

The river approaches the road a time or two, then gathers itself together for a long, straight run (nearly 2 miles) below the mouth of Illabot Slough/Creek. It splits again, turns south through some choppy waves, then curves west once more before splitting into several channels (generally stay right) just above Rockport. Just after the river flows beneath the bridge (S.R. 530), there is a busy boat ramp on the right bank at Howard Miller Steelhead Park, the take-out.

In the spring, summer, and fall this stretch makes a pleasant paddle with a few mild rapids, but from early November through mid-March this stretch is the wintering grounds of bald eagles. Boating is permitted, but paddlers are requested to restrict their river use to specific hours (10:00 A.M. to noon) and to make no stops along the route.

8 SAUK RIVER: DARRINGTON TO SKAGIT

Location	south and west of Rockport
Distance	26 to 27 miles
River Time	5 to 6 hours
Maps	Darrington, Rockport, Finney Peak (7.5'), Lake Shannon (15')
Best Season	all year, except at flood stage
Hazards	sweepers, logjams, cold and fast water, big river
Shuttle	26 miles, S.R. 530 and Sauk Valley Road; 28 miles via S.R. 530 to Rockport, S.R. 20 west
Rating	Class II/II+

The Lower Sauk as it flows into the Skagit is part of the Skagit River Bald Eagle Natural Area. It is well wooded but provides views of several spectacular peaks. Enhanced by a slough system that can be explored at higher water levels, it is a good place for eagle-watching in the winter. Fishing for steelhead, salmon, and sea-run cutthroat trout can be excellent at the mouth of the Sauk, where it joins the Skagit. This short segment of the lower Sauk, coupled with the Skagit immediately below Rockport, is a seldom-paddled stretch that offers a variety of river experiences and changes with each flood.

The upper segment of the Sauk (Darrington to Sauk Park), part of the National Wild and Scenic Rivers System, offers fine views of the North Cascades, especially the peaks around Darrington. A challenging run for canoeists, it has several mild rapids and some interesting chutes, especially at low water. The current is swift, the water clear much of the year, but it turns milky with glacial flour from midsummer through early fall. S.R. 530, which approximately parallels the river, is largely unobtrusive and handy in case of trouble on the river.

Access. The best launching access to the lower stretch of river has disappeared with floods during the 1990s, but it is still possible to launch light canoes and kayaks at Sauk Park, about 5.5 miles south of Rockport. Since the Sauk meets the Skagit less than half a mile below Rockport, it is also possible to access this stretch from Howard Miller Steelhead Park in Rockport, but that means paddling or poling up the Skagit. A take-out can be reached from either John G. Young landing off S.R. 20 about 4.5 miles west of Rockport, or from the Concrete–Sauk Valley Road take-out on the left bank immediately across the river from the Young landing.

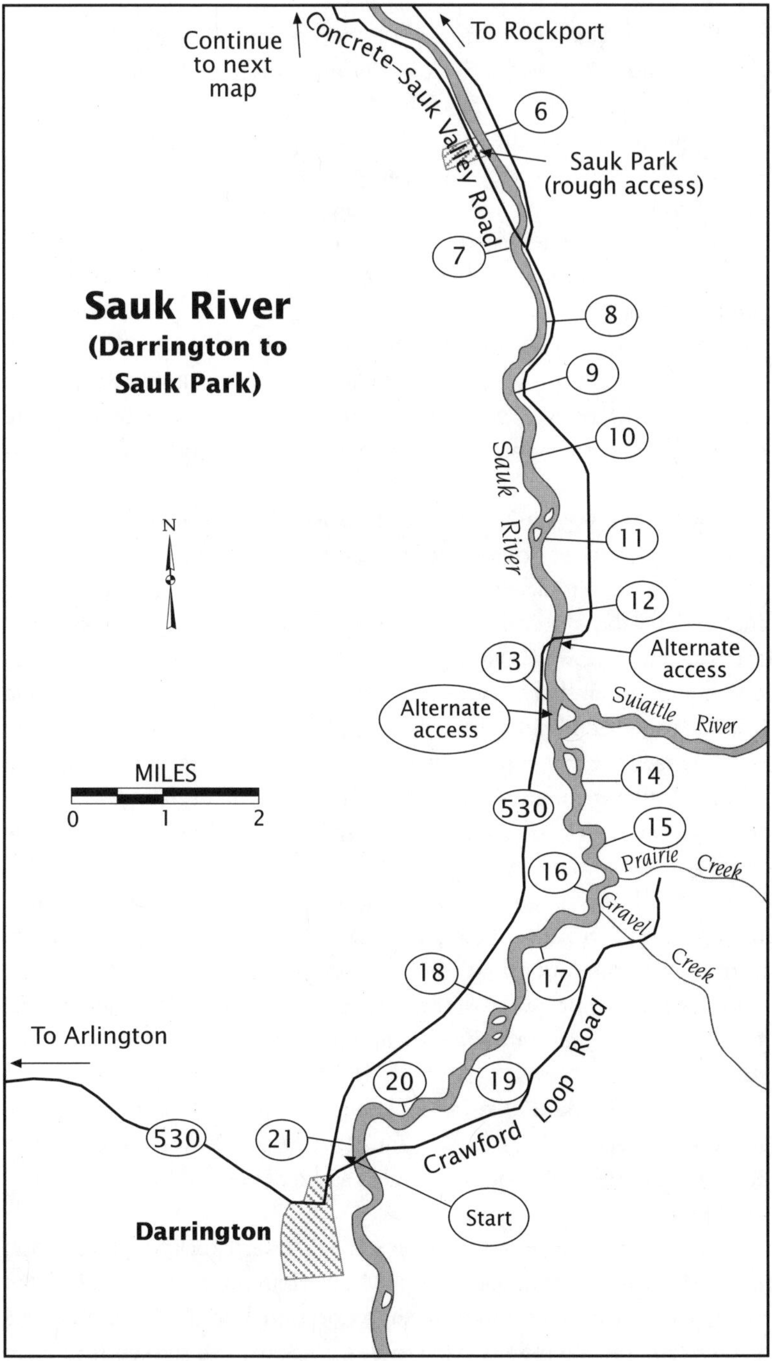

Continue to next map

Concrete–Sauk Valley Road

To Rockport

6

Sauk Park (rough access)

7

8

9

10

Sauk River
(Darrington to
Sauk Park)

Sauk River

11

12

Alternate access

13

Suiattle River

Alternate access

N

14

530

MILES

0   1   2

15

Prairie Creek

16

Gravel Creek

Creek

18

17

To Arlington

20

19

21

Crawford Loop Road

530

Darrington

Start

There are numerous accesses for the lower Sauk, from the put-in by the only bridge across the Sauk in Darrington to the steep, rough take-out at Sauk Park. With S.R. 530 following the entire course of the Sauk in this segment (first on the west bank, then on the east), several points suggest themselves as possible put-in or take-out points. One popular access is across from the mouth of the Suiattle and another at the bridge that carries S.R. 530 across the Sauk. Dories and heavier canoes can be launched at any of these sites except Sauk Park, which has become an impossible access for heavier crafts.

Driving Directions. To reach this portion of the Skagit and its tributary, the lower Sauk, head north on I-5 to Burlington, then take the North Cascade Highway (S.R. 20) east to Concrete. Two accesses on opposite sides of the river a few miles upstream from Concrete offer take-out possibilities.

From Concrete, head east on S.R. 20 about 4 miles to a public fishing access on river right (John G. Young Landing) at RM 62, where a shuttle vehicle can be left (although there is limited parking). For a take-out on the left bank, head south out of Concrete on the Sauk Valley Road across the Skagit River toward Darrington, turning left to a Public Fishing Access about 5 miles southeast of town at RM 62 (immediately across from the John G. Young Landing).

To reach the rough put-in from that location, return to the Sauk Valley Road and turn left toward Darrington. When you reach Sauk Park, turn left into the main entrance and find a spot nearest the river for a rough carry-to-the-river launch.

To reach the rough put-in from a S.R. 20 take-out or from Howard Miller Steelhead Park in Rockport, take S.R. 530 south from Rockport. Turn right at the fork about 6 miles south of Rockport, cross the Sauk River, and head northwest on the Concrete–Sauk Valley Road. In roughly half a mile, turn right into the park and scout out a river access from the campground.

This old standard take-out for the run downstream from Darrington (only for portage-weight boats) is Sauk Park off the Concrete–Sauk Valley Road west of the Sauk, roughly 6 miles south of Rockport (see directions above).

From Darrington, head north on S.R. 530 toward Rockport. After crossing the Sauk (to the east bank), S.R. 530 turns left (north). After 4 miles, the road forks; S.R. 530 continues north to Rockport, and the Concrete–Sauk Valley Road turns off to the left, crosses the Sauk, and passes Sauk Park.

Kayakers enjoy the mild rapids of the Sauk River.

To reach the put-in, drive to Darrington on S.R. 530. North of town, turn east onto Crawford Loop Road (immediately south of the town's major lumber mill) and travel toward the bridge over the Sauk. Just before reaching the bridge, turn left onto a paved road between the lumber mill and the bridge that offers access to the left bank of the Sauk beneath the bridge. This is a common take-out for whitewater trips on the upper Sauk and the put-in for this segment.

For any of the alternate take-outs, drive back to S.R. 530 and turn right, heading north. Six miles north of Darrington there is an access between S.R. 530 and the river, opposite the mouth of the Suiattle—a possible take-out for an 8-mile run. A mile beyond this point the road makes a right-angle turn and crosses the Sauk. Just beyond the bridge on the right shoulder of the road is another access for a take-out on river right just upstream from the bridge.

Description. The lower Sauk is a mellow river in this stretch, isolated from the roads and surrounded by tall timber. It is fast-flowing and may be decorated with sweepers and logjams as it nears the Skagit, depending on the debris left by the last high water. The views of nearby Sauk Mountain (5416 feet) to the north and distant Mount Baker (10,775 feet) to the northwest are well worth the trip.

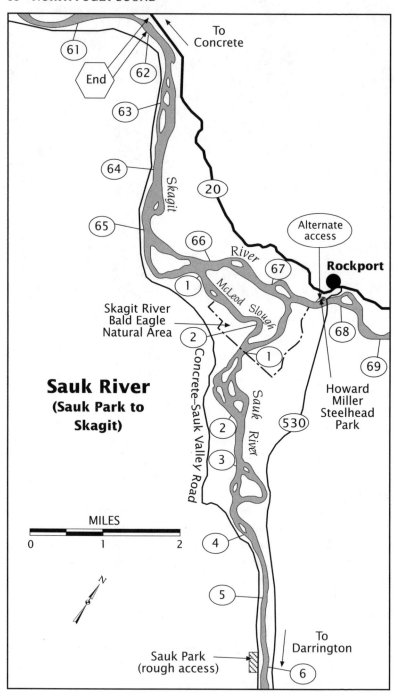

To Concrete

61

End

62

63

64

65

Skagit

20

66

River

67

Alternate access

Rockport

1

McLeod Slough

Skagit River
Bald Eagle
Natural Area

2

1

68

69

Sauk River
(Sauk Park to
Skagit)

Concrete–Sauk Valley Road

Sauk River

530

Howard
Miller
Steelhead
Park

2

3

MILES

0   1   2

N

4

5

To
Darrington

Sauk Park
(rough access)

6

The left bank is relatively low, rising to cut-over mountain land in the Mount Baker–Snoqualmie National Forest. The right bank, also Mount Baker–Snoqualmie National Forest land, is initially steep (except where Hilt Creek comes in at RM 3.3) as the Sauk approaches its delta by breaking through a kind of portal between opposing ridges into the Skagit flood plain. The lower 3 miles of the Sauk is low-lying and marshy.

McLeod Slough branches off to the left, taking 2.2 miles to reach the Skagit at Sauk RM 0.9. The main channel reaches the Skagit at Skagit RM 67.3; McLeod Slough, at Skagit RM 65.9. The delta area changes from year to year as flood waters alter its configuration, but at high water levels it offers some interesting exploration possibilities. The entire mouth, including McLeod Slough, is part of the Skagit River Bald Eagle Natural Area and includes a section of land owned by The Nature Conservancy.

The Skagit itself is a stately river—fast, deep, and powerful, the primary reason for the Class II+ rating of this segment (otherwise it would be simply II). There is a large island just below RM 66, where McLeod Slough enters the Skagit. It is easier to run on the left if reached from the Slough, but it can normally be run on either side. Between the lower end of the island (RM 65), an area commonly known as Mix Master Corner, and the take-out several more small islands split the river. The lower ones, between RM 63.5 and the take-out, are usually run on the right, following the main flow.

From the lumber mill on the north edge of Darrington, the Sauk meanders northeast for 5 miles—dividing around small gravel islands where logjams may pile up, flowing strongly against cut banks where sweepers may overhang, mumbling over shallow bars where stumps and rocks may offer obstacles. Don't forget to look back upstream for the views of Whitehorse Mountain.

The right bank is low, offering views of peaks in the North Cascades and of the massive clear-cuts on Huckleberry Mountain in the Mount Baker–Snoqualmie National Forest, geometric patterns that follow survey lines. Glacier Peak Wilderness lies just beyond; the wilderness can be seen from the river, beyond those ugly clear-cuts.

At RM 16 the Sauk turns north, as Gravel Creek and then Prairie Creek enter from the right. The Sauk still weaves its way among gravel bars, against cut banks, and through timber debris. The views to the east improve as the ridge between the Sauk and the Suiattle descends; and at RM 13, the Suiattle joins the Sauk.

A mile below the mouth of the Suiattle, the river flows under the Sauk River (S.R. 530) bridge, then continues almost due north, still swinging from side to side through its flood plain. At RM 9.6 (where there is a small rapid that at low water offers several chutes), the Sauk brushes the road (indeed, it washed out part of S.R. 530 at this point in the early 1980s) and parallels it closely to the bridge at RM 7, which carries the Concrete–Sauk Valley Road across the Sauk.

There are some large boulders in the river here, creating irregular currents, and there is a small riffle just below the bridge as the river turns left and approaches the rough take-out on river left at Sauk Park. Sauk Mountain looms downstream, as the peaks upstream diminish with distance and the bends of the river.

9 STILLAGUAMISH RIVER

Location	Arlington to Hat Slough
Distance	16 miles
River Time	4 to 5 hours, less at high water
Maps	Arlington, Stanwood (7.5'); NOAA Charts: 18400, 18423
Best Season	early spring through autumn, all year
Hazards	logjams, sweepers, low dam, mild rapids
Shuttle	14 miles on paved roads
Rating	Class I+/II-, Tidal

The Stillaguamish (which means "river people") is a favorite steelhead river that flows through farmlands between Arlington and Port Susan. The Stilly (as it is known in local jargon) is a mellow river, marred in a few places by thoughtless human activity and by barnyard smells, but nevertheless full of wildlife (deer, beavers, and plenty of bird life, including nesting bald eagles). There is a low dam to portage within view of the I-5 bridges, and the lower few miles are tidal. This rural river is picturesque and pleasant, its bottom sandy, and its shoreline well vegetated and marked by a few high bluffs.

Access. Access is available at two parks in Arlington: (1) Haller Park on S.R. 9 immediately below the confluence of the two forks of the Stilly, just north of downtown Arlington; and (2) the park to the east of S.R. 530 just beyond the bridge across the South Fork northeast of Arlington, which provides access to the South Fork 0.5 mile above the confluence.

The logical take-out is south of Stanwood at an access on Hat Slough, the south mouth of the Stilly, just west of Marine Drive off Boe Road.

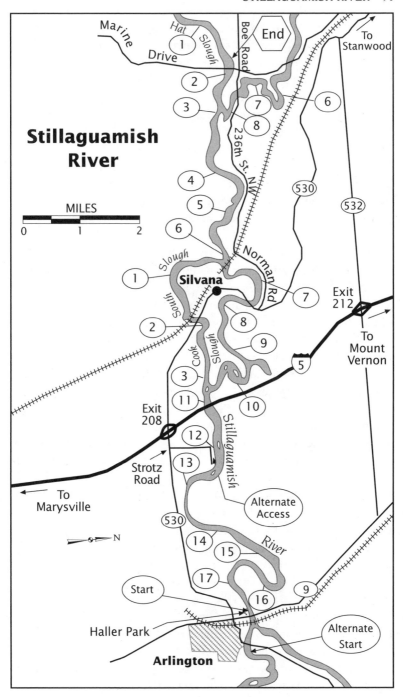

Driving Directions. To reach the take-out, use the S.R. 530 exit (Exit 208) from I-5 and head west toward Silvana through low-lying farming country. Pass through Silvana. Just after crossing the bridge over the North Branch, about 4 miles from I-5, turn left onto Norman Road and follow it west. There is a low-overhead railroad underpass (10 feet 5 inches) that may be a hazard to canoes on van-top carriers. In this case, use the alternative approach described below.

At Marine Drive, go directly across the road (north of the bridge across the Stilly, or Hat Slough, as this south mouth is called) onto the road that parallels Hat Slough on the north bank (Boe Road). The river access (take-out) is left of the road at a boat ramp on river right.

An alternate route for reaching the take-out is to leave I-5 at the Stanwood exit (S.R. 532, Exit 212) and head west toward Stanwood; then take Marine Drive south to 236th Street NW and turn right to the take-out.

To reach the put-in at Arlington, retrace the route to I-5, heading east on S.R. 530 to the Arlington launch site. Turn left onto S.R. 9 and head north a couple of blocks to Haller Park on the left. This access is on the left bank of the Stilly, west of S.R. 9 and immediately below the confluence of the forks that create the Stillaguamish. The old South Fork access beneath the S.R. 530 bridge at the east edge of Arlington has been deleted by the recent development of Twin Rivers Park, which provides plenty of parking but ignores river access; it could still work for light canoes and kayaks.

Description. From the South Fork access, the river flows placidly past a bluff on the left on which part of Arlington is built. After a few riffles and logjams, the South Fork joins the North Fork in a swirl of currents that can be tricky. Less experienced paddlers may want to put in at Haller Park with its boat ramp immediately below this juncture.

From Haller Park (RM 17.8) the river flows slowly over a sandy bottom, past sand and gravel bars and a few riffles, the banks lined with stately cottonwoods. There are rocks and logs in the water (which is clear most of the year), a few tight chutes at low water, a few sweepers at high water. Soon the left bank is encased in concrete. The noise of machinery and barnyard smells invade the river from adjacent gravel pits and dairies; but beaver signs attest to the presence of those primarily nocturnal rodents, and birds are abundant (robins, black-headed grosbeaks, killdeer, mallards, spotted sandpipers, linnets). A pair of bald eagles have built a nest near the river in recent years.

Other river access lies on the left bank along the Dike Road west of Arlington and off Strotz Road a mile east of I-5.

Small sloughs decorate the borders of the lower Stillaguamish, offering unique exploration opportunities.

The Stillaguamish is a broad, slow river lined with grasses, maples, Douglas fir, western red cedar, hemlock, and cottonwoods. At RM 12 (just above the double I-5 bridge) Bed Rock Rapid offers a minor challenge, as do occasional logjams that create tight corners. But the biggest challenge lies just 0.25 mile below I-5: a low diversion dam that may best be portaged or lined. At certain water levels it creates what could be a dangerous hydraulic keeper (reversal current) across the face of the dam. It can be scouted from Gulhagen Road off S.R. 530.

The river begins to swing broadly through its flood plain under bridges (railroad and highway), past a trailer park with a gravel beach (river right) opposite a steep bluff (river left). The river margin is well vegetated with willow, which provides habitat for deer and numerous birds, including the varied thrush and kingfisher. The lower 3 miles are under tidal influence, and marine species begin to appear; at low tide there are mud flats on each shore. The take-out is on river right at RM 1.8.

10 STILLAGUAMISH RIVER: NORTH FORK

Location	between Arlington and Darrington
Distance	8 miles
River Time	2 hours
Map	Oso (15')
Best Season	all year, may be too low August–September
Hazards	sweepers, logjams, Class II rapids
Shuttle	6.4 miles on S.R. 530, ideal for bicycle
Rating	Class II

The North Fork of the Stillaguamish is a lovely stream that flows westward from near the North Cascades timber town of Darrington to Arlington through a bucolic valley of old farms and small homesteads. It offers grand views of the Cascade peaks and, in the winter, a bit of eagle-watching. Its valley is rural enough to foster good wildlife, and its climate mild enough to be runnable any time there is enough water. There can also be too much water, however, for the river floods with heavy winter rains, and boaters don't want to be on it at flood stage.

Access. Since the road (S.R. 530) follows the river and crosses it twice, there are several potential access points. The most appropriate are: (1) the take-out for this segment at the Washington Wildlife Department access off Monty Road at Cicero (near the S.R. 530 bridge, 9 miles east of Arlington) and (2) the put-in at the Evergreen Fly Fishing Club access between the railroad bed (the tracks have been removed, and a trail is planned) and the river on Whitman Road (251st Avenue NE) in Halterman.

Driving Directions. Leave a shuttle vehicle (a bicycle will do nicely) at the Department of Wildlife access off Monty Road, 8.7 miles east of the junction of S.R. 9 and S.R. 530 in Arlington. This is just west of the aesthetically pleasing bridge across the North Fork and north of the highway. The

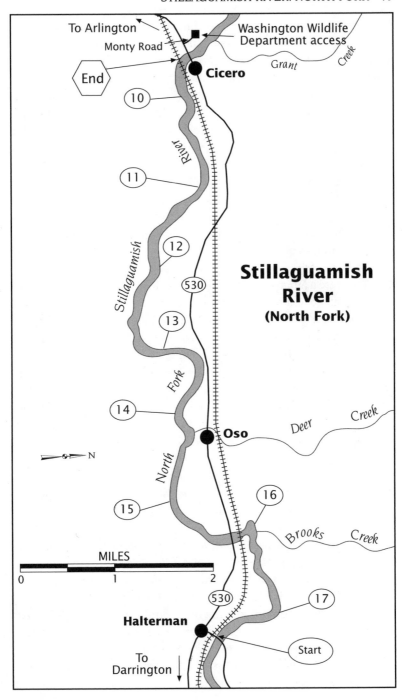

best boating take-out is under the railroad bridge immediately south of the highway (across from the public access area; there is an eddy there, with a nasty logjam just below it). This take-out over the riprapped bank is easier than the often-muddy trail through the brambles below the logjam.

To reach the put-in, drive east on S.R. 530 through Oso for about 7 miles to Whitman Road (251st Avenue NE); turn left (north); and cross the railroad right-of-way. The access, which lies between the railroad bed and the river, is maintained and used regularly by the Evergreen Fly Fishing Club. The put-in is on river left under the bridge.

Description. The North Fork is rocky in its first few hundred yards, with a riffle or two before it reaches a dogleg to the left at the most severe rapid on this segment. Here it runs to the very edge of the Mount Baker–Snoqualmie National Forest (which borders the river for the next mile) before it swings south under the railroad and highway bridges to flow past the foot of Wheeler Mountain on the south side of the flood plain.

There are a number of vacation homes along the southbound stretch of the North Fork. It soon bends west in a broad sweeping curve to the right, leaving a wide gravel bar on the right where steelhead fishermen gather to try their luck. Take care in boating past fishermen. Courteous boaters avoid interfering with the activities of other river users.

The river gets progressively easier downstream, and the views upstream progressively improve. Whitehorse Mountain can be seen from a number of stretches below Oso, which can be recognized by the bridge that crosses the river just south of town (no access here) and by the entry of Deer Creek, which flows into the North Fork just southwest of Oso.

Barnyard smells mingle with the odor of fresh-cut cedar from the small mill near Oso, and you can even smell the raspberries in adjacent fields in midsummer. Spotted sandpipers, kingfishers, great blue herons, robins, and yellow warblers add color and variety to the trip, and old barns offer picturesque views.

There are vacation homes and year-round residences along the river, as well as private picnic areas and trailers. Riverside vegetation includes blackberries, red osier dogwood, tall grasses, and the usual deciduous trees: tall cottonwoods, alders, and maples. The sound of farm machinery and logging trucks intrudes into the river corridor at times, but generally this is a quiet segment with distant views of Cascade peaks and forested hillsides, marred here and there by the inevitable clear-cuts.

The take-out under the bridge is steep, a rough haul over riprap boulders; but the logjam a hundred yards downstream can be hairy in high

At low water, gravel bars force the North Fork of the Stillaguamish into narrow, rocky channels.

water, and its location makes it difficult to land on the left bank, where the access trail is. The eddy under the bridge offers quiet water for a take-out, and there is a small parking area (better used for loading boats than for parking) between the highway and the railroad.

The Monty Road access may also be used for launching a run on the North Fork to Arlington, where the two main forks of the Stillaguamish converge just a hundred yards above the Haller Park access in Arlington. This stretch of river goes through a short, pleasant canyon but adds 9.5 miles to the trip. (Of course, it can be run as an entirely separate trip another day.)

11 STILLAGUAMISH RIVER: SOUTH FORK

Location	between Granite Falls and Arlington
Distance	11 miles
River Time	4 hours
Maps	Granite Falls (15'), Lake Stevens, Arlington (7.5')
Best Season	early spring through summer, all year
Hazards	sweepers, logjams, Class II rapids
Shuttle	8.3 miles, mostly on paved road
Rating	Class II

The South Fork of the Stillaguamish is another favorite steelhead stream flowing through a rural area. Its background bluffs give it the appearance

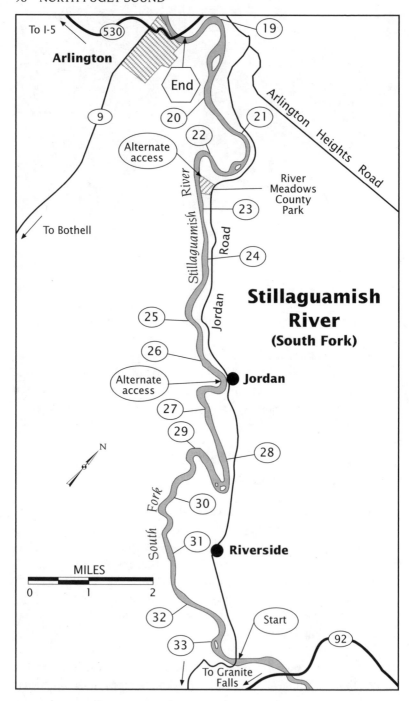

of an Ozark river, but its vegetation is strictly Pacific Northwestern. A broad but lively river, most of its real action comes within the first few miles of the segment. Alternating pools and riffles, the river is rocky: a good poling river challenging enough in its moderate rapids to provide practice in basic canoeing techniques. This segment is a favorite trip for the Paddle Trails Canoe Club.

Access. Three major access points on the South Fork between Granite Falls and Arlington offer opportunities for running several different segments: (1) beneath the bridge across the South Fork just north of Granite Falls; (2) beneath the suspension footbridge at Jordan, about 7 river miles below access 1; and (3) at River Meadows County Park, another 4 river miles downstream. A fourth access is at Haller Park in Arlington that may be used as a launch site for Trip 9.

Driving Directions. Either of the parks in Arlington might serve as take-outs for longer runs. The park to the east of S.R. 530, just beyond the bridge across the South Fork northeast of Arlington, provides access to the South Fork 0.3 mile above the confluence. Haller Park on S.R. 9, immediately below the confluence of the two forks of the Stilly, is just north of downtown Arlington.

To reach River Meadows County Park, take the S.R. 530 exit off I-5 (Exit 208), and head east to Arlington. Go through town as though following S.R. 530 to Darrington, and turn right onto Arlington Heights Road about a mile beyond the bridge across the South Fork. In about a mile, turn right again, onto Jordan Road, and follow it southeast toward Jordan. In about 3 miles turn right into River Meadows County Park, and drive down the hill to the parking area, which is within an easy carry of the riverbank. Spot a shuttle vehicle here.

Eroded bluffs along the South Fork of the Stillaguamish

Drive back to Jordan Road (also known as the Granite Falls–Arlington Road), turn right, and drive the 8.3 miles to the bridge across the South Fork, just north of Granite Falls. The put-in is on the left (that is, the upstream side of the bridge) just before the bridge on river right.

On the drive from River Meadows County Park to the put-in, you will pass through Jordan, a tiny community with a small parking area (six cars at most) on the south side of the road, accessed by way of a suspension footbridge to a small park with a broad beach on river left under the bridge. It makes a strenuous carry, but it is possible to launch or take out here, dividing this run into a 7- and a 4-mile run, above and below this point.

To go more directly to the launch site, take S.R. 92 off S.R. 9 north of Lake Stevens and travel northeast toward Granite Falls. Just before reaching the city streets, turn left onto Jordan Road (Granite Falls–Arlington Road), which jogs around a bit but heads generally north to cross the South Fork. Immediately past the bridge, turn right into a public fishing access area, which lies near a self-help housing development, Housing Partners. The launch site lies on the right.

Description. From the launch site beneath the bridge, the river is clear, rocky, and rapid. Ideal for poling, the river is shallow with a gravel or rocky bottom. There are also lovely deep green pools, followed by a couple of 3- to 4-foot drops, good Class II rapids. Fully half the action of this segment occurs in the first mile.

There are a couple of small islands on the second turn with a third drop (rapid) just below them; then the river mellows out and the wildlife appears (or rather, you have time to notice it). Mergansers, ravens, spotted sandpipers, and great blue herons can be sighted. Houses, a series of miniature waterfalls, and a ledge of fossil shells appear on the left bank. It is a pool-and-drop river with sandy beaches often opposite shallow cliffs.

The banks are lined with vine maple, western red cedar, Douglas fir, hemlock, alder, and (in season) bright yellow monkey flowers. The bird life includes bald eagles, several species of swallows, and more ducks. The suspension bridge at Jordan, throwing its shadow into the deep pools at the edge of the park beach, marks 7 miles from the launch.

Below Jordan the river gets slower, broader, shallower, and more agricultural in the final 4 miles of this segment, a trend that continues all the way to Arlington. Many paddlers take out at River Meadows County Park because it is convenient (though a long carry in late summer, when the gravel bar widens with low water) and because the river slows below the park. To Arlington from the park is another 4 miles, a good hour's hard paddling in slow water.

◆

SOUTH
PUGET
SOUND

◆

12 SNOHOMISH RIVER SLOUGHS

Location	north and east of Everett
Distance	from 3 to 23 miles
River Time	3 miles per hour on average
Maps	Marysville, Everett, Snohomish (7.5'); NOAA Charts: 18423, 18443, 18444
Best Season	all year
Hazards	contrary tides, powerboats
Shuttle	none necessary, paved roads for alternate accesses
Rating	Class I, Tidal

The Snohomish River Sloughs—Ebey, Steamboat, Union, and the mouth of the Snohomish River itself—offer more than 40 miles of paddling potential, a veritable network of waterways in which a paddler could get lost and paddle for days with the tide, moving upstream and down with the ebb and flow. There is industrial development along much of the shoreline, but the area also serves as wonderful waterfowl habitat. The women's Olympic crew team and other rowers use the lower river and some of its sloughs for training; fishermen, many of them in powerboats, make regular use of the slough, as do hunters in waterfowl season.

Access. Amazingly little public access to the lower Snohomish and its sloughs existed before Langus Riverside Park was developed in 1988 on the lower main stem of the river, about 3 miles upstream from its mouth in Everett Harbor. The new facility on the southwestern edge of Smith Island offers the best access with a boat launch, restrooms, picnic areas, and a boathouse.

There is public boating access at the waterfront park in Everett, but it involves paddling across the face of Everett Harbor to reach the mouth of the river or any of the sloughs. There is also a fee for launching.

Other potential accesses are at Lowell Riverside Park, about 7 miles from the mouth (4 miles above the access mentioned above); and about a mile upstream from Lowell at Rotary Park off Snohomish River Road (8 miles from the mouth of the river). A hard-to-find access on Ebey Slough immediately west of the Stillaguamish River (I-5) bridge in Marysville offers limited access but little parking. A Marysville Boat Launch and Waterfront Park on Ebey Slough is presently only a concept.

Driving Directions. To reach the access 3 miles from the mouth of the Snohomish River (at Langus Riverside Park) heading south on I-5,

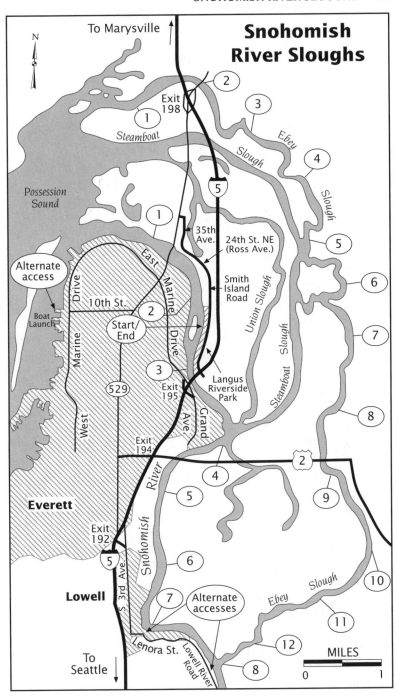

Snohomish River Sloughs

To Marysville ↑

N

To Seattle ↓

Possession Sound

Alternate access

Boat Launch

Exit 198

Steamboat Slough

Ebey Slough

Exit 195

Start/End

10th St.

East Marine Drive

Marine Drive

West Marine Drive

35th Ave.

24th St. NE (Ross Ave.)

Smith Island Road

Langus Riverside Park

Union Slough

Steamboat Slough

529

Grand Ave.

Exit 194

Everett

Snohomish River

Exit 192

Lowell

S. 3rd Ave.

Alternate accesses

Lenora St.

Lowell River Road

Ebey Slough

MILES

0   1

1 2 3 4 5 6 7 8 9 10 11 12

take the S.R. 529 exit off I-5 (Exit 198); head south off S.R. 529, following first Frontage Road, then 24th Street NE (also Ross Avenue) to Smith Island Road. Follow the signs to Langus Riverside Park (formerly Smith Island Park), developed and maintained by the Everett Parks Department. To reach this access from the south (driving north on I-5), take Exit 195 and turn left on Marine View Drive to S.R. 529 heading north. Then turn right onto 28th Place; turn right again onto 35th Avenue to Smith Island Road; and turn left, following it to the park and access.

To reach the 10th Street waterfront park in Everett, take I-5 Exit 195 heading north onto Grand Avenue, which becomes East Marine Drive under I-5 as it swings northwest to loop around the north end of the peninsula on which most of north Everett is built. It becomes West Marine Drive as it swings south and the cross-street numbers begin to climb. At 10th Street turn right into the waterfront park and boat launch.

To reach Lowell, take I-5 south to Exit 192 (Broadway/Lowell Road) and head south; turn left on Lenora Street and head for the river on what becomes Lowell River Road. At the edge of Lowell there is a steep, rough access on the left bank of the river bend left of the road. A mile beyond this access (southeast) is a water pipeline crossing and a public access left of Lowell River Road on the left bank of the river—just downstream from Ebey Slough (which branches off the lower Snohomish River just above this access).

Description. From the launch site at the Smith Island Public Boat Launch at Langus Riverside Park, paddlers may head downstream toward the Everett waterfront to paddle south to the Port of Everett or turn north, to paddle the sloughs. Careful scrutiny of tide charts will make this an easier and more pleasant trip. It is possible to paddle up Steamboat Slough, the first major waterway north of the river mouth, or Ebey Slough, which flows into Possession Sound a mile north of the river mouth. Union Slough splits off Steamboat Slough about a mile from its mouth.

The waterfront is developed and industrial, a port for some large ocean-going vessels (and it will become more so as the Navy develops its homeport here). To the north there is a storage area for millions of logs, largely at the mouths of the sloughs. Despite the development, this is good wildlife habitat for shorebirds, waterfowl, and bald eagles. The farther up the sloughs you paddle, the farther you get from industrial development and the background noise of I-5 traffic (which dominates their lower 2 or 3 miles).

Ebey Slough and Steamboat Slough entwine twice at RM 5.2 and RM 6.4 at high water levels (high tide). Union Slough and Steamboat Slough,

Crew racing on the Snohomish River and its sloughs has become popular since the development of Langus Riverside Park.

having run 4.4 and 6.2 miles respectively, join at RM 4 on the lower Snohomish. Ebey Slough splits off the river at RM 8.1, flowing 12.4 miles to the Sound, a decided longcut (a long way around).

Going upriver from the Smith Island launch site (again with careful study of tide charts), paddlers pass under the double span of the I-5 bridge; skirt the industrial northeast edge of Everett; meet the take-off point of the twin sloughs, Union and Steamboat, at RM 4; then skirt the ridge carrying I-5 and much of southeast Everett until they reach Lowell. Here the river turns abruptly away from the ridge and heads eastward (remember, you are going upstream).

Ebey Slough, a mile above Lowell, is controlled by floodgates. This barrier can be portaged and—if the tide is right—this slack-water route can be followed to the Sound, using the tide to increase the craft's speed.

It is also possible to paddle downstream on the Snohomish from Cady Park in Snohomish (see Trip 13) to either of the take-outs suggested above. It is a 10-mile run (a 3-hour paddle) from Cady Park to Langus Riverside Park.

13 SNOHOMISH RIVER: CONFLUENCE TO SNOHOMISH

Location	Snohomish, southeast of Snohomish
Distance	8 miles
River Time	2 to 3 hours
Maps	Snohomish, Maltby (7.5'), Everett (15')
Best Season	all year, especially summer
Hazards	logjams, sweepers, powerboats
Shuttle	13 miles by main roads
Rating	Class I+/II-, Tidal

The Snohomish River begins where the Snoqualmie and the Skykomish join, roughly 20 miles from its mouth. More than half its length is under tidal influence, which reaches well above the town of Snohomish. This segment is mellow—a cool, clear green river easy to paddle for its slow current and braided channel full of islands. Its backdrop changes by slow degrees from forested and mildly isolated, through agricultural, to developed. It offers good birding (especially Canada geese and killdeer) and an opportunity to watch skydiving and biplane acrobatics.

Access. There is an excellent take-out for this segment at Cady Park in Snohomish. Three possible put-in points suggest themselves (see Map 14 also): (1) Gus Pedersen's Three Rivers Mobile Park on the left bank about a mile below the confluence (within sight of the Snohomish River (S.R. 522) bridge); (2) the public boat launch on the Skykomish immediately south of Monroe, 4 miles upstream from the confluence; (3) the High Bridge public fishing access on the Snoqualmie, 2.8 miles upstream from the confluence.

Driving Directions. To reach the take-out at Cady Park in Snohomish, drive to the town of Snohomish on US 2 or S.R. 9. From US 2, take the exit east of town, head west on 92nd Street SE (which becomes Second Street in Snohomish), turn left onto Maple Street, and follow it to its end at Cady Park. From S.R. 9, take the exit west of town (Foster Slough/River Road), head east into town, take the fork to the right (First Street), turn right onto Maple Street, and follow it one block to its end at Cady Park.

To find the access south of Monroe (see Map 14), take US 2 east toward Stevens Pass, turning right in Monroe onto S.R. 203 and heading south toward Duvall, Carnation, and Fall City. Just before the bridge across the Skykomish immediately south of town, turn right onto a dirt road that

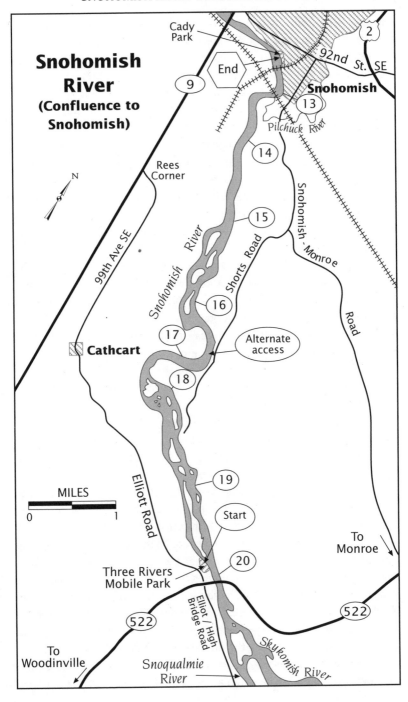

Cady Park

End

Snohomish

Snohomish River (Confluence to Snohomish)

N

Rees Corner

99th Ave SE

Snohomish River

Shorts Road

Snohomish - Monroe Road

Pilchuck River

92nd St. SE

Alternate access

Cathcart

MILES

0   1

Elliott Road

To Monroe

Three Rivers Mobile Park

Start

Elliot / High Bridge Road

To Woodinville

Snoqualmie River

Skykomish River

constitutes a public boating access. This shuttle is roughly 14 miles. This upstream extension of Trip 13 is described in Trip 14.

Reaching the High Bridge access on the Snoqualmie or Three Rivers Mobile Park on the Snohomish is complicated. From Snohomish head south on S.R. 9, turning left at Rees Corner onto Broadway (called 99th Avenue SE and also S.R. 96) to Cathcart, where 164th SE coming in from the right eventually becomes Elliott Road (Connelly Road on some maps). It winds around, approximately paralleling the river and heading upstream. Just before you reach the S.R. 522 bridge overhead, you'll see Three Rivers Mobile Park on the left, a good put-in after a 9-mile shuttle. Some 3 miles after Elliott Road passes under S.R. 522 at Three Rivers Mobile Park (stay left at the fork 1.5 miles beyond), turn left onto High Bridge Road. Just past the bridge, turn left into a public fishing access to launch. This shuttle is roughly 12 miles.

Description. The 4-mile run on the Skykomish from Monroe to the confluence can be tricky at low water, when the current flows strongly beneath sweepers in a place or two. The Skykomish meanders from bank to bank, with large gravel bars forcing the current back and forth into sweepers. (On one river trip, my canoe capsized beneath a sweeper near the left bank about 3 miles below Monroe on this stretch.)

The 2.8-mile lower stretch of the Snoqualmie is like a Southern swamp, except for a riffle a few hundred yards above the confluence with the Skykomish; it is slow and sluggish (except at high water) and heavily forested. At the confluence, the two rivers meet then flow around an island. Depending on water levels and the action of the last flood, the island may be in any one of the three rivers that meet here, the Skykomish and Snoqualmie joining to create the Snohomish.

From the confluence of the Skykomish and the Snoqualmie, the Snohomish River passes under the long angular bridge of S.R. 522, then flows placidly past forested banks with cottonwoods along the river, and Douglas fir, hemlock, and western red cedar on the ridges. There are some farmhouses and rural residences and, on the left bank, Three Rivers Mobile Park, a private access. For 3 miles the river flows fairly straight, the channel braiding among islands; then it takes an abrupt turn to the right, the beginning of a huge S where the river spreads out. Here there is much timber debris in the river, well anchored in a sandy bottom. Shorts Road provides rough access along the final bend of the S at RM 16.3-16.5.

The river continues to split around islands, the water level determining how navigable any channel may be. A private beach offers swimming

Canada geese rest on a Snohomish River gravel bar.

and sunbathing opportunities at roughly RM 15 as the farmlands begin to become evident. Flocks of Canada geese and coveys of killdeer frequent the gravel bars, and powerboats begin to appear. On sunny days you may be able to observe skydivers and biplane acrobatics at the local airport just south of Snohomish (river left).

As paddlers approach the town of Snohomish, they may notice the mouth of the Pilchuck River coming in on the right just after they pass beneath the first of two railroad bridges. The second railroad bridge announces the take-out 0.25 mile downstream on the right bank at Cady Park.

14 SKYKOMISH RIVER: MONROE TO CONFLUENCE

Location	southwest of Monroe
Distance	4 miles
River Time	1 hour
Maps	Monroe, Maltby (7.5')
Best Season	all year, especially summer
Hazards	logjams, sweepers
Shuttle	4 miles on paved roads and city streets
Rating	Class II

This short segment of the lower Skykomish is a delightful run and can easily be coupled with a run up the Snoqualmie to the High Bridge access (see Trip 13) or a run all the way (8 more miles) to Snohomish. The area through which it flows is agricultural (but unobtrusively so) and full of wildlife. At high water it is a flush down a big river with few obstacles; at low water it requires more maneuvering because a few bends carry most of the flow under some serious sweepers.

Access. The only logical take-out for this run is the boat ramp at Three Rivers Mobile Park on the left bank, a mile or so below the confluence with the Snoqualmie that forms the Snohomish River. The only logical launch site is off South Lewis Street at the south edge of Monroe.

Driving Directions. To reach the take-out at Three Rivers Mobile Park, head south from Snohomish on S.R. 9. Turn left at Rees Corner onto Broadway, called 99th Avenue SE or S.R. 96 on some maps. Follow that road to

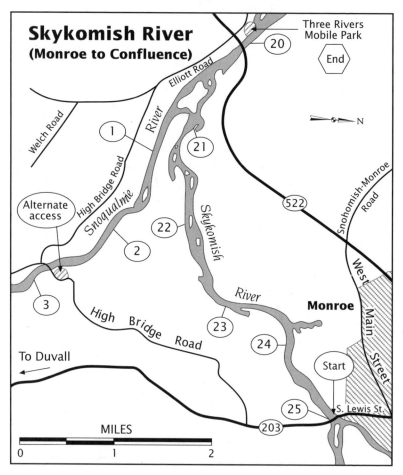

Skykomish River
(Monroe to Confluence)

Deer can be seen along many western Washington rivers.

Cathcart, where 164th SE comes in from the right, eventually becoming Elliott Road (also called Connelly Road). It winds around, approximately paralleling the river and heading upstream. Just before you reach the S.R. 522 bridge overhead, you should see Three Rivers Mobile Park off to your left.

To reach the launch site, retrace the route to US 2 and take it east into downtown Monroe; turn right onto South Lewis Street (also S.R. 203); and drive south to the edge of town. Before reaching the bridge, turn right onto a dirt road, which offers access to the Skykomish River's right bank below the bridge.

Description. The Sky (shorthand for Skykomish) is broad and deep here, and green most of the year. It soon shallows and, at low water levels, meanders from bank to bank between gravel bars. Farms line the banks, but agricultural activities do not intrude into the river corridor, and the area is full of wildlife (deer, beavers, raccoons, and numerous bird species, including ospreys and eagles).

At low water levels the river seems to disappear downriver; then the channel swings off to the left, where it hugs the bank after running over a shallow bar that pinches the current into a narrow chute. The current swings back to the right for a time, clear and green as it ripples over the shallows, then swings again hard against the left bank under a sturdy sweeper that has upset a number of paddle craft over the years. Inexperienced paddlers may want to portage or line at certain water levels or take a different channel, even if the craft has to be walked through. Islands occur at higher water levels; in selecting routes, it is generally best to follow the stronger current.

Within sight of the confluence there is a rocky promontory on the left bank that makes a nice lunch stop. From the rock, which makes a good diving platform for the adjacent deep pool, the summer sunbathers and swingers of ropes from the downstream bridge can be observed at the beach on the right. The take-out at Three Rivers Mobile Park lies on the left bank, downstream from the S.R. 522 bridge.

15 SKYKOMISH RIVER: SULTAN TO MONROE

Location	east of Monroe along US 2
Distance	9.5 miles
River Time	2 to 3 hours
Maps	Sultan, Monroe (7.5')
Best Season	all year, especially summer
Hazards	sweepers, narrow chutes at low water levels
Shuttle	9 miles on paved roads
Rating	Class I+/II-

The Skykomish between Sultan and Monroe offers excellent steelhead fishing. It sweeps widely within its flood plain, meandering between huge gravel bars, the shoreline protected by giant cottonwoods. As it hugs the south side of its flood plain, it embraces steep hills that leave the river in shadow much of the year, a cold river where steelheaders gather to try their luck. The adjacent agricultural lands through which the river meanders are hardly noticed from the river, so dense is the streamside vegetation in most of this stretch.

Access. The obvious access for the put-in is the small park on the lower Sultan River just west of the town of Sultan. A good take-out lies just south of Monroe on the right bank below the Skykomish River (S.R. 203) bridge. An alternate access point, heavily used by fishermen, lies about 2 miles upstream from the S.R. 203 bridge on Ben Howard Road, which parallels US 2 on the south side of the river.

Driving Directions. To reach the take-out, drive east on US 2 into Monroe, and turn right (south) on S.R. 203 to the south edge of town. Just before the bridge across the Skykomish, turn right onto a dirt road paralleling the river. This road provides public fishing and boating access.

The standard launch site lies at the mouth of the Sultan River just west of Sultan. To reach it from the Monroe take-out, head north on

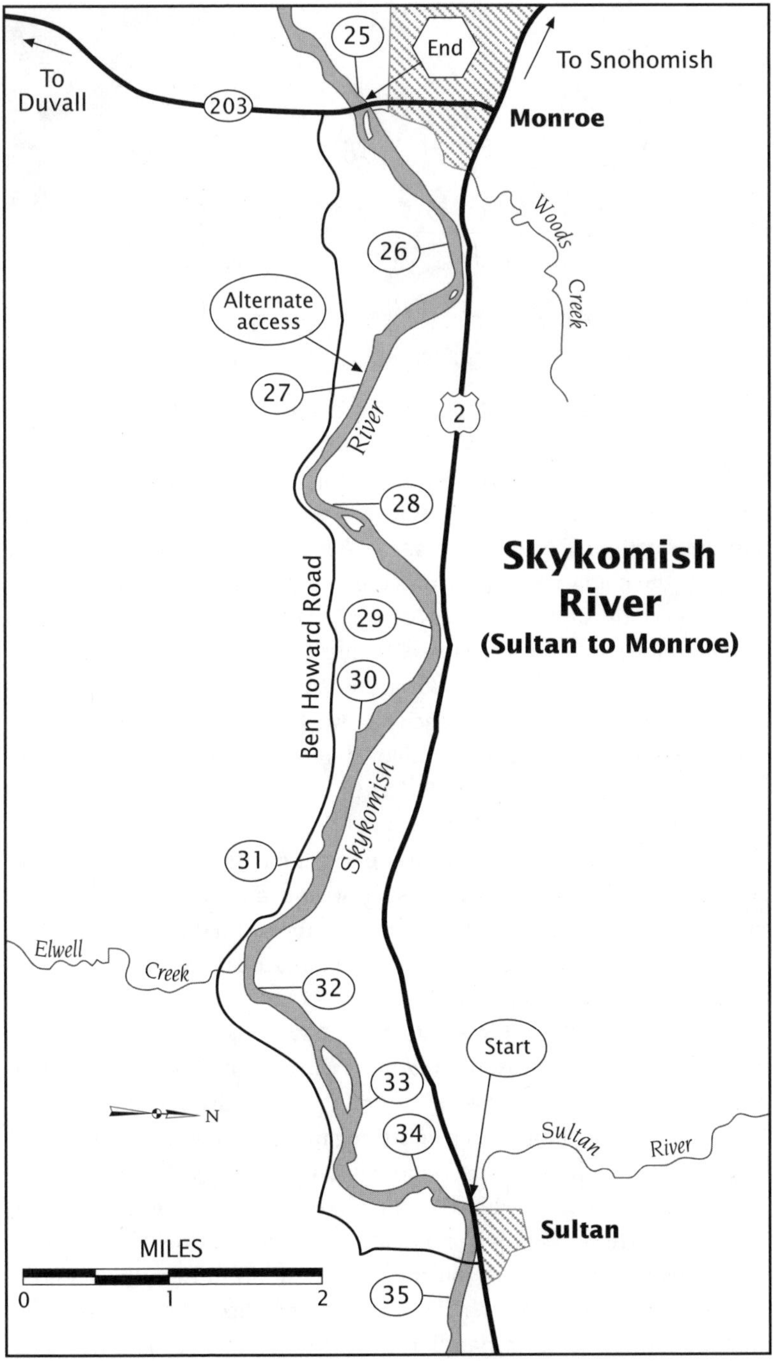

To Duvall

203

25

End

To Snohomish

Monroe

26

Woods Creek

Alternate access

27

River

2

28

Ben Howard Road

29

30

Skykomish

Skykomish River
(Sultan to Monroe)

31

Elwell

Creek

32

Start

33

Sultan River

34

Sultan

N

MILES

0   1   2

35

A *dory fisherman hauls his boat out of the Skykomish.*

S.R. 203 through town, turn right onto US 2, and head east to the west edge of Sultan. Just before the bridge across the Sultan River, turn left into the small park. The launch site is beneath the railroad bridge that parallels the highway bridge across the mouth of the Sultan River.

To reach the alternate access on the left bank 2 miles above Monroe, take Ben Howard Road, which essentially parallels US 2 south of the river. To reach the east end of Ben Howard Road, take the bridge across the Sky in downtown Sultan. To reach the west end of Ben Howard Road, cross the bridge over the Sky south of Monroe and take the first left. The access lies 2 miles from the S.R. 203 bridge south of Monroe, about 8 miles from the access in Sultan.

Description. From the launch site at the mouth of the tributary Sultan River (RM 34.4), the Sky flows southwest in a huge open S to accept the offerings of Elwell Creek flowing in from the south (RM 31.7). The river is broad and swift, especially just before it reaches the south side of its flood plain against a steep hillside.

From the mouth of Elwell Creek the Sky angles west-by-northwest for 2 miles until it bumps into the ridge carrying US 2 between Monroe and Sultan. This section is well wooded to screen the agricultural lands that flank the Sky through this entire segment. In summer, broad gravel bars are ideal for lunch stops; paddlers can pick sun or shade.

From its encounter with US 2, the Sky makes a beeline to the southwest again. It runs headlong into that same steep hillside, which turns it west-by-northwest again, bouncing it back and forth between its flood plain barriers. In less than a mile the fishermen's access on the left bank offers an out to the weary paddler.

The Sky approaches the highway again in another mile, then turns southwest for a 2-mile run past Monroe, where the take-out lies on the right (north) bank, just below the S.R. 203 bridge. Paddlers who have planned a longer run can continue to Three Rivers Mobile Park below the confluence of the Sky with the Snoqualmie 4 miles downstream.

16 SKYKOMISH RIVER: BIG EDDY TO SULTAN

Location	east of Sultan along US 2
Distance	9 miles
River Time	2 to 3 hours
Maps	Sultan (7.5'), Index (15')
Best Season	all year, but especially summer
Hazards	logjams, sweepers, rapids, clay ledges
Shuttle	8 miles on paved roads
Rating	Class II

The Skykomish River from the Big Eddy beneath the Skykomish (US 2) bridge east of Gold Bar to the small park west of Sultan is a favorite segment for paddlers who like a little action. Most of it comes in the first quarter mile in the form of a Class II rapid that can be seen from the launch site. There are a few other minor rapids and a series of waves, and one chute caused by gray mud ledges about halfway down the run. The adjacent highway and farmlands are unnoticeable, for the most part, and the wildlife is plentiful—a great picnic run with several massive gravel beaches.

Access. The obvious take-out for this run is the small park off US 2 at the west edge of Sultan. The put-in is just south of US 2, 8 miles east at the Big Eddy—a huge, deep green, mildly swirling pool. The Big Eddy is visible from the US 2 bridge 2 miles east of downtown Gold Bar.

Driving Directions. The take-out lies beneath the railroad bridge adjacent to the US 2 bridge, at the park on the Sultan River just west of Sultan. Drive east on US 2 to the edge of Sultan. Turn left into the park immediately east of the Sultan Waste Water Treatment Plant.

To reach the put-in, drive back to US 2, turn left (east), and drive through Sultan, Startup, and Gold Bar. A mile beyond Gold Bar, the highway crosses the Skykomish on a high bridge. Just beyond the bridge, turn right down a bumpy dirt road to an access on the left bank of the river between the railroad bridge downstream and US 2.

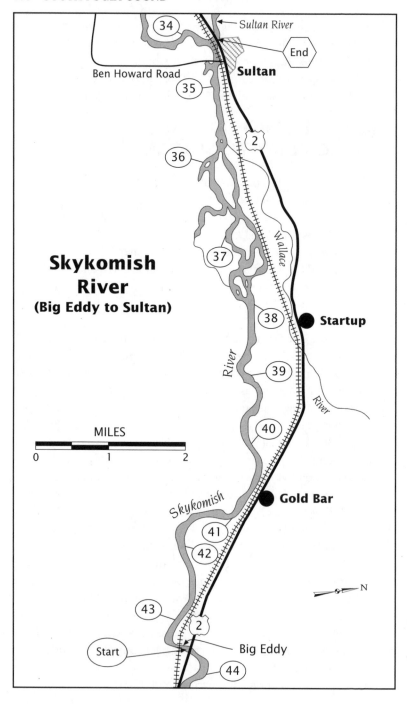

Sultan River

34

End

Ben Howard Road

Sultan

35

2

36

Wallace

37

Skykomish River
(Big Eddy to Sultan)

38

Startup

River

39

River

MILES

0   1   2

40

Skykomish

Gold Bar

41

42

N

43

2

Start

Big Eddy

44

Description. From the Big Eddy (a good place to practice paddling technique), the river dives under the Burlington Northern Railroad bridge and immediately enters a Class II rapid. Below the rapid, the river doglegs to the right, moving quickly into a second, less-severe rapid. (**Caution:** One canoeist who failed to wear a PFD drowned in the first half mile of this river segment.)

The river broadens and shallows, becoming mellow for the next 3 or 4 miles, its banks lined with tall trees, its waters full of fish that entice fishermen, kingfishers, great blue herons, mergansers, and ospreys.

A blue-gray claybank appears on the left, marking a peculiar geologic feature that manifests itself in a series of waves and strange currents that have flipped a few canoes. The hard clay bottom is very near the surface at low water levels, but the water is difficult to read.

A few homes appear along the shore as the river splits around islands; paddlers generally take the right-hand channels. Either of the two big islands at RM 36 and RM 37 will serve as a lunch stop, but the second island is especially popular, summer or winter. It is a great place to skip rocks, and the big logjam offers some protection from the wind if there is any. In the summer it makes a good swimming beach as well.

A dory rests on the bank at the Big Eddy, launch site for the run downriver to Sultan.

The Wallace River enters from the right just below the second big island as the river gathers itself together for the parade through town. Numerous houses line the right bank as the river approaches Sultan. After passing beneath the bridge across the Skykomish in Sultan—the one that leads to Ben Howard Road—there is only 0.25 mile to make the landing on the right, just below the mouth of the Sultan River, which makes a tricky landing at times.

17 SNOQUALMIE RIVER: TOLT MOUTH TO CONFLUENCE

Location	Lower Snoqualmie Valley
Distance	25 miles
River Time	6 to 7 hours
Maps	Carnation, Monroe, Maltby (7.5')
Best Season	all year, but autumn is recommended for colors, blackberries
Hazards	floods, sweepers, and logjams in the first half of the trip
Shuttle	26 miles on paved road
Rating	Class I

The bucolic character of the lower Snoqualmie River dominates this segment. Dairy farms line the river (adding to its nutrient base, especially during periodic winter flooding) and decorate the banks with farm litter and used equipment. Holstein cattle graze its banks and water at the river, breaking down the banks and leaving droppings. Distant mountains, snow-clad in winter and spring, rise in the distance beyond forested hillsides periodically scarred with clear-cuts. This stretch of river is popular with fishermen.

The final few miles of this trip flow through an isolated, heavily forested area reminiscent of a southern swamp. Ideal for summer and early fall paddling—rope swings hang from riverside trees, sandy beaches invite swimming and picnicking, blackberries ripen in August and September—this segment offers placid paddling through private lands (but the river below mean high water is for public use).

Access. Easy access exists at the mouth of the Tolt River near John MacDonald Park at the edge of Carnation. Farther downriver is a put-in from a public fishing area called Taylors Landing, at the north edge of

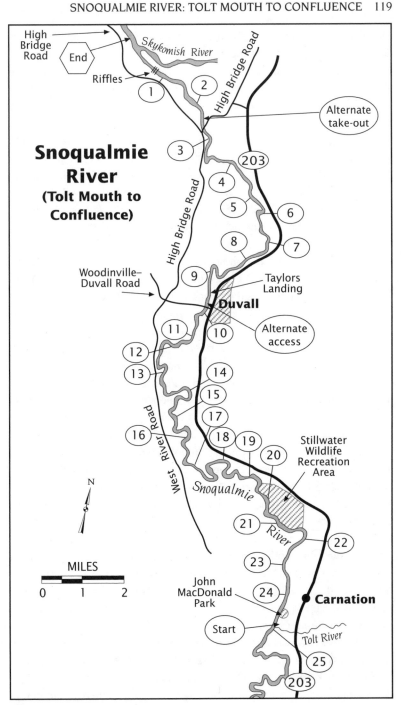

Duvall on the right bank of the river. Both accesses can be reached from S.R. 203 between Fall City and Monroe.

The take-out is on the left bank just below the confluence at Three Rivers Mobile Park, within view of the S.R. 522 bridge across the Snohomish River. An alternate take-out at the High Bridge access shortens the trip by about 3 miles.

Driving Directions. To reach the take-out at the Three Rivers Mobile Park, head south from Snohomish on S.R. 9. Turn left at Rees Corner onto Broadway (99th Avenue SE) to Cathcart, where 164th SE coming in from the right eventually becomes Elliott Road (Connelly Road on some maps). It winds around, approximately paralleling the river and heading upstream. Just before you reach the S.R. 522 bridge overhead, you'll see Three Rivers Mobile Park on the left.

An alternate take-out at the High Bridge public fishing access can be reached by taking High Bridge Road east off West Snoqualmie Valley Road NE, which roughly parallels the river on the west bank and intersects the Woodinville-Duvall Road. High Bridge Road (Tualco Valley) can also be reached from the east off S.R. 203 a mile south of Monroe.

To reach the Tolt launch site, drive to Carnation on S.R. 203 between Fall City and Monroe. Just south of Carnation, at the bridge across the Tolt River, turn west onto a dirt road immediately north of the bridge. This road leads to the mouth of the Tolt, where a convenient rough access offers a reasonable launch on the right bank just below the Tolt.

For an alternate launch site, Taylors Landing, drive to Duvall in the lower Snoqualmie Valley: 8 miles south of Monroe, 14 miles northwest of Fall City on S.R. 203. Woodinville-Duvall Road reaches Duvall from the west, crossing the Snoqualmie River just before entering town. Turn left onto S.R. 203, head north (toward Monroe), and drive 0.2 mile to the public fishing access left of the highway.

Description. From a launch at the mouth of the Tolt River, the Snoqualmie runs swift and deep past King County's Tolt River John MacDonald Park, which includes a suspension footbridge across the river from which it is possible to watch salmon swimming upstream during their spawning runs. You can see them from your boat as well. This stretch is a popular steelhead fishing area.

After two relatively straight miles, the river makes a tight turn to the left and flows past Stillwater Wildlife Recreation Area on the right bank. Stillwater Park lies just below the wildlife area.

The flow slows, as the name "Stillwater" suggests. The river meanders

Steelhead fishermen, some in high waders and others in a powerboat, test the waters of the Snoqulamie River.

widely through its flood plain, creating numerous oxbows and abandoned meanders that decorate the river valley, providing important wildlife habitat as well as hunting and fishing opportunities. As the river nears Duvall, it swings toward the east side of the valley and straightens for a mile or so past Duvall. Taylors Landing lies at the north edge of Duvall.

From Duvall (RM 10) the river is deep, diked, and riprapped but placid and peaceful; an easy river to paddle, with little current, ideal for beginning paddlers. The river makes a straight run for a mile north, then doubles back upon itself in a tight S at RM 8.7. For the next few miles, it passes through pasturelands (adjacent to dairy farms) on the east side of the valley. At RM 6.2 the river crosses the King-Snohomish County Line.

Nothing much changes on the river in Snohomish County except that the river widens and begins a gradual snaking movement toward the west side of the valley. At RM 3.6 it makes a sharp turn to the north and picks up a little speed around a small island where the river both narrows and shallows. In less than a mile (at RM 2.8) the river passes under High Bridge Road, a possible take-out, then enters its "southern swamp" stage for the next mile or so before breaking out into a lively little riffle less than a mile above the confluence.

The river straightens for its last mile as it runs past the promontory that separates it from the Skykomish; the two rivers run almost parallel for their final mile. Where they join, the Snohomish River is born. Almost immediately they split again around an island created by silt from both rivers. Just below the island, the S.R. 522 bridge becomes obvious. The take-out lies on the left bank off the road that creeps beneath the bridge.

18 SNOQUALMIE RIVER: FALL CITY TO TOLT MOUTH

Location	between Fall City and Carnation
Distance	11 miles
River Time	4 hours
Maps	Snoqualmie, Fall City, Carnation (7.5')
Best Season	all year except at flood stage
Hazards	pilings in the river, sweepers, logjams
Shuttle	8 miles
Rating	Class I

The Snoqualmie River between Fall City and Carnation is a bucolic stretch of river perfect for novice paddlers. It may be bound by dikes much of the way, but the river is well forested, offers views of its agricultural valley and distant peaks, and gives the beginning paddler few worries. There are occasional riffles, sweepers, and logjams; but the current is so slow, for the most part, that they serve as good training for more rambunctious river segments. There is an alternate take-out 3 miles into the trip for anyone who wants a shorter run.

Access. There are four accesses: a boat ramp on the left bank in Fall City near the entrance to a private campground; a steep boat ramp in Fall City immediately below the Snoqualmie River (S.R. 203) bridge; a boat ramp 3 miles downstream on Neal Road just off S.R. 203; and a good take-out at the mouth of the Tolt River near John MacDonald Park (King County) at the edge of Carnation.

Driving Directions. To reach the take-out, drive to Carnation on S.R. 203 between Fall City and Monroe. Just south of Carnation, at the bridge across the Tolt River, turn west onto a dirt road immediately north of the bridge. This road leads to the mouth of the Tolt, where a convenient rough access offers a reasonable take-out on the right bank just below the Tolt.

A few dozen yards downstream there are possible take-out points beneath the suspension footbridge across the Snoqualmie on the right bank, near the parking area in John MacDonald Park, but they require long carries. To reach this area, take the turnoff for the park, between Carnation and the Tolt Bridge (north of the Tolt River).

To reach the suggested launch site, drive south on S.R. 203 to Fall City, crossing the bridge over the Snoqualmie into town. There are two alternatives: (1) turn right, park along the road within the next few dozen

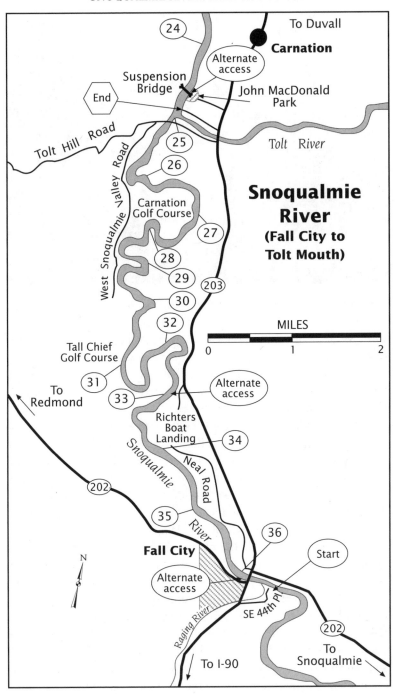

The Snoqualmie River sweeps quietly through its agricultural valley east of Seattle.

yards (if there is room), and launch from the gravel bar beneath the bridge on river left; (2) keep going straight through Fall City toward Preston. Just after crossing the bridge over Raging River, turn left onto SE 44th Place, which leads to a boat ramp and a campground at the river's edge on the left bank. Either access is a good launch site.

The intermediate alternate access, Richters Boat Landing, requires a state Access Stewardship Decal; it lies just off S.R. 203, 2.5 miles north of Fall City, at the northern terminus of Neal Road (which has its southern terminus less than 0.25 mile north of the S.R. 203 bridge over the Snoqualmie, at the north edge of Fall City). Neal Road roughly parallels the river between the river and S.R. 203.

Description. From either Fall City launch site (RM 36.1 or 36.3), the river flows northwest for a little over 2 miles between riprapped banks overgrown with blackberry bushes and lined with native vegetation. Adjacent farms go largely unnoticed. There are a few mild riffles and one stretch where old pilings in the river require some maneuvering.

At RM 33.7 the river turns abruptly to the right and in less than a mile passes the boat ramp at Richters Boat Landing. S.R. 203 comes close enough to be visible from the river twice in the next mile, and there is another area where old pilings create a potential hazard. Farms begin to encroach on the river corridor, and the banks in places are beaten down by cattle.

The river meanders widely for the next several miles, looping back and forth on the west side of the valley. It comes close to both the Tall Chief Golf Course and the Carnation Golf Course, some 5 river miles apart. The river first aims at Tall Chief (RM 31), then runs north for a mile through farmlands. At RM 30 it begins a series of three east-west hairpin bends in the next 2 miles, all through pasture- or croplands.

Through most of this segment the river is slow and deep, full of snags and tree trunks anchored in the sandy bottom. At RM 28 it begins a loop to the north, then abruptly south, and finally, northeast for 0.5 mile before it swings west again past Carnation Golf Course (river left). Once more it turns abruptly north in a big bend adjacent to West Snoqualmie Valley Road. For the last mile of this segment, it flows almost due north to the Tolt Mouth take-out.

19 SNOQUALMIE RIVER: FALLS TO FALL CITY

Location	southeast of Fall City
Distance	4 miles
River Time	1 to 2 hours
Maps	Snoqualmie, Fall City (7.5')
Best Season	all year
Hazards	rapids, especially above Tokul Mouth
Shuttle	3 miles on paved road, ideal for a bicycle shuttle
Rating	Class II; upstream, Class III

The stretch of Snoqualmie River between Snoqualmie Falls and Fall City is short (about 4 river miles), but it offers good variety. Many experienced paddlers go upstream from the boat launch to play in the Class II rapids above (within sight of the falls). Polers like to practice their skills in the rocky rapids of this upper section, but even novice paddlers can negotiate the river downstream (though at low water levels the rapids become rockier and tighter). Blackberries festoon the banks to provide succulent snacks, bird life is abundant, and fishing is often good.

Access. Excellent access to this segment of river is available at two possible take-outs in Fall City and at the logical put-in on river right, a public fishing access area just below the mouth of Tokul Creek, along Fish Hatchery Road. Kayakers often drive to the end of Fish Hatchery Road, to the power plant at the foot of the falls, and launch from the trail immediately below the powerhouse.

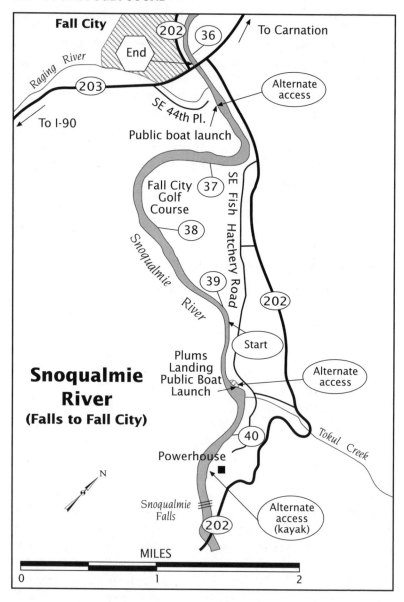

Fall City

202   36

To Carnation

Raging River

End

203

SE 44th Pl.

To I-90

Alternate access

Public boat launch

Fall City Golf Course   37

38

Snoqualmie River

SE Fish Hatchery Road

39

202

Start

Plums Landing Public Boat Launch

Alternate access

Snoqualmie River
(Falls to Fall City)

40

Tokul Creek

Powerhouse

N

Snoqualmie Falls

Alternate access (kayak)

202

MILES

0   1   2

Driving Directions. Drive to Fall City, taking S.R. 202 (from the west or from the south, off I-90 through North Bend and Snoqualmie) or S.R. 203 (from the north). To reach the take-out below the bridge in Fall City, turn west just south of the S.R. 202/203 bridge (at the junction of S.R. 202 and S.R. 203). The take-out is under the bridge and can be accessed from roadside parking between the river (left bank) and the road (S.R. 202 from Redmond).

To reach the boat ramp 0.25 mile upstream, take S.R. 203 south from the junction of S.R. 202 and S.R. 203, cross the bridge over Raging River, and turn left immediately past the bridge onto SE 44th Place, which follows Raging River to its confluence with the Snoqualmie. The boat ramp lies on the dike left of the river a few dozen yards above the confluence, near the entrance to a riverside campground.

To reach the launch site from Fall City, cross the S.R. 203 bridge heading north, then turn right immediately and follow S.R. 202 toward Snoqualmie and North Bend. After a mile, turn right onto SE Fish Hatchery Road, which angles off S.R. 202 toward the river. Follow the road along the river to Plums Landing Public Boat Launch to the right of the road, on the right bank of the river.

To reach the kayakers' launch area, continue on the same road, cross Tokul Creek, and drive up the hill and around a bend or two to the small parking area by a gate (usually locked) at the powerhouse. Follow a trail to the river to the right of the fence around the power plant facility.

Description. This segment gets progressively tougher heading upstream from the boat ramp, and progressively easier using the kayakers' launch at the powerhouse and heading downstream. Below the boat ramp the river has a couple of mild rapids and a few rocks to dodge at low water levels. The river broadens, deepens, and slows as it approaches Fall City.

Negotiating a shallow stretch of riffles on the Snoqualmie River below the falls

There are a few riffles in low water as the current swings from one side of the river to the other, but once the river flows into its big bend to the right, around Fall City Golf Course, it is almost like a lake: a long, narrow stretch of deep green water. The river turns abruptly to the left as it approaches S.R. 202 a mile east of Fall City; then it hugs that road for the rest of the way. A few ancient pilings line the right bank. The left bank is busy with the campground, which covers the promontory around which the last bend of the river is made.

The recommended take-out is on the left just above the mouth of Raging River. At this writing, a commonly used rough take-out for canoes and kayaks lies just below the mouth of Raging River, but the land is privately owned and likely to be developed. A canoe/kayak take-out below the bridge is also on the left, a hundred yards below the mouth of Raging River.

20 SNOQUALMIE RIVER: ABOVE THE FALLS

Location	North Bend to Snoqualmie
Distance	3.5 miles
River Time	1 to 2 hours
Maps	North Bend, Snoqualmie (7.5'), Bandera (15')
Best Season	all year
Hazards	sweepers, logjams, rapids, major falls downstream
Shuttle	4 miles on paved road, ideal for bicycle shuttle
Rating	Class II- first mile, Class I below

This section of the river is obvious from the road, but difficult to get to. It has few real access points, all of which have limited parking. But the river is a real gem, involving all three major forks of the Snoqualmie above the falls. It lies right under Mount Si, which provides a spectacular background for the entire run. The river itself is delightful, with a few riffles, lots of deep pools, a largely natural shoreline, and numerous sand and gravel bars much used by fishermen and picnickers. It is also a favorite for tubers and air-mattress floaters. This area is part of the Three Forks Natural Area of the Mountains to the Sound Greenway, but there is precious little river access.

Access. Although this segment lies in a mixed rural-urban area with lots of roads in the vicinity, viable access to the river is limited. Rough

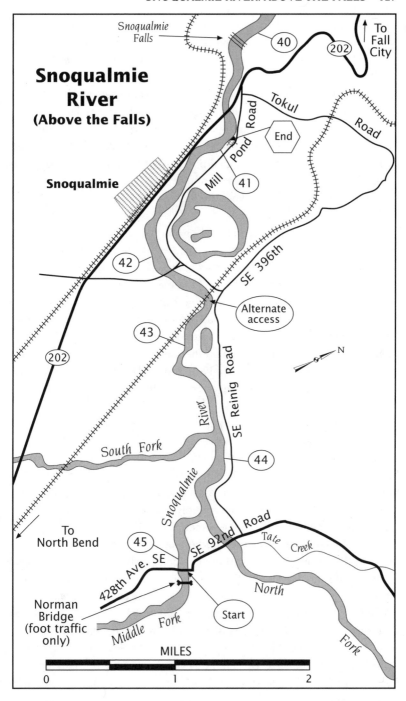

Snoqualmie River
(Above the Falls)

Snoqualmie

Snoqualmie Falls

To Fall City

Tokul Road

Pond Road

End

Mill

SE 396th

Alternate access

SE Reinig Road

River

N

South Fork

Snoqualmie

To North Bend

SE 92nd Road

Tate Creek

428th Ave. SE

North

Norman Bridge (foot traffic only)

Middle Fork

Start

Fork

40 · 41 · 42 · 43 · 44 · 45

202

MILES

0   1   2

but adequate access lies adjacent to Mill Pond Road, 0.5 mile above the falls, and roadside or trail access is available from Reinig Road. A good but limited launch site lies beneath the bridge on 428th Avenue SE, northeast of North Bend.

Driving Directions. To reach the take-out, drive east on S.R. 202 from Fall City toward Snoqualmie and North Bend. At the top of the falls at the northwest edge of Snoqualmie—just beyond Snoqualmie Falls Lodge and before crossing the Snoqualmie River—turn left onto Mill Pond Road. The take-out lies to the right of the road, just beyond the bend of the river, at a small informal access point that may require roadside parking. (A small parking area lies across the road on the north side of Mill Pond Road at the Weyerhaeuser mill.)

To reach the launch site, drive east on Mill Pond Road to SE Reinig Road, which continues east (upstream) alongside the river. SE 396th may seem like the continuation of the main road here, but SE Reinig Road turns right at the next intersection, at a bend of the river where rough access exists on river right at a favorite summer play spot for swimmers and waders.

Continue east on SE Reinig Road to a T intersection, turn right (south), go 0.6 mile to SE 92nd Road (a dead-end road) and turn left, then immediately right onto a rough dirt road that once led under the abandoned Norman Bridge across the Middle Fork. Today vehicles cannot access the river, but a short carry to the river offers launching possibilities. Parking is highly limited.

Description. At the launch site, the river is pleasant and picturesque: Mount Si looms over the paddler's shoulder, and downstream the river is wild in its scenic beauty but mild in its flow. At the first bend of the river, however, the river turns a bit wild in its flow. After a little jog to the left, it makes a sharp swing to the right against a gigantic logjam that at high water could be a terror. At low flows it is merely a hazard to maneuver past, but there are numerous snags in the sometimes swift water in this first mile.

Just below the logjam, the Middle Fork meets the North Fork head-on and the currents swirl together off a long sandy point bar. With a trail coming into this vicinity on the right, fishermen and picnickers use the area heavily. The deep pools begin just below the confluence with plenty of debris in the river, but the current is so slow that the logs and snags offer few real hazards; they're just obstacles to maneuver around.

Pools and riffles alternate to the mouth of the South Fork on the left, which is totally blocked by fallen trees at this writing but may open to winter floods. Reinig Road runs along the right bank, offering possible access at a couple of points. A few rural homes line the bank as the river becomes one big, slow, deep channel.

As it turns left in a big bend beneath a railroad bridge, the river passes the swimming hole on the right at the junction of SE 396th and Reinig Road, a possible launch or take-out point. Soon the river swings back to the right under a bridge. The edge of the town of Snoqualmie lines the left bank of the river; a thin fringe of timber between the river and Mill Pond Road lines the right.

This slow, deep stretch continues around moderate bends, the river passing under the railroad bridge that serves the Weyerhaeuser mill. Soon the protective railing

View of Mount Si from the Middle Fork of the Snoqualmie

along Mill Pond Road comes into view—the sign that it is time to look for the take-out on the right, just upstream from the railing.

21 SAMMAMISH RIVER

Location	between Redmond and Kenmore
Distance	13 miles
River Time	4 to 5 hours
Maps	Redmond, Kirkland, Bothell (7.5'); NOAA Chart: 18447 (lower river)
Best Season	all year
Hazards	trash and debris in the river
Shuttle	12 miles on paved roads and streets, bicycle shuttle ideal
Rating	Class I

The Sammamish River, which links Lake Sammamish with Lake Washington, creates a passage between the lakes for boats as well as for anadromous fish. The Sammamish River Trail runs all the way from Marymoor County Park to Kenmore. The river flows slowly through an urban area that supports beavers, muskrats, and numerous species of nesting birds, including many ducks and geese. It offers nearby access to fine restaurants, shopping areas, two wineries, and a brewery as it passes through Redmond, Hollywood Corner, Woodinville, Bothell, and Kenmore.

Access. Abundant access to the Sammamish River suggests numerous short sections of this segment for brief after-work runs. There is easy access in Marymoor County Park and from West Lake Sammamish Parkway south of Redmond, from several points in downtown Redmond, from every bridge crossing in the valley (and there are several), from both sides of the river in Bothell, and at a public boat ramp in Kenmore. Additional access is available at several parks on both Lake Sammamish and Lake Washington if a longer run is sought and if paddlers are willing to travel upstream against the usually mild current.

Driving Directions. To reach the last take-out before Lake Washington, take NE Bothell Way (S.R. 522), the route that follows the north end of Lake Washington, eastbound into Kenmore. At 68th Avenue NE, turn right, cross the Sammamish River, and immediately turn right again into a public fishing access on the left bank of the river beneath the bridge (Kenmore County Park). There is substantial parking here, but the area is heavily used by powerboats and is often crowded with vehicles and boat trailers. The nearest auxiliary parking is blocks away.

To reach the Bothell accesses, return to NE Bothell Way (S.R. 522) and head east. As it enters Bothell, the road curves left (north). Just as it begins to curve back to the right (east again), turn right onto Wilson Avenue into the park at Bothell Landing, an access on river right with parking and several nice shops and restaurants nearby.

The other Bothell access is just across the river on the left bank. Turn right off Main Street (a block north of NE Bothell Way and S.R. 522) onto 102nd Avenue, heading south over the Sammamish River. Take the first right just past the bridge approach on the south side of the river, turning into a large parking area that offers access to the river's left bank—a good take-out or put-in point.

To reach the access points in the Sammamish Valley, retrace the route to S.R. 522, which soon becomes a freeway. Turn right toward Woodinville, then take the Woodinville exit and follow S.R. 202 south, first along the west side of the river, then along the east side after it crosses the river on NE 145th Street. Between Woodinville and Redmond it is possible

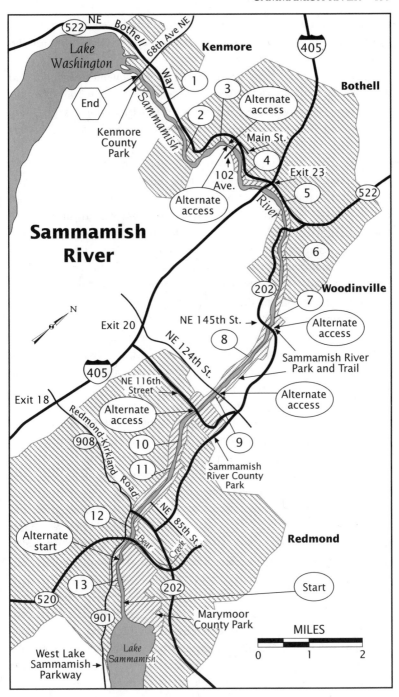

Sammamish River

to access the river at any of the crossings that intersect with S.R. 202: 154th Place NE, NE 145th Street, NE 124th Street, or NE 116th Street (in Sammamish River County Park).

In Redmond itself you can access the river at several street ends and at NE 85th Street, all of which abut the Sammamish River Trail. The better accesses, however, lie in Marymoor County Park immediately south of Redmond. These are reached from West Lake Sammamish Parkway (S.R. 901) south off NE Redmond Way (S.R. 908).

One access lies between West Lake Sammamish Parkway and the river, 0.2 mile south of the red light at the entrance to Marymoor County Park; but it is rough, unpaved, and somewhat steep at low water. The better access (though it requires a carry of several dozen yards) lies in the park. Turn east at the red light on S.R. 901, follow the main road into Marymoor County Park, and turn right toward the Pea Patch Picnic Area and Dog Training Area. Park in the large parking lot as near the river as possible, and carry the craft to the river (which is swift in this vicinity near the outlet of Lake Sammamish).

Description. Launching at the outlet of Lake Sammamish requires an upriver carry of a couple hundred yards but gives a swift start on the run to Bothell or Kenmore. Below the fast water, the river swings along the edge of Marymoor County Park adjacent to the Sammamish River Trail, which parallels this segment all the way to Bothell.

Bear Creek comes in on the right about a mile below the lake outlet. The river passes beneath the Sammamish River (S.R. 520) bridge high overhead, enters Redmond (flanked by condominiums), passes under the NE Redmond Way (S.R. 908) bridge and a railroad bridge, then passes an office park and the Redmond City Hall. There are a number of good restaurants within easy walking distance of the river.

Channelized for most of this stretch to Lake Washington, the Sammamish runs northward out of Redmond. However, the fact that it lies in a uniform-sided trough does not detract from its aesthetic quality or its wildlife and natural beauty. There are views of Mount Rainier upstream, and beavers and muskrats live in this stretch.

Ducks and geese nest here, along with red-winged blackbirds and marsh wrens. There are swallows, spotted sandpipers, northern harriers, red-tailed hawks, kingfishers, killdeer, grebes, great blue and green herons, as well as yellow iris and wild sweetpeas that bloom in summer, cattails and blackberries, ripe in late summer. A few noisy electric pumps drain water from the river in late summer for nearby irrigation.

Well-kept homes and boat docks line the Sammamish River in Bothell.

The water is slow, even sluggish, but there is always a perceptible flow and a sense of the natural. The river passes open meadows, ball fields, turf farms, dairies, and scattered condos. It passes within 0.25 mile of rural shopping centers as well as two wineries and a brewery. Bikers, runners, fishermen, hikers, skaters, hot air balloonists and ultralight fliers, even dogsledders (with sleds on wheels) may be seen from the river.

As the river passes the Tolt Pipeline Trail, it swings northwest toward Woodinville, scrapes the edge of that growing community, and turns westward through a light industrial area. Even as it approaches the noisy overpasses that carry I-405 overhead, the river is flanked by small farms and residences. Soon it begins to curve past suburban homes, nurseries, golf courses, and a couple of mobile parks.

The river widens, making room for powerboats tied up at private docks. Canada geese mob the river in this area. Always there is activity along the trail that parallels the river, and the closer the river gets to Bothell, the more the urban environment encroaches upon the natural. The take-out on the left bank in Bothell is a good place to stop after a 10-mile run. Bothell Landing on the right just beyond offers a pleasant park, more urban than bucolic.

The last 2.5 miles are largely urban-industrial, and powerboats ply this stretch so continuously (especially on weekends and after-work hours) that it is less than pleasant for paddling. Still, it can be delightful in the early mornings and whenever you can have the river to yourself.

22 ISSAQUAH CREEK

Location	south end of Lake Sammamish, north of Issaquah
Distance	1 to 2 miles
River Time	1 to 2 hours
Map	Issaquah (7.5')
Best Season	all year
Hazards	debris from human activity, natural debris
Shuttle	none necessary, 2 miles at most
Rating	Class I

One of the smallest streams covered in this book, Issaquah Creek is perhaps the most intimate. It requires no shuttle because it involves paddling up a creek from an access on the lake into which it flows, then returning. The creek offers a natural area in the midst of rapid urban development.

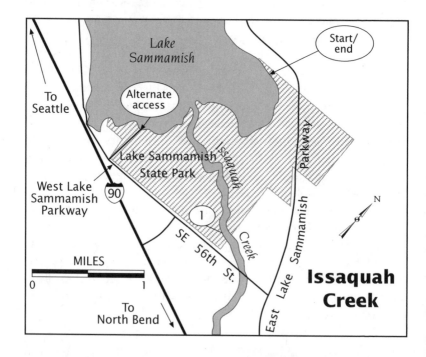

A *wooden footbridge over* Issaquah Creek *in* Lake Sammamish State Park

It has a salmon run, muskrats, beavers, deer, coyotes, and abundant bird life, from bald eagles to marsh wrens, from green herons to nesting ducks. It is protected, after a fashion, by Lake Sammamish State Park.

Access. The best access is from the boat launch area at the southeast end of Lake Sammamish in Lake Sammamish State Park. An alternate access, which involves a longish carry, is from the swimming beach area of Lake Sammamish State Park at the south end of the lake.

Driving Directions. Take I-90 east to the second Issaquah exit (Exit 17). Take the East Lake Sammamish Parkway north about 3 miles to the Lake Sammamish State Park boat launch area, turn left into that facility, and launch onto the southeastern lobe of Lake Sammamish.

To reach the Lake Sammamish State Park swimming beaches, take I-90 east to the first Issaquah exit (Exit 15), go north 0.25 mile to SE 56th Street, turn left, and after 0.5 mile, turn right into the park entrance. Follow the signs to the swimming beach and park as close as possible, because the carry will be a couple of hundred yards. The area may be crowded in summer.

Description. Between the boat launch at Lake Sammamish State Park southwest and the low-lying delta of Issaquah Creek, paddlers may encounter a few powerboats; but once into the creek mouth and heading upstream, the noise (as well as the wind and most of the people) will be left behind. A few trails in the vicinity may have hikers, but within 0.25 mile (shortly after passing beneath the footbridge across the creek), they too should be left behind.

The channel may be blocked by natural debris from recent storms, but boaters can generally make their way up the creek with either pole or paddle—though the pole may get snagged in overhead vegetation at times, for the river flows through a virtual tunnel of trees and shrubs. Blackberry vines hang over the water in places but can easily be avoided. They can also be sought out for snacks in the late summer or early fall.

The creek winds along through the trees and shrubs, gradually increasing in speed as it breaks into an opening here and there. At a sharp turn on the left, about half a mile from the mouth, there is a strong current around a little island that may call for portaging or lining. However, especially with a pole, it is usually possible to work your way upstream. A few fishermen or a pair of lovers may be seen along the bank.

Steep cutbanks a few feet high mark the creek's course through the meadows as it approaches SE 56th Street. In the summer these meadows are full of wildflowers and goldfinches feeding on thistle seeds. In late spring the creek abounds with families of ducks, mostly mallards. Fall brings the salmon runs, fun to watch as they work their way up to the hatchery in Issaquah. Paddlers can turn around at this point and drift back down to the mouth, then paddle across the lake to the launch site, which is also the take-out.

23 CEDAR RIVER

Location	Maple Valley to Renton
Distance	14.5 miles
River Time	3 to 4 hours
Maps	Maple Valley, Renton (7.5')
Best Season	all year, great in summer
Hazards	logjams, sweepers, rapids, one headwall
Shuttle	12 miles by paved road
Rating	Class II

The Cedar River flows under the Renton Library and can be seen from the I-405 S curves. A raging Cascade river in its youth, its final few miles offer an active paddling experience through a bucolic semirural area. The river is small and intimate, a rocky run with brushy bends, an occasional high bluff, lots of gravel bars, numerous species of birds (including mallards and mergansers), and evidence of beavers and muskrats. Its run through downtown Renton is unique, with anadromous fish visible in the clear cool water, even under the library. The Cedar—along with the Missouri, the Yellowstone, the Lower Snake, and several other rivers—made American Rivers' list of the 10 Most Endangered Rivers in 1999 due to urban sprawl and water withdrawals. (American Rivers is North America's leading river conservation organization.)

Access. The last mile of the Cedar River before it flows into Lake Washington is flanked on the right by parklands with an excellent take-out across the river from the Renton Airport. The logical launch site is a rough, often-rutted access at the edge of Maple Valley, within sight of the S.R. 18 overpass.

Driving Directions. To reach the take-out, find the Cedar River Trail and Park in Renton off North 6th Street from Logan Avenue North in the midst of the Boeing Complex. NE Park Drive, which becomes Lake Washington Boulevard North, is a good way to get there from Exit 5 off I-405. (S.R. 900 to Issaquah goes off at this same exit.)

Lake Washington Beach Park, which has abundant parking, is another potential take-out, but it involves paddling a mile across the lower end of Lake Washington (which can be an interesting run through an industrial area).

To reach the launch site at Maple Valley, take the Enumclaw exit off I-405 to the Renton–Maple Valley Highway (S.R. 169). Heading east on this route, paddlers can scout much of the river, especially if they take the Jones Road cutoff that crosses the river, parallels it, and recrosses it again well below Maple Valley.

In Maple Valley, turn left off S.R. 169 just after crossing the river, then left again into an unpaved, unmarked riverside access between the highway and the railroad tracks. This is the launch site, unpretentious but adequate. It is 12 miles from the I-405 exit.

Description. From the launch site on river left (RM 14.7), the river is fast and rocky. It passes beneath S.R. 169 and S.R. 18 in quick succession, runs a fast mile through a brushy corridor, then passes under S.R. 169 again and the adjacent railroad bridge a mile northwest of Maple Valley (RM 13.5) to run north of the highway for several miles.

The river has a rural flavor. Well-wooded banks hide most, but not

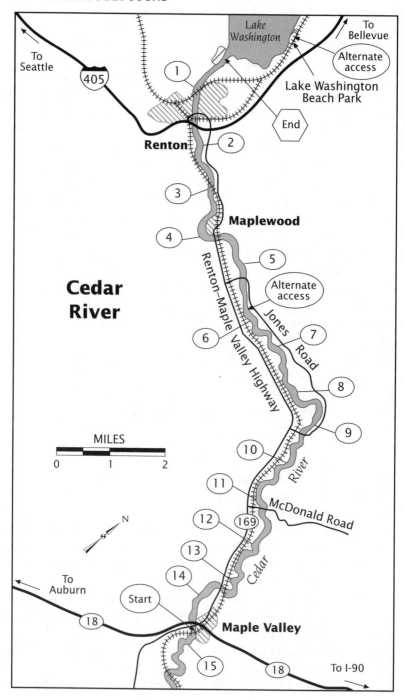

all, of the surrounding homes. Some short, simple rapids and the speed of the current keep paddlers busy as the river swings back and forth across its flood plain. At one moment it nudges the railroad embankment on the left; at the next it nibbles at the base of the bluff on the right; and at one point (near RM 12) it drives into the headwall on the right.

The Cedar flows beneath a bridge (McDonald Road) at RM 11.1, parallels the railroad for a few hundred yards, swings back toward the bluff, back again toward the railroad, and repeats this performance to slide beneath the Jones Road bridge at RM 9.3. Just below this point, the highway and the railroad (which have been heading north-northwest) turn due west, still paralleling one another quite closely; whenever you near the railroad tracks, the highway is immediately adjacent.

At RM 5.8 there is access off Jones Road on river right in an area that is frequently used during summer months by air-mattress and inner-tube

The Cedar River

floaters. Jones Road kisses the riverbank between RM 5 and 6. The river flows beneath the western Jones Road bridge at RM 5.3, then becomes more debris-ridden as the gradient mellows. A mile downstream the river curves left under both the railroad and the highway to make a big loop around Maplewood. It remains south of the highway for the rest of its course to Renton, but the railroad crosses to the south side of the river at RM 2.9.

The Cedar River mellows as it approaches Renton, getting slower, a little deeper, less rambunctious. Development intrudes here and there (a sand and gravel works on the left from which silty water trickles into the river, concrete or asphalt banks in places, buildings), but parklands also embrace much of the riverbank in the lower few miles. Once the river passes beneath the twin spans of I-405, the banks are concrete, the scene urban, including the river's passage beneath the library.

For the last 1.5 miles there will be people watching, waving, having their lunch along the river. Fish can be seen in the river, and gulls overhead, but it is an urban world, and not a bad place to stop for a drink or something to eat. Paddlers could even exit the river at one of the cross streets, but that might tie up traffic—better to go on the last mile to the take-out suggested above.

24 DUWAMISH RIVER/WATERWAY

Location	Fort Dent Park to Elliott Bay
Distance	12 miles
River Time	4 to 5 hours
Maps	Seattle South, Des Moines (7.5'); NOAA Charts: 18448, 18449, 18450
Best Season	all year
Hazards	snags, tidal currents, powerboats, large ships, a major rapid (Class II) at low tide below Pacific Highway South bridge (S.R. 99)
Shuttle	12 miles on paved roads, city streets, none necessary
Rating	Class I, Tidal

The Duwamish River and the waterway at its mouth provide a unique paddling experience, from fast-water chutes when the tide is going out to dodging ocean-going vessels around Harbor Island while admiring views

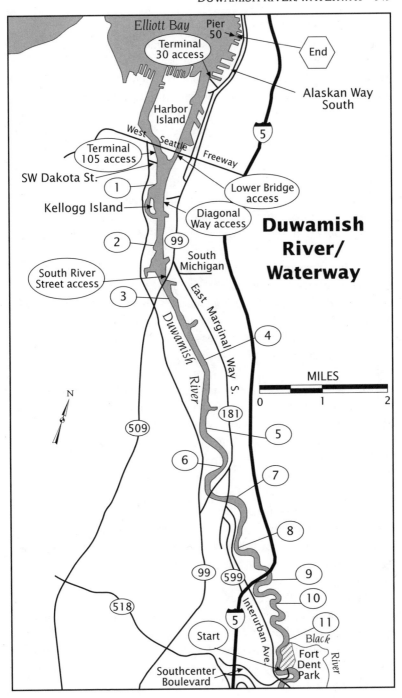

Elliott Bay

Pier 50

Terminal 30 access

End

Alaskan Way South

5

Harbor Island

West Seattle Freeway

Terminal 105 access

SW Dakota St.

1

Lower Bridge access

Kellogg Island

Diagonal Way access

Duwamish River/ Waterway

2

99

South Michigan

South River Street access

3

East Marginal Way S.

Duwamish River

4

MILES

0   1   2

N

509

181

5

6

7

8

99   599

9

10

518

5

11

Start

Interurban Ave.

Black River

Fort Dent Park

Southcenter Boulevard

of the Seattle skyline. The Green River becomes the Duwamish just below Fort Dent Park, where the Black River draining out of Lake Washington once joined it. The Lower Duwamish is almost totally industrial, yet it harbors a great blue heron colony, and fishermen still line the low-level Spokane Street bridge to try for a variety of salt- and freshwater fish.

Access. Numerous accesses exist for launching a small paddle craft onto the Duwamish River or Waterway, from the poor put-in at Fort Dent Park on the last mile of the Green (before it becomes the Duwamish) to public access on Elliott Bay, below the artificial saltwater mouth of the river. (It has been totally channelized, and its banks have been altered.)

Most of the alternate accesses lie in the saltwater reaches of the river (perhaps more properly called a waterway, since it is virtually all paved over and developed). They consist of six public accesses, five of them reached from either East or West Marginal Way.

Driving Directions. The ultimate access—that is, the farthest downstream—is just south of Pier 50 on the Seattle Waterfront. A trip from Fort Dent Park to the Seattle Waterfront makes a run of slightly more than 12 miles.

There are six other public accesses:

(1) Jack Perry Memorial Viewpoint (Terminal 30 Access) is the lowest one on the river itself, at the lower end of the East Waterway where Alaskan Way South becomes East Marginal Way South. This is south of the Coast Guard Station (south of Massachusetts Street), where the huge orange cranes can be seen to the west rising into the sky at the edge of the waterway. Driving south, turn right immediately south of the tank farm (fuel storage structures) at an area marked "Terminal 30, East Waterway, Interim Public Access Site." This is a Port of Seattle access with ample parking that marks the end of an 11-mile trip from Fort Dent Park.

(2) Lower Bridge Site on the east shore of the East Waterway lies a few dozen yards below its split from the West Waterway, but it can be reached only from the eastward traffic on the lower bridge from West Seattle (beneath the new West Seattle Bridge). The access ramp is so close to the bridge you can't see it until you are there: immediately after the guardrail ends on the bridge over the East Waterway. There is room for only five vehicles to park at this take-out—the end of a 10-mile trip from Fort Dent Park—or the launch site for local exploring. (During my last two visits to the site in 1999, transients were living there.) An outgoing tide causes significant current through the bridge pilings. On high tides there is no clearance beneath the bridge.

(3) Diagonal Avenue South Public Shoreline Access (Diagonal Way Site) is probably the best take-out (or launch site, for local exploration) on the entire waterway. There is plenty of parking, and the access is protected by a small indentation at the southwest end of Diagonal Way. Launch along the fence at the south edge to protect fragile intertidal habitat. The turnoff to Diagonal Way is the second stoplight south of the viaduct carrying Old S.R. 99. It is located just opposite the lower (downstream) end of Kellogg Island.

(4) South River Street Site consists of a boat ramp almost directly beneath the First Avenue South Viaduct, just south of the South Michigan Street ramp onto the viaduct. Turn west onto South River Street, a very short street that bisects East Marginal Way a block south of South Michigan. The boat ramp (but little parking) is just east of the Viaduct over the

The little-used boat ramp beneath the First Avenue South Viaduct off South River Street can be hard to find.

Duwamish. This take-out point serves to terminate an 8-mile trip from Fort Dent Park.

(5) Terminal 105 Viewpoint lies on the west bank of the Duwamish just as the West Waterway splits around Harbor Island. Located off West Marginal Way, it is a tiny park provided by the Port of Seattle. Just north of Southwest Dakota Street, this access is marked "Duwamish Public Access—Public Shore." A trip from Fort Dent Park ending here would be 10 miles long. (This access is not intended as a boating access, but it can serve that purpose.) Parking is limited.

(6) The public access at Fort Dent Park (RM 11.7) is no more than a trail leading to a sandy beach (at low water levels) or an eddy (at high flows). To reach Fort Dent, get on southbound I-5 any of several different ways: (1) West Seattle Freeway, (2) Old S.R. 99, or (3) East Marginal Way S. Travel toward Southcenter or the juncture of I-5 with I-405. East Marginal Way S. (also S.R. 181) may be the best bet, because it puts you on Interurban Avenue, which crosses Southcenter Boulevard at the right place: at the left turn to Fort Dent Park. Heading south on I-5, take the Interurban exit (Exit 156), follow Interurban to the Southcenter Boulevard junction, and turn left. Crossing the lower Green River, enter Fort Dent Park and turn left at the south end of the parking area adjacent to an open field. The access is on the point of land at the south edge of the park, where the river loops back in a great horseshoe. Check it out on foot before you carry the craft and gear all over the park looking for the right place. A dedicated boat-launching site (not a boat ramp) at Fort Dent Park would greatly enhance boating use of the lower Duwamish—a highly developed but nonetheless interesting stretch of river.

Description. From the launch site in Fort Dent Park the river heads northwest, skirting the park and forming its western boundary. A fringe of trees on the left bank of the river thinly veils development. Within a mile a slough comes in from the right—all that remains of what was once the Black River, the historical outlet of Lake Washington. The confluence of the Green and the Black historically created the Duwamish, named for an Native American tribe that no longer exists.

For the next 2 miles—to the I-5 crossing—the Duwamish meanders through Foster Golf Links, a lovely run and a good access site as well. At the I-5 crossing overhead there is traffic noise. If the tide is going out, there is a strong pull by the river, gurgling past snags anchored in the muddy bottom. Earlington County Park embraces the right bank. There are bridges galore: 42nd Avenue South, East Marginal Way S. (S.R. 181),

Pacific Highway. Some of this stretch of river is lovely, almost isolated by the dikes raised to control its flooding. Beware of commercial traffic on the river. Groups of paddlers should stay together along one shore or the other.

From RM 5 the Duwamish is an industrial river, but nonetheless interesting and paddle-worthy. Late in the afternoon and on weekends and holidays it can be a delightful place to explore, though powerboats often create an atmosphere less than desirable for paddle craft. At RM 0.8 the Duwamish splits around Harbor Island, creating a pair of busy waterways where paddling may not seem appropriate during the working day, but where it can offer unique paddling opportunities.

25 LOWER GREEN RIVER

Location	Kent to Tukwila
Distance	6.5 miles
River Time	2 hours
Maps	Renton, Des Moines (7.5')
Best Season	all year
Hazards	none
Shuttle	8 miles on paved roads, city streets
Rating	Class I

This is a short stretch of placid but relatively fast water bound by dikes on both sides. A worthwhile segment to consider, much of it is flanked by parklands, both in west Kent and in Tukwila. It begins in a rural area marked by nurseries, berry fields, and old barns; traverses several miles of what was once fertile farmland but is now devoted to housing developments; passes through Tukwila's industrial and commercial heart; then ends at Fort Dent Park after passing beneath I-405. It provides a link between the Green River in the Auburn-Kent area and the Duwamish River, allowing a continuous trip of more than 30 miles. Salmon enhancement projects and Native American fishing activities have discouraged development of additional river access for recreational boaters.

Access. Access is limited to the take-out at Fort Dent Park (RM 11.7) and a choice of two possible put-ins almost opposite one another (RM 18.1 and 18.3) in west Kent, just south of South 212th Street.

Driving Directions. Take the S.R. 181/Interurban Avenue exit from I-405 (Exit 1) a mile east of the I-5/I-405 interchange, and head north on

Interurban. Turn right onto Southcenter Boulevard, which crosses the lower Green as it enters Fort Dent Park. Turn left at the first intersection in the park and stop as far south and as close to the open field on the southwest as possible. The take-out lies at the bend of the river a hundred yards below the bridge but is reached by a long carry from the south parking area. (See map for Trip 24.)

To reach the put-ins, retrace the route to I-405 but do not get back on the freeway. Go straight ahead on S.R. 181 (Interurban Avenue, which soon becomes West Valley Road South) heading south. It touches bends of the river at three points and parallels it for several hundred yards. It can be scouted from the road. Turn right at South 212th Street in Kent, and follow it to the river.

To launch on the east side of the river, turn left onto Russell Road just before reaching the river and follow the river south to Van Dorens Landing, the best access on the river in this vicinity. To launch on the west side of the river, cross the Green, turn left onto Frager Road, and follow the river south to an unmarked access around the bend and upstream of Van Dorens Landing. A four-wheel-drive vehicle can get you closer to the river, but it's a short carry either way. There is also an access a mile above I-405 on the west shore near RM 13.

Description. The Green River is usually clear in the area of both launch sites, swift and sandy-bottomed. Its grassy dike blocks out much of the surrounding development, but there are domestic geese in the river and enough wild birds to make it worth the effort for birdwatchers. The river meanders in slow, easy curves, passing beneath bridges at South 212th Street and South 176th Street, where it begins a brief love affair with West Valley Road, which it hugs for half a mile.

Christensen Road embraces the left (west) bank. A greenbelt park, then a Bicentennial park, help preserve the natural aspect of this stretch of river as it cuts through industrial back yards and commercial enterprises. A major manufacturer of paddle craft has its headquarters less than a quarter mile from the river as it swings back and forth just west of the former Longacres Race Track, approaching I-405.

After passing beneath the freeway, the lower Green leaves behind much of the developed world and takes on a more natural tone as it approaches Fort Dent Park. It makes a big horseshoe bend, flows beneath the bridge that leads into the park, and bends to the right. The take-out appears on the right, just around the bend.

The lower Green River flows through a protected parkway in Tukwila.

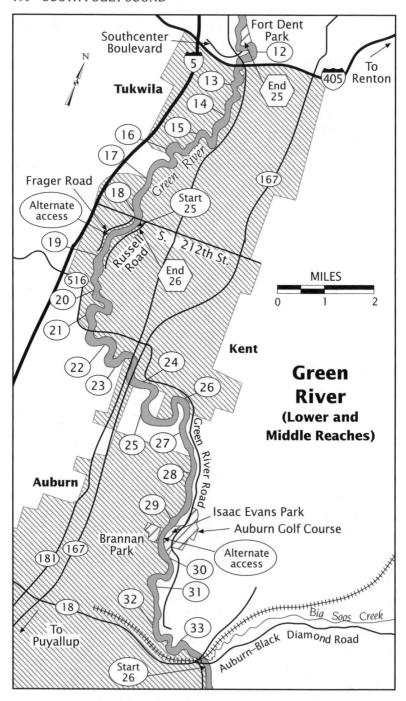

Southcenter
Boulevard

Fort Dent
Park

12

5

To
Renton

405

13

Tukwila

14

End
25

15

16

Green River

17

167

Frager Road

18

Start
25

Alternate
access

19

S. 212th St.

Russell Road

516

End
26

20

21

Kent

22

24

Green River

23

26

Auburn

25

27

28

29

Isaac Evans Park

Auburn Golf Course

Brannan
Park

Alternate
access

167

30

181

31

18

32

To
Puyallup

33

Big Soos Creek

Auburn-Black Diamond Road

Start
26

MILES

0   1   2

N

Green River
(Lower and Middle Reaches)

26 GREEN RIVER: MIDDLE REACH

Location	Auburn area to west Kent
Distance	15.6 miles
River Time	4 to 5 hours
Maps	Des Moines, Renton, Auburn (7.5')
Best Season	all year
Hazards	logjams, sweepers in upper mile
Shuttle	15 miles, paved roads
Rating	upper mile, Class II; remainder, Class I

The Green River from the mouth of Big Soos Creek 2 miles above Auburn through west Kent changes from a rural river, where steelhead fishermen dominate the scene, to a suburban river that nibbles the edges of two towns (Auburn and Kent) while following a natural course through agricultural lands and residential fringes. Much of the riverbank is riprap overgrown with blackberry bushes, natural grasses, and shrubs—ideal habitat for the many species of birds that live here.

Access. Several rough accesses exist between the proposed launch site opposite the mouth of Big Soos Creek 2 miles above Auburn and the proposed take-outs in west Kent, but most of them are in the Auburn vicinity. Adequate public access in or near downtown Kent is badly needed for appropriate utilization of this segment.

Driving Directions. To reach the proposed take-outs in west Kent, find S.R. 181 south of I-405 (Exit 1); go south on West Valley Road (S.R. 181) to South 212th Street; and turn right (west). At the Green River bridge, either (1) turn left onto Russell Road east of the river to Van Dorens Landing, or (2) turn left onto Frager Road west of the river to an unobtrusive, unmarked access left of the road on the left bank of the river.

To find any of the suggested launch sites, go back to South 212th, turn right (east) back to S.R. 181, and turn right again (south) to S.R. 516 (Kent–Des Moines Road South). Then either (1) turn left to S.R. 167 heading south to Auburn, where you take S.R. 18 (a freeway of sorts) to the proposed launch site; or (2) turn left, then go straight ahead under the S.R. 167 overpass on West Meeker Street to Central Avenue in downtown Kent, turn right, go south to 259th Street, and turn left onto what becomes the Green River Road east of the river.

Green River Road offers several possible rough access points as it parallels the river upstream (south) toward Auburn. Isaac Evans Park at the northeast edge of Auburn is one of these points. This route into Auburn has the advantage of permitting the paddler to scout the river from the road.

The uppermost launch site can be reached by continuing along the Green River Road into Auburn until it becomes 104th Avenue SE, and turning right (west) onto SE 320th (which becomes 8th Street NE after crossing the Green River). By weaving around through Auburn—taking Harvey Road south to Main, Main east to R Street SE, and following it until it becomes the Auburn–Black Diamond Road—paddlers can reach the proposed launch site described below.

To reach this launch site from S.R. 18, turn right about 3 miles east of Auburn at the exit to the Auburn–Black Diamond Road. Just before that road crosses the Green River, turn right onto the road to Flaming Geyser State Park (SE Green Valley Road), then left into a public fishing access just upstream from the bridge carrying the Auburn–Black Diamond Road across the Green River. The launch site is on the left bank.

Description. Big Soos Creek's entering the Green River from the right is the first notable natural feature, but man-made structures dominate the first couple of hundred yards: the Green River (Auburn–Black Diamond Road) bridge, the Burlington Northern Railroad bridge, and the

The Green River's course through Auburn

S.R. 18 bridge. The first mile of river seems like wilderness, with natural islands and forest debris (sunken logs, stumps, sweepers, and logjams). The river swings to the left around a bend full of downed trees. At times the river may be entirely blocked, but a portage around the obstacle is usually short and simple, especially at low water.

The river runs into the riprapped railroad embankment to the south as it gathers itself into one channel for an S turn at the eastern edge of Auburn. Soon houses begin to appear on the left bank, though the right bank remains forested. The diked banks are overgrown with blackberry bushes, natural grasses, and shrubs. Bird life abounds: great blue herons, spotted sandpipers, kingfishers galore, several species of swallows, many mallards and mergansers, frequently with young in late spring and early summer.

The trip through east Auburn is delightful, as one of the nicer parts of town smiles on the river (rather than turning its back on the river, as Kent seems to). The river flows beneath Porter Bridge (8th Street NE and SE 320th Street); loops past an undeveloped park (Isaac Evans) on the right bank, where access to the river is possible; then runs north out of town past Brannan Park on the left and the Auburn Golf Course on the right.

Between Auburn and Kent the river is much used by tubers, rafters, and air-mattress floaters who gain access from Green River Road east of the river. The river is clear and shallow, with a few riffles and some deep pools—an ideal poling stream. The banks are natural enough to attract such bright-colored birds as orioles, goldfinches, and western tanagers.

In 2.5 hours from the proposed launch site, a paddler can reach Kent at the intersection of 78th Avenue South and South 259th Street. But there is no real access, even though you can read the street signs from the river: a pity, for the paddler gets hungry and thirsty about this time, and South Kent stores suffer the loss of potential business. Tall grass and blackberry bushes dominate the landscape, and it is possible to discern a small dairy farm.

Below the Green River (S.R. 167) bridge, the Green is largely a big ditch—but it is a delightful ditch, its banks covered with eye-pleasing vegetation, its waters full of fish (salmon and steelhead), wildlife (beavers and muskrats), and birds. Domestic ducks and geese join their wilder cousins, while hikers, cyclists, and joggers join the parade along riverside trails. The take-out on the left at RM 18.5 lies a few hundred yards downstream from Cottonwood Grove. Van Dorens Landing lies a few hundred yards downstream on the right bank at RM 18.2.

27 GREEN RIVER: RURAL REACH

Location	east of Auburn, along Green Valley Road
Distance	7 miles
River Time	2 hours
Maps	Auburn, Black Diamond (7.5')
Best Season	all year
Hazards	logjams, sweepers
Shuttle	8 miles, paved road
Rating	Class I+/II-

The Green River between Whitney Bridge (RM 40) and the mouth of Big Soos Creek (RM 33.6) flows through the bucolic Green Valley east of Auburn, an area similar to the Skykomish Valley between Sultan and Monroe. It meanders through croplands, orchards, and pastures between forested slopes. Ancient evergreens stand as sentinels here and there, remnants of early days before the valley was cleared.

Access. Access to the river at Whitney Bridge (the launch site) and across from the mouth of Big Soos Creek (the take-out) is quick and easy by the paved but winding Green Valley Road.

Driving Directions. To reach the launch site at Whitney Bridge Park, take S.R. 18 about 3 miles east of Auburn, then turn right at the exit to the Auburn–Black Diamond Road. Just before that road crosses the Green River, turn right onto SE Green Valley Road. Signs suggest this is the way to Flaming Geyser State Park.

Eight miles from the turnoff, turn right onto SE 219th Street. Within a hundred yards, turn right into the parking area at Whitney Bridge Park.

Taking S.R. 18 east of Auburn also brings you to the take-out, where Big Soos Creek flows into the Green River (see put-in for Trip 26).

Description. While the launch site on river right at Whitney Bridge Park involves a short carry, there is plenty of parking. A big barn across the river just upstream of the bridge marks the location. Downstream a half mile the river bends left, then runs straight between well-vegetated banks for another mile before it splits around an island (RM 38) where fishing access extends for a half mile along the right bank.

Below the island the river bends right, straightens for another mile, then is augmented by creeks entering—first from the right, then from the left. There is walk-in access on both sides of the river at RM 36 as the river bends first right, then left. The river courses through pastures of dairy

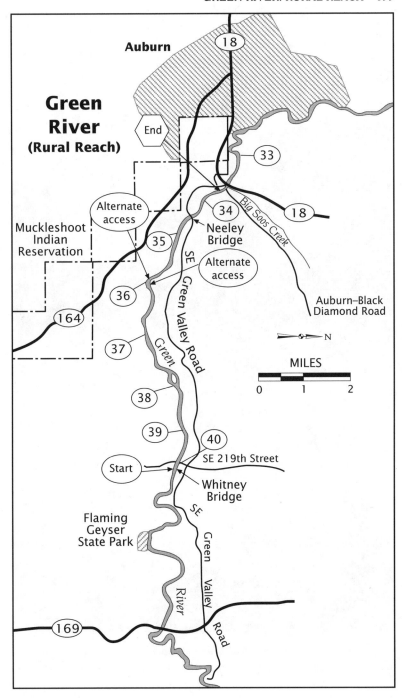

Auburn

18

Green River
(Rural Reach)

End

33

18

Alternate access

34

Neeley Bridge

Big Soos Creek

35

Muckleshoot Indian Reservation

Alternate access

36

Auburn–Black Diamond Road

164

SE Green Valley Road

37

Green

N

MILES
0   1   2

38

River

39

40

SE 219th Street

Start

Whitney Bridge

Flaming Geyser State Park

SE Green Valley Road

169

A fisheries biologist awaits his shuttle in a rural setting on the upper Green River at the Whitney Bridge near Flaming Geyser State Park.

cattle and horses, past neatly kept houses and vivid barns. Planted flowers grace many of the homes along the river. The checkerboard lands of the Muckleshoot Indian Reservation lie above the river on the left. Most are above S.R. 164, which parallels the river for the final 3 miles. Fishing access to the river above and below Neeley Bridge often leaves the banks littered, but the river flows clean and clear with strong current between sometimes forested banks, a pleasant float. The take-out has been badly littered in recent years by fishermen and transients who have taken up residence near the boat ramp.

28 GREEN RIVER: YO-YO STRETCH

Location	east of Auburn, Flaming Geyser State Park to Whitney Bridge
Distance	3 miles
River Time	less than an hour
Map	Black Diamond (7.5')
Best Season	all year
Hazards	Class II rapids, logjams
Shuttle	less than 2 miles on paved roads
Rating	Class II

A short and varied section of river, this segment is known to local paddlers as the Yo-Yo Stretch: it is a favorite with paddlers who make the same run down and up several times a day for practice. It is ideal for poling. Polers can work their way up from Whitney Bridge into the park and back down again in 2 hours for a good workout. It has small rapids, one short but serious Class II rapid, one interesting bedrock riffle, and a few deep pools with fine beaches and well-forested banks.

Access. There is excellent access at the Whitney Bridge take-out and at several places within Flaming Geyser State Park. One or two roadside accesses are also possible, and (with special permission) a few private accesses—all within a very short run.

Driving Directions. From S.R. 18, about 3 miles east of Auburn, turn right at the exit for Auburn–Black Diamond Road. Just before that road crosses the Green River, turn right onto SE Green Valley Road. Signs suggest this is the way to Flaming Geyser State Park.

Eight miles from the turnoff, turn right onto SE 219th Street. Within a hundred yards, turn right into the parking area at Whitney Bridge Park. Leave a shuttle vehicle (possibly a bicycle locked to a pole) here.

To reach the put-in, retrace the route to SE Green Valley Road and turn right, continuing toward Flaming Geyser State Park. The road crosses a bridge in less than a mile and then enters the park. Follow the road to its end, park, and explore the area for river access. The river is to the north; there are several points along a half mile of riverfront where a craft may be launched.

Description. From any of the launch sites in Flaming Geyser State Park, the stream is clear with just enough action to keep paddlers on their toes. In midsummer it is crowded with tubers and sunbathers, kids floating on air mattresses and riverside picnickers. Drifting through the park, boaters pass a few rock gardens and mild rapids, occasional beaver cuts, and (during the fishing season) frequent steelheaders—fishermen after the prize game fish of the Northwest.

Horses on the Yo-Yo Stretch of the Green River

At the big bend of the river above Flaming Geyser Bridge, there is a deep pool—so deep that even in the clear water you cannot see the bottom. A rope tied to an overhanging tree tells of summer swimming here. A long rock garden (merely shallow water at highwater flows) leads to the bridge. There is an exposed gravel-and-sand bar at river left, a swimming beach in the summer, and a year-round take-out for those who want to go up and do it again.

Below the bridge the river splits around a series of islands, the flow on either side runnable at any level above absolutely low water. At low water levels it can be shallow, and the current can take a craft into sweepers along the shoreline. Around the bend is a small rapid, followed by a deeper section of river, then a bedrock area where the river shallows over sandstone and consolidated mud. It drops again into a deep pool, then shallows out, deepens around a bend visible from the road, and gets ready for an honest Class II rapid.

The head of the rapid can be seen, but it can't really be scouted from the road. The river splits around a small island, at least at higher water levels, and drops a few feet in 50 yards over a "bouldery" stretch of fast water. It can be lined on the right from a point that is ideal for scouting the river. Stop and have a look at it if you are uncomfortable with the rapid, but it is fairly straightforward. It is tough to pole up.

From the foot of the rapid to the take-out bridge, the river is broad and shallow, ideal for poling. The take-out is under the bridge, on river right within a 100-foot carry of the parking area.

The river from this access to the mouth of Big Soos Creek just east of Auburn is a 7-mile Class II run (Trip 27) through a rural valley full of horse farms and pastureland, a delightful trip that will challenge beginning paddlers. The river is lined with huge trees and offers excellent habitat for birds and other wildlife as well as excellent fishing.

29 NISQUALLY RIVER DELTA/ McALISTER CREEK

Location	between Olympia and Tacoma
Distance	8 miles combined
River Time	3 to 4 hours
Maps	Nisqually (7.5'), Anderson Island (15'); NOAA Charts: 18440, 18445, 18448
Best Season	all year
Hazards	logjams, contrary tides, fog, storms
Shuttle	none necessary, up to 10 miles on paved roads
Rating	Class II, Tidal

The Nisqually Delta, one of the richest wildlife habitats in Puget Sound, is protected as the Nisqually National Wildlife Refuge. McAlister Creek and the Nisqually River—two major streams that created the delta—offer unique paddling experiences. More than 200 species of birds have been seen in the refuge, which also harbors numerous species of mammals, reptiles, amphibians, and fish, as well as such saltwater species as crabs, clams, and oysters—even seals. McAlister Creek, once known as Medicine Creek, was the site of early Native American treaties in western Washington.

Access. Luhr Beach on Puget Sound is the nearest public boat launch. It offers access to both McAlister Creek, which flows past it, and the mouth of the Nisqually itself, a mile or so across the tidal flats. Access to the

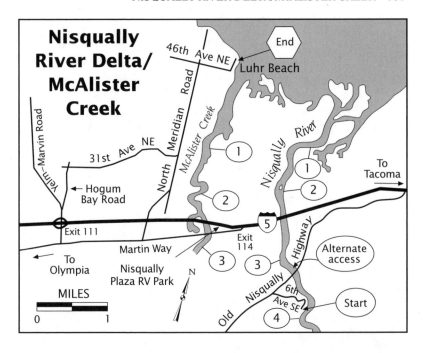

lower Nisqually is available at RM 2.3 and 3.7 from public boat accesses just upstream from the twin I-5 bridges, one off Old Nisqually Highway, the other off 6th Avenue SE at the north edge of Nisqually. Private access is available to McAlister Creek at Nisqually Plaza RV Park at the bottom of Nisqually Hill off I-5 (Exit 114); be prepared to pay a small fee for the convenient access.

Driving Directions. To reach Luhr Beach, take Exit 111 (Yelm-Marvin Road) off I-5 between Tacoma and Olympia, and head north toward Tolmie State Park. In only 0.1 mile turn right onto Hogum Bay Road; then, in less than a mile, turn right onto 31st Avenue NE. After 1.3 miles turn left onto North Meridian Road heading north. In another mile turn right onto 46th Avenue NE, and follow the public fishing signs that direct you to turn left onto D'Milluhr Road, then right to Luhr Beach. The Nisqually Beach Nature Center also resides here.

A simpler way to reach Luhr Beach is to take Exit 114 off I-5 just west of the Nisqually River crossing. Turn right to follow Martin Way west toward Lacey, turn right onto North Meridian Road, then follow the signs to the public fishing access (Luhr Beach).

To reach the access on the lower Nisqually at RM 2.3, take Exit 116 off I-5 and head for Nisqually. At this writing, the bridge on the Old Nisqually Highway is being rebuilt. However, the rough and unmaintained access on the right bank of the river below the bridge still exists.

To reach the access at RM 3.7, return to the Old Nisqually Highway and turn right, cross the river, and continue for 0.5 mile to 6th Avenue SE (marked by a public fishing access sign). Turn left and go to the end of the road, where a public handicapped fishing area lies on the left bank of the Nisqually. The parking area is 0.1 mile from the access. To access McAlister Creek near Exit 114 on I-5, take the exit and drive to the RV park behind the service station.

Description. Launching at RM 3.7 poses an immediate problem in the form of a nasty logjam on the left bank, into which the whole river

The Nisqually Delta National Wildlife Refuge

seems to flow at low water. (This minor rapid can be, and perhaps should be, lined at low water.) At higher flows there is plenty of room to negotiate on the right of what becomes a mere riffle. A few residential back yards line the riverbank, largely ignoring what the river has to offer. In about a mile the river flows beneath the Old Nisqually Highway bridge, and another access lies on the right bank at RM 2.3.

From this point the river is tidal and mellow with a few riffles at low tide. The houses disappear as a Native American fishing camp appears; the tribe for whom the river is named still fishes the streams in accordance with the Medicine Creek Treaty of 1854, signed on what is now McAlister Creek only a few miles away. The twin spans of the I-5 bridge loom ahead as the roar of freeway traffic intrudes into the river corridor—but not for long.

The river slows, both banks are wooded, and the river takes on a mellow mood, creating a placid presence that one paddle partner suggested "could be in Guilford, Connecticut." Soon the protection of the Nisqually National Wildlife Refuge makes its impact; the world grows still, natural, and wholesome, and the sound of freeway traffic subsides.

Depending upon the tide level, the river may be tearing along to reach the Sound or backed up in a slow lake, but the setting is pleasant, calm, and quiet except for the sounds of nature (or an occasional power-boat carrying Native American fishermen to set or check their nets). There are gulls overhead, mallards and wood ducks in the eddies. A trail along the left bank spawns people, bird-watchers hiking through the refuge. Blackberry bushes and beaver cuts mark the shoreline; Native American gill nets mark the river's surface.

Soon the craft reaches the open water of the Sound. A seal's head pops up. Duck blinds appear—yes, hunting is allowed on the refuge, but only during the open season, and gunners are required to use nontoxic shot. The dock at Luhr Beach is visible to the west. Shore birds and many ducks and geese frequent the area; bald eagles, great blue herons, and numerous gulls feed on the mud flats and in the nearby Sound.

The mouth of McAlister Creek can be reached by paddling a few hundred yards west; and if the tide is right, paddling upstream is not difficult. The lower creek is broad, but a mile upstream it narrows and begins to meander, nuzzling the west bank where a steep, forested hillside turns it back to loop through the meadows to the east. The tide mark shows on the vegetation; salt burn kills leaves of vine maple but doesn't seem to bother the sturdy trees that grow right to the water's edge.

It is possible to paddle or pole right up McAlister Creek to I-5, though the outgoing tide creates a fierce flow in the channelized creek where it has been forced by humankind to loop around the bridge supports. Above the I-5 bridge there will be placid water (if the tide charts have been used wisely), but having left the refuge behind, the river is now in agricultural land. It may be best to head back downstream to the take-out at Luhr Beach.

OLYMPIC
PENINSULA

30 LOWER CHEHALIS RIVER AND SLOUGHS

Location	Montesano to Hoquiam-Aberdeen-Cosmopolis area
Distance	13.3 miles
River Time	3 to 4 hours
Maps	Montesano (15'), Aberdeen, Hoquiam (7.5'); NOAA Chart: 18502
Best Season	possible all year, but best in summer months
Hazards	contrary tides, big ships, powerboats
Shuttle	15 miles on paved roads, none necessary
Rating	Class I, Tidal

The lower Chehalis and its associated sloughs combine a logging town and seaport with some amazingly pristine backwater paddling. The lower 3 miles of the river are almost totally urban, commercially developed, and export oriented; but above the 3-mile mark, six sloughs branch off into picturesque bayous reminiscent of Southern swamplands (except for the vegetation, which is strictly Northwestern). Three major tributaries covered by this book enter the Chehalis in this segment: the Hoquiam, the Wishkah, and the Wynoochee.

Access. Several boat launches provide abundant access to the lower Chehalis: one on the Aberdeen waterfront, another across the Chehalis from the mouth of the Wishkah, a third at RM 3, and a fourth 1 mile south of Montesano just above the mouth of the Wynoochee. Paddle-craft access can also be negotiated from Morrison Waterfront Park at RM 1, just below the mouth of Elliott Slough—the only one of seven sloughs that joins the river below RM 3.

Driving Directions. To reach the westernmost access, take US 101 (Sumner Street) west through Aberdeen. After entering Hoquiam, turn left (south) onto 28th Street to the Port of Grays Harbor boat ramp (gravel) by the Observatory (hours 7:00 A.M. to dusk).

To reach the boat ramp across from the mouth of the Wishkah, take US 101 south across the bridge over the Chehalis River (a sign says "to Westport and Raymond"). Turn left at the first stoplight (H Street; the main flow of traffic goes left at this light) and left again onto Boone Street as the road bends right just before the South Aberdeen Fire Station appears on the left. (This is an awkward turn in heavy traffic; it may be best

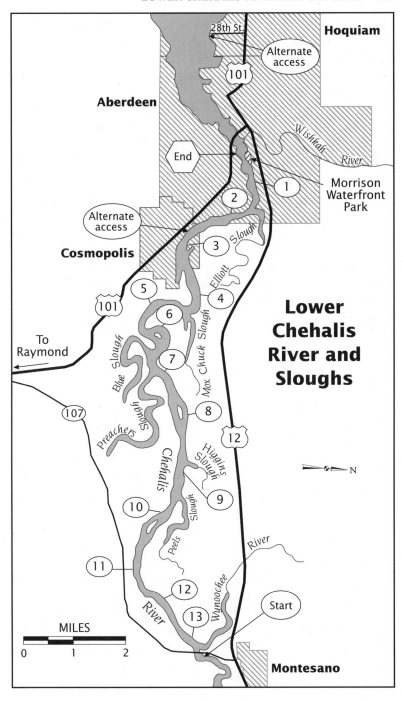

Lower
Chehalis
River and
Sloughs

to go beyond it, turn around somewhere, and approach it from the other direction so a right turn will be easier.) This is the old West Bridge approach. There is no sign, no dock, and little parking.

To reach the third access, in south Cosmopolis, return to US 101 and turn left past the South Aberdeen Fire Station, toward Raymond. Turn left at F Street and drive to the waterfront access provided by Weyerhaeuser.

To reach the boat ramp south of Montesano, return to US 101. At this point there are two options. The first is to turn left and continue toward Raymond, but in a few miles to turn left on S.R. 107 to Montesano on the South Bank Road. This location provides a look at Blue Slough and Preachers Slough, both south of the river. After S.R. 107 forks left and crosses the Chehalis River, 0.1 mile above the mouth of the Wynoochee River, turn right at a public fishing access sign into a parking area with a boat ramp.

The second option (after you return to US 101) is to turn right and return to Aberdeen, turning right again in downtown Aberdeen onto US 12, heading east. At Montesano, turn right onto S.R. 107, drive a mile south of town (past a lumber mill), and turn left into the public fishing access (the launch site).

Morrison Waterfront Park, another launch site, is located at what was the dock for the local fishing fleet until 1956. Traveling east on Wishkah Street (US 12), turn right onto Fleet Street just past the shopping mall at the east end of Aberdeen (just before US 12 starts to climb the hill east of town). This area offers access to the right bank of the Chehalis, less than 0.25 mile above the mouth of the Wishkah.

Description. The Chehalis is tidal throughout this segment: a big, deep river impacted by logging activities and heavily used by power-boats, many of which launch at the boat ramp south of Montesano at RM 13.3. Launching here, paddlers immediately pass beneath S.R. 107, then under the railroad bridge. The Wynoochee enters on the right, flushing the Chehalis with fresh mountain water.

The river flows southwest until it bumps into the railroad embankment (RM 11.6). Then it hugs that embankment for a mile before swinging slowly toward the north and encountering sloughs on the right: first Peels at RM 9.5, then Higgins at RM 8.7. The river narrows, divides around an island (RM 8), and swings toward the south again.

At RM 6.8, Preachers Slough enters from the left (offering a side trip of more than 2 miles up the slough if the tide is high and there are no

The Chehalis River

barriers); at RM 6.4, Blue Slough enters, also from the left (a side trip of nearly 3 miles up this one). Below Blue Slough, the river enters a tight S bend that takes it 1.5 miles to complete. Mox Chuck Slough enters from the right at RM 4.4, as the river bends left. The river straightens as it enters Cosmopolis (with the Weyerhaeuser mill visible on the left bank) and greets one more small slough on the left.

Slough exploring can take a lot of time. Just be aware that such side trips add to paddle time. Keep in mind too that tidal influence will alter tour time on the river; it is slow going against an incoming tide, but fair time can be made paddling upstream with the incoming tide.

From RM 3 the river is flanked on the left by the back yards of Cosmopolis, on the right by log export activities and facilities. The river here heads north and then makes a sharp left turn as Elliott Slough enters on the right at RM 1.3. Elliott Slough is largely a log-storage facility, and the Chehalis River from this point is totally engulfed by Aberdeen. In another mile the river gives up its ghost to Grays Harbor.

31 | HOQUIAM RIVER: EAST AND WEST FORKS

Location	Hoquiam and Aberdeen, north of Hoquiam
Distance	5 miles, East Fork; 9 miles, West Fork
River Time	2 hours, East Fork; 3 hours, West Fork
Maps	Hoquiam (7.5'), Humptulips (15'); NOAA Chart: 18502
Best Season	all year, but rainy in winter
Hazards	contrary tides, waterfront traffic at end
Shuttle	7 miles, East Fork; 9 miles, West Fork on paved roads
Rating	Class I, Tidal

The Hoquiam River proper, only 2.5 miles long, is totally urban; but at the point where it splits into East and West Forks, it becomes almost rural—nearly primitive. Both forks have lives and accesses of their own, as they loop widely back and forth in sinuous curves through marshy lands that protect the rivers from greater development. They offer peaceful paddling on tidal waters that are disturbed only by such commercial activities as log storage (more historical than current) and sports fishing.

Access. The most logical take-out access is on the Grays Harbor waterfront in southwestern Aberdeen. Developed boat launches exist on both major forks of the river and on the Little Hoquiam (see Trip 32), from US 101 on the West Fork and from East Hoquiam Road on the East Fork.

Driving Directions. To reach the waterfront take-out in southwestern Aberdeen, from US 101 as it goes through Aberdeen turn south (left) onto 28th Street; then head south past a log storage yard to the Observatory, a pointer to the Port of Grays Harbor boat ramp, which is the take-out. This boat ramp is only a few hundred yards east of the mouth of the Hoquiam River.

To reach major access points on the West Fork, go back to US 101 (Lincoln Street) and follow it north out of Hoquiam toward either of two put-in points: (1) only 2.4 miles north of the ancient steam engine at Last Spur Park in north Hoquiam, turn onto a spur road that veers off to the right (Fairfield Acres Access), then turn right again down a residential road and drive to its dead end, where a log boom serves as a possible public put-in at RM 5.3; (2) 5 miles north of Last Spur Park, right of the highway,

Second-growth timber lines the banks of the Hoquiam River, marked by pilings used to anchor rafts of old-growth timber cut decades ago.

there is a facility known as Green Banks, dedicated to public fishing access by ITT Rayonier, Trout Unlimited, and the Northwest Steelheaders Association. Green Banks has parking and a covered picnic table (RM 8.7).

To reach a boat ramp at RM 4.6 on the East Fork (7 miles from the mouth of the Hoquiam), go back to US 101 from the 28th Street take-out, then follow it west to 16th Street (a few blocks after the highway begins to parallel the left bank of the Hoquiam River). Turn right (the sign says "Woodlawn") onto 16th Street (which soon becomes Broadway) and follow it through Woodlawn, turning right onto East Hoquiam Road. This road follows the river (more or less) to a boat ramp 5 miles from the turnoff from US 101.

Description. Both forks of the Hoquiam offer interesting and contrasting paddling; both are tidal throughout these segments; and both can be paddled or poled upstream and down if tidal charts are consulted and followed.

From the boat ramp on the **East Fork**, the river is lined by mud banks at low tide; at high tide, it is lined by brushy shorelines with occasional stands of tall trees (even in this heavily cut-over logging land). Fisherman traffic attests to the aquatic life, as do kingfishers and great blue herons. There are a few homes along the bank, a number of pilings from earlier log storage areas, and more commercial development downstream as the river meanders through a marshy flood plain.

At RM 2.7 the river kisses the road, as it does again at RM 1.5. At RM 0.5 commercial development begins in the form of forest products and industrial facilities on the left bank. The East Fork joins the West Fork at the north edge of Hoquiam, 2.5 miles from Grays Harbor. From RM 0.5 on the East Fork, paddlers are still 3 miles from the waterfront take-out.

The **West Fork** plays hide-and-seek with US 101 from the put-in at RM 9 to RM 3, only 0.5 mile above the confluence of the East and West Forks at the north edge of Hoquiam. It is probably more heavily fished than the East Fork because of its proximity to the major highway and the developed fishing facilities. But for all of its access, it is still a pretty primitive paddle; few boats make use of it.

For its first 2 miles, the West Fork parallels the highway, passing between towering trees and along shrub-lined banks. Its Middle Fork joins it from the left just above RM 7, opposite the entrance of Bernard Creek from the right.

The river moves away from the highway below RM 7, swinging back to parallel the highway for nearly a mile (RM 6.5 to RM 5.7) before making the big loop on which access #1(the log boom) is located on the right bank at RM 5.3. It loops back near the highway at RM 4.8, then takes a long loop to the east side of its marshy flood plain before making one more move toward the highway to parallel it coming into town at RM 3. Here the Little Hoquiam joins it from the right.

Half a mile below its entry into Hoquiam, the West Fork is joined by the East Fork from the left. Totally tidal and surrounded by commercial and residential development for its last 2.5 miles, the Hoquiam flows into Grays Harbor at the west end of Rennie Island. To reach the take-out, paddle 0.5 mile to the Observatory on the Aberdeen waterfront.

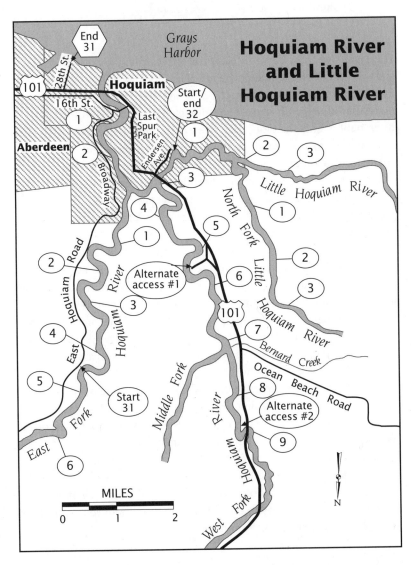

32 LITTLE HOQUIAM RIVER

Location	west of Hoquiam
Distance	3 miles
River Time	2 to 3 hours
Map	Hoquiam (7.5'); NOAA Chart: 18502
Best Season	all year, but lots of rain in winter
Hazards	contrary tides, powerboats
Shuttle	none necessary
Rating	Class I, Tidal

This small river may be badly clear-cut at this writing, but its atmosphere suggests "wild" and its waters are full of life. Its access is from an isolated little park, and its upstream reach offers one of the most peaceful experiences paddlers could seek. Even though a new road and bridge have been built over its first fork, many nearby sounds are blocked off by the ridge to the south. Even at tidal flux, it is so still and quiet that you can see insects alight on its surface and watch fish take them. Birds in flight can even be identified by their reflection on the river's surface.

Access. The only access necessary (because a craft can easily be paddled up this little river, then back down it) is at a small park in northwest Hoquiam.

Driving Directions. To reach the access park, head north out of Hoquiam on US 101 (Lincoln Street), which turns left (west) near the north edge of town and then swings right at an angle to the northwest just before crossing the Little Hoquiam River. As the highway completes its swing to the northwest, turn left onto Queen Avenue, which becomes Endersen Avenue at the first curve west of US 101. Follow it southwest to a bend in the Little Hoquiam River, where there is a small park and a boat landing. This is the put-in and take-out.

Another way to reach this put-in is to cross the Hoquiam River on US 101, turn left onto S.R. 109, and head west toward Ocean Shores. In a little more than a mile, turn right onto Spencer Street and follow it over the hill to Lions City Park. Turn right to skirt the park, then left onto the other end of Endersen Road (a road at one end, an avenue at the other).

Description. From the launch site, the river is reflection-still except for the occasional stirring by powerboats that also use the boat ramp. Around the first bend upstream, the man-made world is left behind and paddlers enter a kinder, softer realm.

The placid Little Hoquiam serves as a reflection pond.

Wonderful woodsy smells take away the exhaust fumes, and bird songs nibble away at the fading echoes of the motors' roar. Hundreds of swallows fill the air at dusk or before a rain, and the only sounds are natural ones as the river weaves its way into the wilderness. Clear-cut scars dominate the landscape, but nature was here first and will endure. Even in the battle-scarred landscape, there are great blue herons, spotted sandpipers, kingfishers, green herons, gulls, nighthawks, robins—and a huge nest of white-faced hornets.

The river loops quietly into the darkening landscape. An insect hatch in the happening: the surface of the river is alive with the multi-strikes of tiny fish. Their feeding frenzy makes more noise than passing paddlers. A new bridge looms ahead, and the river splits beyond it. The right-hand fork is blocked by fallen trees a few hundred yards in.

The main river meanders and curves for another mile. Then paddlers can head back down the quiet river toward the landing, moving with the tide, watching reflections in the water and nighthawks flit and dive and swoop, gathering insects. It's that kind of river.

33 WISHKAH RIVER

Location	Aberdeen, north and northeast
Distance	7.5 miles
River Time	2 hours
Maps	Aberdeen (7.5'), Humptulips (15'); NOAA Chart: 18502
Best Season	all year, rainy in winter
Hazards	contrary tides, powerboats
Shuttle	6.2 miles on paved roads
Rating	Class I, Tidal

The Wishkah River flows into the Chehalis River in the latter's last mile, virtually at the point where the Chehalis gives up its ghost to Grays Harbor. One of several tidal rivers in the Grays Harbor area, the Wishkah offers exploratory paddle trips on different branches, providing different insights into the area. The Wishkah, which circles through northeastern Aberdeen, flows out of the timbered forestlands from an area that hosts two units of the Olympic Wildlife Area. It is a slow, narrow river, ideal for beginning paddlers.

Access. The best access to the take-out is from the south side of the Chehalis River opposite the mouth of the Wishkah. The launch site is from a public boat ramp at RM 7.2 on Wishkah Road, which closely parallels the river on the right bank (west of the river).

Driving Directions. To reach the take-out across the Chehalis River from the mouth of the Hoquiam, follow US 101 south from H Street across the bridge over the Chehalis River. (Highway signs suggest that this is the way to Raymond and Westport.) Turn left at the first stoplight (the main flow of traffic goes this way) and left again in a few hundred yards onto Boone Street as the road bends to the right, just before the South Aberdeen Fire Station appears on the left. (Since this may be a difficult turn to make in heavy traffic, it may make sense to go beyond the turnoff, double back wherever it is convenient and legal, and, as you head back toward Aberdeen, make the right turn.) Boone Street leads to the take-out at the Hoquiam River bridge approach, a public boat access.

To reach the launch site, several miles up Wishkah Road, take US 101 (G Street) straight ahead to Market. Turn right onto Market to B Street; turn left on B Street; and follow it north. It forks right to become Wishkah Road. Follow it out of town along the river to the boat ramp (5 miles from the left turn onto B Street).

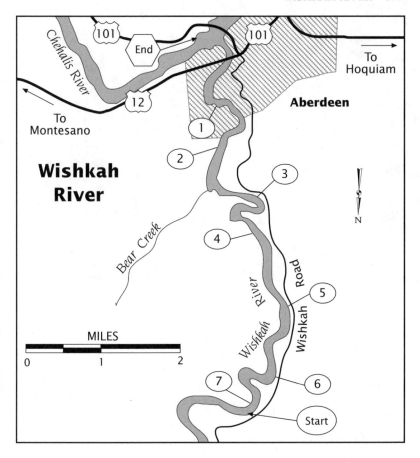

Description. The Wishkah River is a small, intimate stream. It seems to have been diked at some time in the past, but whatever human control existed is so far removed in time that it appears natural enough; the banks are well vegetated and the bends seem appropriate. It is mostly a rural river, with a few big trees along its banks and a house or two along the way. A slow-moving fishing boat may come putting along upstream, but there are few powerboats in so narrow a river.

The river swings left, then sharply right through marshy lands. It hugs the road between RM 5.4 and RM 5, then swings away into the marsh—only to return for another kiss at RM 4.3. At RM 4 it begins a sharp S that ends only as Bear Creek comes in from the left and the river approaches Aberdeen. The last 2 miles of this route flow through an urban area; the final 0.5 mile, through downtown. US 12 crosses the river only a hundred

Log storage pilings on the lower Wishkah River

yards from its mouth. The take-out involves paddling across the mouth of the Chehalis as it flows into Grays Harbor.

34 WYNOOCHEE RIVER: LOWER MAIN STEM

Location	north, northwest of Montesano
Distance	16 miles
River Time	4 to 5 hours
Maps	Montesano, Wynoochee Valley (15')
Best Season	all year, due to reservoir release
Hazards	timber trash, sweepers, diversion structure (RM 8.1)
Shuttle	15 miles on paved roads
Rating	Class II

The Wynoochee River flows south out of Olympic National Park, but a major dam that makes this river runnable throughout the year (though it may get a bit lean in late summer and early fall) creates a barrier between the pristine and the merely scenic. Several segments of the upper river are run by kayakers, and canoeists run a 19-mile segment above this lower 16-mile stretch, which is broken by a diversion structure near RM 8. This segment flows through a broad farming valley to the Chehalis just south of Montesano. It is a pool-and-riffle river with plenty of gravel bars and fine views of low, timbered hills.

Access. The best take-out is at a public fishing area south of Montesano on the Chehalis River, 0.25 mile above the mouth of the Wynoochee. There are three accesses along the Wynoochee Valley Road north of Montesano: one about 4 miles northwest of town at the mouth of Black Creek (RM 5.5); another at the Cutover Bridge (RM 13.7); and a third at the Old White Bridge Site (RM 16).

Driving Directions. To find the take-out on the Chehalis River a mile south of Montesano, take US 12 to Montesano and turn off onto S.R. 107 toward Raymond. Less than a mile south, just past a lumber mill, turn left onto a narrow road that leads to a public fishing access on the right (north) bank of the Chehalis River, 0.25 mile above the mouth of the Wynoochee.

To reach any of the accesses on Wynoochee Valley Road, return to Montesano, head west on US 12 to Wynoochee Valley Road (which leads toward Wynoochee Dam), and turn right, following it northwest 3 miles to the Black Creek boat ramp left of the road on river left. A run from here to the take-out is less than 6 miles.

To locate the access at the Cutover Bridge Site (a shortcut to the Wishkah River), continue north on the Wynoochee Valley Road another 6.2 miles, then turn left on Wishkah-Wynoochee Road to an access on the left bank (east side) at RM 13.7. The river is actually accessible from either side of the river at RM 15.7. To reach the right bank (west side) of the river, turn west on Wishkah-Wynoochee Road, which crosses the river on the Cutover Bridge toward Aberdeen. Turn right almost immediately and follow the road 2 miles to the west side of the Old White Bridge Site at the end of the road. To reach the left bank (east side of the river), return to Wynoochee Valley Road, turn left, and drive 2.5 miles to a public fishing access sign. Turn left again, following the road to the riverbank.

Description. From the Old White Bridge Site the river flows relatively straight for nearly 3 miles, its banks overgrown with grasses, native shrubs, wildflowers, and the ubiquitous blackberry. There is an island at RM 14.8, with two small creeks entering the river from opposite sides at the island. The river flows beneath the Cutover Bridge at RM 13.6, bends sharply left at RM 13.2, and begins a series of slow meanders that continue for the next 6 miles. A diversion structure at RM 8.1 may have to be portaged.

Several times the river kisses Wynoochee Valley Road east of it from

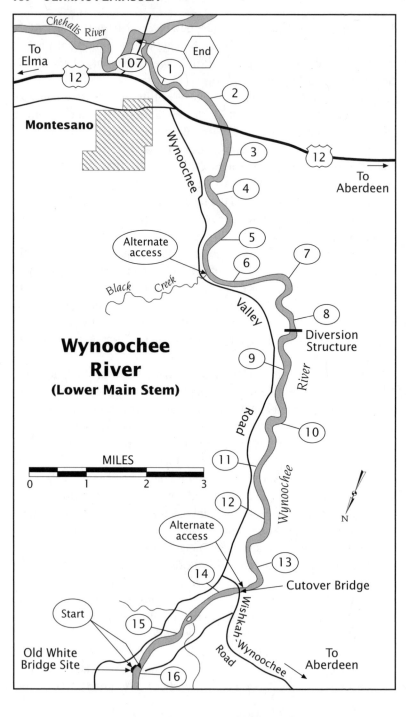

Chehalis River

To Elma

107

12

End

1

2

Montesano

Wynoochee

3

12

To Aberdeen

4

5

Alternate access

6

7

Black Creek

Valley

8

Diversion Structure

Wynoochee River
(Lower Main Stem)

9

River

Road

10

MILES

0   1   2   3

11

Wynoochee

12

N

Alternate access

13

14

Cutover Bridge

Start

15

Wishkah-Wynoochee Road

To Aberdeen

Old White Bridge Site

16

Low water and gravel bars on the lower Wynoochee River

RM 12 south to RM 2.5, where US 12 crosses the Wynoochee. Throughout this segment the river flows through farmlands, and an occasional barn or farmhouse is visible from the river; but the agricultural scene rarely intrudes upon the river corridor. Wildlife occurs along the river (bird life, raccoons, deer), and fishermen often ply their sport during their season.

Despite the obvious rural and urban scene of Montesano and the traffic of US 12 (which it roughly parallels for a mile or so), the Wynoochee remains relatively wild all the way to its meeting with the Chehalis, south of Montesano. The boat ramp that serves as the take-out for this segment is just a brief paddle to the left (0.25 mile up the Chehalis) from the mouth.

35 SATSOP RIVER: LOWER MAIN STEM, EAST AND WEST FORKS

Location	between Aberdeen and Olympia, north of US 12
Distance	10 miles, East Fork; 11 miles, West Fork; 4 miles, main Satsop
River Time	3 to 4 hours each
Maps	Elma (7.5'), Wynoochee (15')
Best Season	all year, except late summer or early fall
Hazards	timber debris, sweepers, pilings in fast water
Shuttle	11 miles, East Fork; 12 miles, West Fork on paved roads
Rating	Class II-

The lower Satsop and its lower East and West Forks constitute a network of small, intimate clear-water streams that flow out of the southern

Olympics through rain-forest vegetation. The area is largely cut over, but the second-growth areas still offer high-quality habitat for paddlers. One of the launch sites is in a state park, another in one of Weyerhaeuser's premier parks. The pool-and-drop character of the river offers challenges to the paddler, and the scenery provides an exciting and varied backdrop.

Access. The two uppermost accesses (one on each fork) lie in parks, one of which offers a steep but manageable launch. The two suggested take-outs (both on paved roads) have boat ramps, one off US 12 near the town of Satsop (within sight of the defunct nuclear power plant cooling towers).

Driving Directions. To reach the take-out boat ramp, travel east on US 12 between Montesano and Elma near Satsop. The boat ramp, on river left below the US 12 bridge, is accessible only from the eastbound lane, but there are several traffic crossovers. A shuttle vehicle can be left here if you plan to paddle the main stem river from the forks, a 4-mile run. An alternate take-out lies on the Chehalis River, 0.25 mile above the mouth of the Satsop. Take Keyes Road south off US 12, just east of the bridge, and follow it 1.3 miles to a public fishing access with a boat ramp.

The boat ramp on the lower West Fork lies less than a hundred yards above the forks and can readily be used as a take-out for runs on either fork or as a launch site for the short run to US 12 or the Chehalis River.

To reach this handy access, head east from the boat ramp on US 12 to the next exit (Satsop), and turn left (north) toward Satsop. Then turn left again into that small town and head west to Brady, another tiny town. In Brady, turn right onto West Satsop Road and drive about 3.5 miles to the boat ramp (a public fishing access right of the road, on the right bank of the West Fork).

To reach either of the two put-in points from this access, return to West Satsop Road and turn right (heading north). To reach the West Fork put-in, stay left at the fork in the road in 0.25 mile and follow this narrow, winding road to Weyerhaeuser Timber Company's Swinging Bridge Park (the last 0.5 mile is through a tunnel of trees). Launch at RM 7.2 on the right bank of the West Fork, for a 7-mile run to the forks access or an 11-mile run to US 12.

To reach the East Fork put-in, turn right from the forks access and head north on West Satsop Road. At the fork in the road 0.25 mile north of the forks access, turn right and follow the signs 4.7 miles to Schafer State Park. It is possible to launch from the park with a short carry to the river. (The park can also be reached by taking the East Satsop Road north from

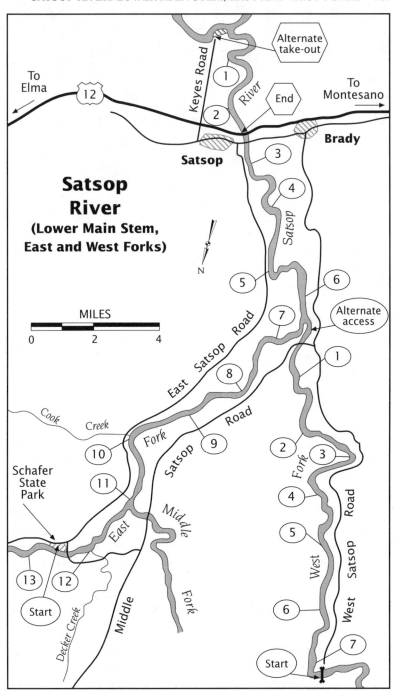

The launch site in Schafer State Park, along the East Fork of the Satsop River

the Satsop-Brady Road just west of Satsop, east of the bridge across the Satsop.)

Description. The East Fork in popular Schafer State Park is lean in late summer, but most of the year it is readily runnable by canoe or kayak. It will be challenging at times because of the tight corners, timber debris, and sweepers, but it offers an insight into an isolated, intimate rain-forest river.

Almost immediately paddlers will float beneath the bridge that brought them to the park. As the river bends out of sight of the bridge, a tiny creek enters on the right, followed by Decker Creek also on the right (RM 12). The river corridor is lined with tall trees; even though roads parallel the river on opposite sides, they rarely intrude upon the river itself.

Below Decker Creek the river makes a jog to the right, then a quick jog to the left over a rocky bed, to meet the Middle Fork, which enters from the right at RM 11. A long, gradual curve to the left and the mouth of Cook Creek appears on the left, at RM 10. At this point East Satsop Road is near enough to touch as the river curves back to the right for a straight mile.

A trio of tiny creeks enters from the right between RM 9.2 and 8.2, as the river meanders through its flood plain for the final 2 miles to a confluence with the West Fork at RM 6.4. The 4-mile run from here to the US 12 take-out will be described later in this section.

The West Fork put-in at RM 7.2 is marked by a footbridge across the river, the namesake of Swinging Bridge Park. Almost immediately there is a sharp turn to the right, and the park is lost from sight in a narrow gorge overhung with huge rain-forest trees. The road is very near the river for the next 5 miles, but so far above it that it never really intrudes.

Three small streams enter from the left in the next 3 miles. The gorge and forest end, and meadows appear. Deer may be seen, as well as raccoons and muskrats—even foxes—and numerous species of birds, especially in late spring and early summer. At RM 3.7 the river makes a sharp bend to the right, then at RM 3, an even sharper bend back to the left. The final 3 miles of the West Fork meander through meadowlands, as the river takes on a pool-and-drop character; flows beneath Middle Satsop Road (which leads to Schafer Park); and enters a small gorge in its last 0.5 mile to join with the East Fork in a huge, deep pool.

From the forks down, the river slows, meanders more widely through its flood plain, creates a few islands, and flows through farmlands. At RM 3 it straightens for a run through some old bridge pilings just above the Satsop-Brady Bridge, then a railroad bridge and the double span of the Satsop River (US 12) bridge. The take-out is on the left bank immediately below the highway bridge.

36 CHEHALIS RIVER: PORTER TO MONTESANO

Location	between Olympia and Aberdeen
Distance	20 miles
River Time	5 to 6 hours
Maps	Montesano, Malone (15')
Best Season	all year
Hazards	sweepers, logjams, high water
Shuttle	18 miles, all paved road
Rating	Class I+/II-

This long, looping stretch of the Chehalis offers excellent paddling on a clear-water river with numerous gravel bars for fishing, picnicking, or camping. For the most part it flows through private property, so be sure to camp below mean high water level or obtain permission from the local landowner. An easy river flowing through a broad valley, this segment provides good fishing as well as occasional views of distant mountains and nearer, forested (and clear-cut) hillsides. Several of its tributaries can also be canoed.

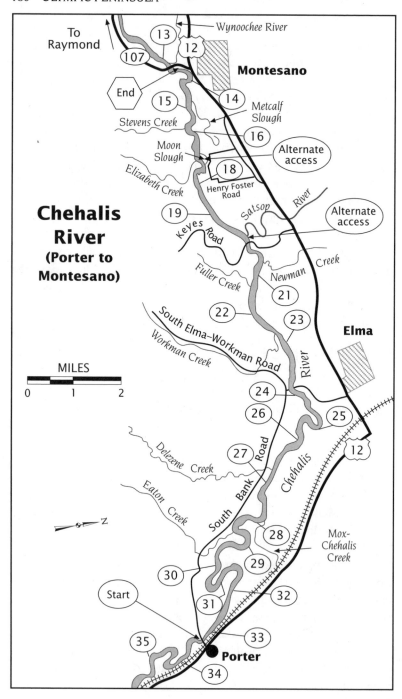

To Raymond

(13) ← Wynoochee River

(12)

(107)

Montesano

End

(15)

(14)

Metcalf Slough

Stevens Creek

(16)

Moon Slough

Alternate access

Elizabeth Creek

(18)

Henry Foster Road

Chehalis River
(Porter to Montesano)

(19)

Keyes Road

Satsop River

Alternate access

Newman Creek

Fuller Creek

(21)

(22)

(23)

Elma

South Elma–Workman Road

Workman Creek

River

MILES

0   1   2

(24)

(26)

(25)

(12)

Delezene Creek

(27)

South Bank Road

Chehalis

N

Eaton Creek

(28)

Mox-Chehalis Creek

(30)

(29)

Start

(32)

(31)

(35)

(33)

Porter

(34)

Access. The best access lies at the put-in near Porter and at the take-out south of Montesano. But additional access is possible at at least two points in the lower 7 miles of this run: at the mouth of the Satsop (RM 20.5) and at RM 17.3, off Brady Loop Road (if anyone has recently cleared the trail from the road to the river).

Driving Directions. From US 12 at Montesano, take S.R. 107 south toward Raymond. Less than a mile south of town (immediately after passing a lumber mill on the left), turn left to a public fishing access on the right bank of the Chehalis, 0.25 mile above the mouth of the Wynoochee River. Leave a shuttle vehicle here.

Return to US 12 and head east toward Elma, then southeast toward Porter. Turn right (south) at the northwest edge of Porter, toward Rony and South Bank Road, crossing the railroad tracks and the Chehalis River. As the bridge grade drops, turn left into the public fishing access parking area. The launch site (boat ramp) is on the southwest bank of the river beneath the bridge at RM 33.2. (**Note:** this is also the take-out for Trip 37.)

To reach the access at the mouth of the Satsop, take US 12 to the Satsop exit (north to Satsop, south to the access) and turn off onto Keyes Road. Access lies less than 2 miles from US 12.

To reach the Brady Loop Road access, turn off at the Brady exit, about 2 miles west of the Satsop exit. Head south (Brady is north) on Henry Foster Road, which turns right to become Valentine (all part of the Brady Loop Road). Public fishing access exists (if the trail has been cleared) near a farmhouse south of the loop road.

Description. In this stretch the Chehalis River is slow and lazy with a few easy drops. From the launch site on the left bank, the river flows northwest for almost 2 miles, gradually leaving the highway and flowing through farmlands. A short distance below RM 32 it starts a big S curve left, then right, approaching the left edge of its flood plain. It curves less sharply for another big S bend—right, left, right—as Eaton Creek enters on the left (RM 28.6) and Mox-Chehalis Creek enters on the right (RM 27.8).

The river straightens for more than a mile, paralleled by South Bank Road and the railroad. Delezene Creek enters from the left (RM 26.8). At RM 26—just after a powerline crossing—a third big S bend begins just south of Elma. Although the river is crossed by a bridge carrying the South Elma–Workman Road at RM 23.8, there is no access.

The river flows almost due west as it passes beneath this bridge, curving in gradual bends for the next 3 miles. Workman Creek enters from the left at RM 22.7, Fuller Creek from the left at an island at RM 21.4, and

The bridge across the Chehalis River south of Elma is not an access.

Newman Creek from the right at RM 20.8. Just after the river flows beneath the bridge carrying Keyes Road across the Chehalis, the Satsop River comes in from the right. The access here is between the Satsop mouth and the bridge.

The river has been gaining volume; it has gradually become bigger and broader. From the mouth of the Satsop, the Chehalis again flows along the south edge of the valley, paralleling the railroad for more than 2 miles before making a sharp right turn into a broad area, from which Moon Slough loops around an island in the vicinity of RM 17. The access off Brady Loop is onto the right bank of Moon Slough.

Elizabeth Creek enters from the left, opposite the island (RM 17). Stevens Creek enters from the left on a sharp bend at RM 15.8, where the river touches the railroad embankment. Another mile of relatively straight river, and Metcalf Slough enters from the right (RM 14.7). This area is tidal, and at extremely high tides the impact can be felt. One more big, sweeping bend—right, then left—and the river parallels S.R. 107 south of Montesano, makes a final sharp right, and flows beneath a pair of bridges. Take out at the boat ramp on the right before reaching the bridge.

37 CHEHALIS RIVER/LOWER BLACK RIVER: OAKVILLE TO PORTER

Location	southwest of Olympia, near Oakville
Distance	9.2 miles; from Black River, 18 miles
River Time	3 hours; from Black River, 6 hours
Map	Malone (15')
Best Season	all year, but best spring through fall
Hazards	sweepers, logjams
Shuttle	8 miles, paved road
Rating	Class I+

The Oakville-to-Porter run is a pleasant paddle on a moderate-sized river that flows through a broad, undeveloped agricultural valley. The banks are well vegetated with shrubs, grasses, second-growth timber, and non-timber species. The lower Black River is shallow and narrow, with a gravel bottom and abundant aquatic vegetation; its lower 2 miles revert to southern swamp—slow with heavily wooded banks. The Chehalis between the mouth of the Black River and the Oakville access flows through farmlands with fields often nudging the river itself. It has plenty of gravel bars and lots of timber trash as well.

Access. All three accesses are easy to find; two are just off US 12, and one is only a mile by paved road from this main highway. The take-out is just northwest of Porter; the launch site is just northwest of Oakville. The launch site on the Black River (take-out for Trip 38) is at the US 12 bridge crossing, west of Rochester and east of Oakville.

Driving Directions. To reach the take-out for this segment (which is the launch site for Trip 36), turn west from US 12 just northwest of Porter, cross the river, and turn left into a public fishing access parking area. Leave a shuttle vehicle here, return to the highway, and turn right, heading southeast toward Oakville.

There are two ways to reach the put-in, roughly one mile northwest of Oakville:

(1) Go to the outskirts of Oakville and turn right (near Oakville High School) onto Elma-Gate Road, which doubles back along the northwest between the highway and the river. The put-in is an undeveloped public fishing access on a slough that communicates with the Chehalis (at low water it may be blocked by a beaver dam). The access is left of the road traveling northwest from Oakville, on river right.

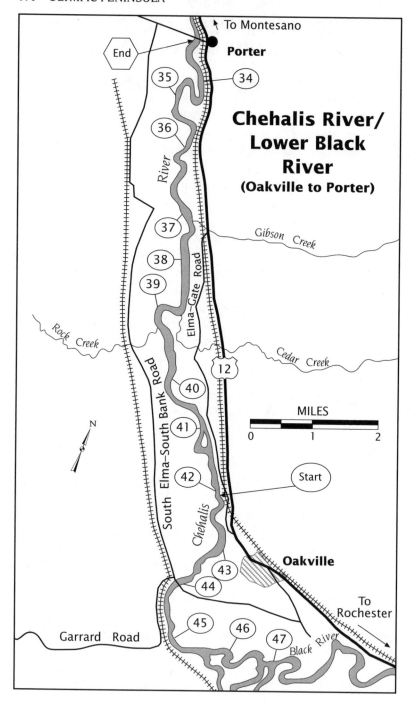

To Montesano

End

Porter

35   34

36

River

Chehalis River/
Lower Black
River
(Oakville to Porter)

Gibson Creek

37

Elma–Gate Road

38

39

Rock Creek

Cedar Creek

12

MILES

0   1   2

40

N

41

Start

42

South Elma–South Bank Road

Chehalis

Oakville

43

44

To
Rochester

45   46   47

Garrard   Road

Black River

(2) Heading southeast from Porter to Oakville on US 12, just after crossing Gibson Creek turn right 3 miles southeast of Porter onto Elma-Gate Road. This will save a couple of miles and provide an opportunity to see the river, which it parallels for a mile or so.

To reach the Black River access off US 12 (for the longer trip on the lower Black and a longer stretch of the Chehalis), drive through Oakville, heading east toward Rochester; about 2 miles east of Oakville, immediately after crossing the Black River, turn right into a small parking area by a boat ramp on the left bank of the river.

Description. At the launch on the Black River, masses of aquatic vegetation almost obstruct a paddle route down its narrow course through this section. Some route-finding may be necessary at the low water levels of late summer. The river flows past farmhouses and barns, past pastures and clearings. After a couple of miles of extreme meandering over a shallow gravel bottom with occasional riffles, the river slows to sluggish, winding between steep, thickly wooded banks.

From the mouth of the Black at RM 47, the Chehalis flows through a broad, intensively farmed valley where some fields extend right to the river's edge. It meanders widely, involving a sloughlike backwater on the right 0.25 mile below the confluence, and another on the left 1.5 miles

A well-used boat ramp near Oakville is a logical take-out or launch site for trips on the middle Chehalis.

below the confluence. At RM 45 the river reaches the left (southwest) aspect of its flood plain to parallel the railroad and Garrard Road for a mile, then flows beneath the bridge (RM 44) that carries South Elma–South Bank Road into Oakville.

From the bridge, the river curves toward the northeastern edge of its flood plain through a heavily wooded area on the outskirts of Oakville. At RM 42.2 the undeveloped access (which may be difficult to see from the river unless it's been scouted carefully beforehand) lies on the right bank of a slough (it may be a beaver pond at low water levels).

For the next mile, the river hugs the northeastern side of its flood plain (except for a loop to the left), then makes a sharp turn back toward Elma-Gate Road. It then swings slowly to the west, running along the south-western edge of the flood plain for a mile (RM 40 to RM 39) not far from Cedarville Road. Then it loops back to the middle of the valley to flow northwest for several miles through alternating open areas and forested stretches, with pastureland and farms on either side.

Rock Creek enters from the left at RM 39.2, just as the river bends east. Cedar Creek enters from the right at RM 38.7, and Gibson Creek enters from the right at RM 37.2. The broad valley is full of isolated oxbow lakes and gravel deposits left by an earlier river. At RM 36 the river again hugs the northeastern edge of its flood plain briefly, paralleling the Burlington Northern Railroad tracks for 0.25 mile; then it begins a major double loop just south of Porter, to again nudge the railroad for 0.25 mile at RM 34. It loops left around Porter, and the take-out lies on the left bank (across the river from Porter), upstream from the bridge.

38 BLACK RIVER

Location	southwest of Olympia, near Rochester
Distance	12 miles
River Time	5 to 6 hours
Maps	Rochester, Oakville (7.5'), Rochester (15'); DNR Map: "Capitol Forest"
Best Season	all year
Hazards	vegetation masses, fallen trees, sweepers
Shuttle	10 miles on paved roads, ideal for bicycle
Rating	Class I

The Black River southwest of Olympia is unique: a southern river placed in the Pacific Northwest, a placid fairyland stream, full of beautiful butterflies and bird life during the summer months, fantastic colors in autumn, and wildflowers in spring and summer. Even in winter this black-water river suggests *The Hobbit* or *Willow* in its scenic beauty. Curling around the southeastern base of the Black Hills below Capitol Forest, it has excellent access, yet remains one of the most remote rivers in the state. Even in this 12-mile segment it offers great variety.

Access. There is public access on S.R. 121 south of Littlerock, at the oxbow bend of the river off Moon Road west of Rochester, and on US 12 between Rochester and Oakville. There is also access to the Chehalis River 1.5 miles northwest of Oakville, about 5 miles below the mouth of the Black River for anyone who wants to make a longer run.

Driving Directions. To reach the take-out on US 12 about 3 miles east of Oakville (4 miles west of Rochester), take I-5 Exit 88 south of Olympia and head west on US 12 toward Aberdeen and "Ocean Beaches." The boat ramp lies on the left bank, south of the highway before it crosses the Black River bridge—immediately downstream from the bridge at RM 4.2.

To reach the modest boat ramp off Moon Road, return to US 12 and head east 2 miles to Moon Road, which T's in from the left. Turn left onto Moon Road, then right in 0.25 mile onto School Land Road and head east toward Rochester for 0.25 mile. The access is to the left of the road on the left bank of the river at RM 8.7.

To reach the access on S.R. 121 south of Littlerock, continue east on School Land Road into Rochester, then turn left onto S.R. 121 and head north toward Littlerock for about 5 miles. The put-in for this trip is at a public fishing access left (west) of the highway, about 2 miles south of Littlerock, at RM 16.2.

(To reach the alternate access on the Chehalis River northwest of Oakville, return to US 12 and head west. Just west of Oakville, turn left onto Elma-Gate Road, which follows the river more closely than does US 12; within a mile there is an access point left of the road on the right bank of the river. See the map for Trip 37.)

Description. Protected by marshes and pasturelands, both public and private, the Black River barely flows for the first 5 miles of this 12-mile segment. It is a long, deep lake fringed by water lilies, often overhung by streamside vegetation. Carved by the massive glacial melt in the Cascades at the end of the last ice age, the Black River takes its name from its dark water (stained with the tannin of its decaying vegetation) and from the Black Hills (its source).

The first 3 miles hug the east side of the valley, never more than 0.5 mile from the highway and the adjacent railroad. (They are hidden by dense

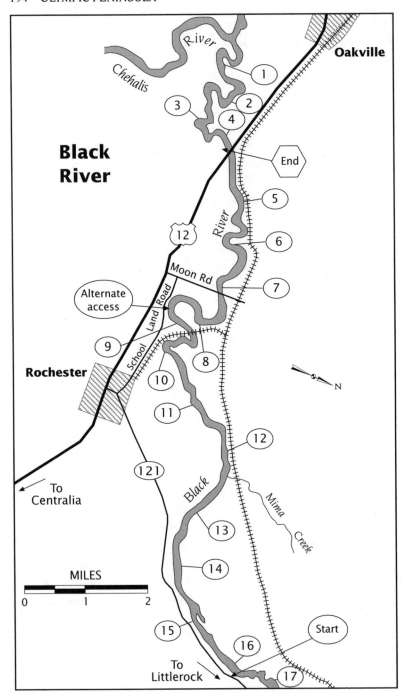

Black River

vegetation that screens all but the sound of an occasional logging truck.) At RM 13 there is a private boat ramp on the left bank without an access road; crayfish sun themselves on the corrugated concrete.

From this point the river swings gradually toward the west side of the valley. Mima Creek enters from the right at RM 12.3, 0.5 mile before the river nudges the Burlington Northern Railroad (RM 11.8) near the Black River Wildlife Area. From that point it heads southwest for 1.5 miles, past isolated homes and tall conifers, one on the right sporting an active osprey nest.

The river skirts a couple of farms near the northwest edge of Rochester and changes character completely at RM 10. It begins to loop

An osprey nest sits in a tall conifer along the Black River.

in sharp, sudden curves, its bottom shallows into a series of dips, and the current picks up. The bottom is covered with thick mats of aquatic vegetation; in some places the clumps actually interfere with navigation, forming obstacles that nearly block the river.

Passing beneath a spur railroad bridge at RM 9.3, the river goes into its oxbow between RM 9 and RM 8. The access at RM 8.7 is so subtle that paddlers may miss it unless they are looking carefully. The river is less than a dozen yards wide here. At RM 7 it passes beneath Moon Road between US 12 and Gate, which lies only a few hundred yards from the river.

The river continues its looping course, hemmed in by dense vegetation. Its bottom is shallow, full of aquatic growth in places but scoured clear in others. The current increases from time to time (thus the scouring effect). Rafts of water crowfoot, forget-me-nots, and wild mint grow in the water during the summer. Ancient pilings and dead logs host lush gardens of grasses, wildflowers, and shrubs.

When the Black River (US 12) bridge comes into view, it is time to take out unless paddlers plan to continue downstream another 4 miles to the Chehalis (the lower Black embraces the Chehalis Indian Reservation, and paddlers may encounter fish nets), and 5 more miles on the Chehalis River to the access northwest of Oakville. This is farming country, with some fields extended to the water's edge. There are small drops and deep pools, a few trashy corners with sweepers and snags, but lots of gravel bars.

39 HUMPTULIPS RIVER: WEST FORK

Location	north of Hoquiam/Aberdeen, southwestern Olympic Peninsula near Humptulips Store
Distance	6.5 miles
River Time	1 to 2 hours
Map	Quinault Lake (15')
Best Season	all year, but best at high water, November to May
Hazards	logjams, sweepers
Shuttle	4.5 miles on paved roads, mountain bike ideal
Rating	Class II-

A rain-forest river rising along the southern boundary of Olympic National Park, the Humptulips River is charming for its name as well as its lush vegetation and pristine character—even in an area where the forests have been butchered for decades. This short segment of the West Fork flows past steep bluffs of conglomerate and sandstone, alternating between pools and shallows with occasional modest drops. There are logjams and sweepers, sometimes a tree across the river, but such obstacles can be portaged. There is disagreement over the meaning of Humptulips—either "cold area" or "tough to pole."

Access. Access to the take-out is off Donkey Creek Road east of US 101, north of the Humptulips crossing. The launch site is off Fish Trap Road (FR #2360), a logging road branching off Donkey Creek Road a few miles north.

Driving Directions. To reach the take-out, turn right (north) off US 101 onto Donkey Creek Road (FR 22) about 3.5 miles north of where 101 crosses the Humptulips River near the village of Humptulips. Drive 4.9 miles to a bridge across the West Fork of the Humptulips; just beyond the bridge, turn left onto a dirt road that gives access to the river. Leave a shuttle vehicle here; a mountain bike is ideal for the short shuttle.

To reach the launch site, return to Donkey Creek Road and turn left.

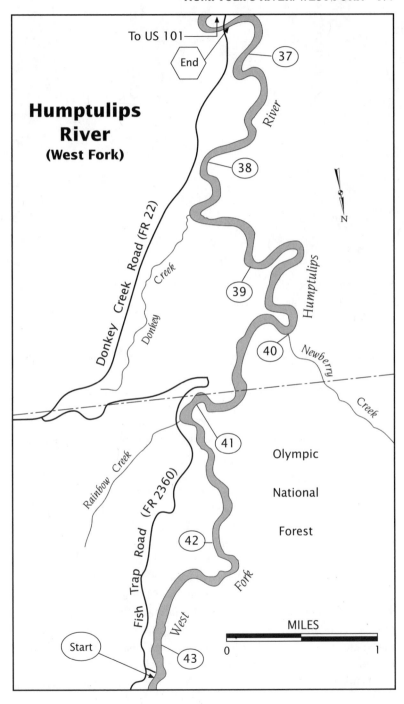

Humptulips River
(West Fork)

Sun and shadow and shallow water on the Humptulips typify late-summer paddling on the southern Olympic Peninsula.

Drive 2.9 miles to Fish Trap Road (unmarked), and turn left again. Follow this road to a river access in about two miles to put in on the left bank of the river (RM 43.2).

Description. The West Fork of the Humptulips flows south from the launch site (RM 43.2) over a shallow, gravelly bottom, through lush rainforest vegetation (big-leaf maples festooned with ferns overhanging the river, hemlocks and western red cedar). It pools occasionally, swinging back and forth between gravel bars and dropping over minor rapids. After a few hundred yards it bends right, then sharply left to serpentine southward for a mile to the mouth of Rainbow Creek entering from the left (RM 41.2). Fish Trap Road (FR 2360) crosses Rainbow Creek by a bridge adjacent to the river; the river turns abruptly right, then right again in two sharp bends to form three sides of a square box between dense streamside vegetation.

The river then loops north for a final bend through Olympic National Forest and flows southwest. The hidden bluffs begin to emerge to form vertical riverbanks of conglomerate. Tiny falls and dripping springs water the ferns and flowers that grow on the bluffs, a spectacular sight. Newberry Creek enters from the right (RM 40). The river loops its way south, then east in two big horseshoe bends, and approaches Donkey Creek Road.

Donkey Creek enters from the left (RM 38.4), and the river bends southward again. At RM 38 it nudges the road (unnoticeable because it is well above the river and screened by vegetation) before swinging back to the west for 0.25 mile to the mouth of a tiny tributary creek (RM 37.7). Then the river swings south again for its last meandering mile to the take-out. The bluffs have been left behind, and on the flats the river swings between gravel bars and overhung banks, where a tree occasionally falls to block the entire river or create a sweeper.

The take-out lies at a wide gravel beach on the left bank as the river swings east to flow beneath the Donkey Creek Road bridge (RM 36.7).

From this point it is possible to continue downstream all the way to Grays Harbor. Many of the river access points in the next several miles (not shown on map) have been closed off by local landowners to protest a county ban on gravel mining (intended to protect water quality and enhance the river's ability to propagate anadromous fish). There is rough access beneath the Humptulips (US 101) bridge, on the north bank of the river (RM 23.1), and a good public access less than a mile downstream, off a spur road from 101 marked "Public Fishing Access" that turns west about a mile south of the Humptulips Store.

40 QUEETS RIVER: SAMS RAPID TO HARTZELL CREEK

Location	southwestern Olympic National Park
Distance	12 miles
River Time	3 to 4 hours
Map	Salmon River (15')
Best Season	all year, but best at high water, November to May
Hazards	Class II rapids, sweepers, logjams
Shuttle	12 miles by gravel road, mountain bike
Rating	Class II+/III- (the most difficult in this book)

The Queets is a big, fast, cold river flowing out of the Olympic Mountains through coastal rain forest. Its frequent winter floods rearrange the logjams and create new sweepers. Its serious Class II rapids challenge paddlers, but it is the best wildlife river in the Northwest with elk, deer, otters, beavers, minks, coyotes, ospreys, and eagles as well as an occasional bear. Its meandering flood plain offers spectacular views of the Olympic peaks (its ultimate source), and its waters are milky with rock flour from its headwater glaciers.

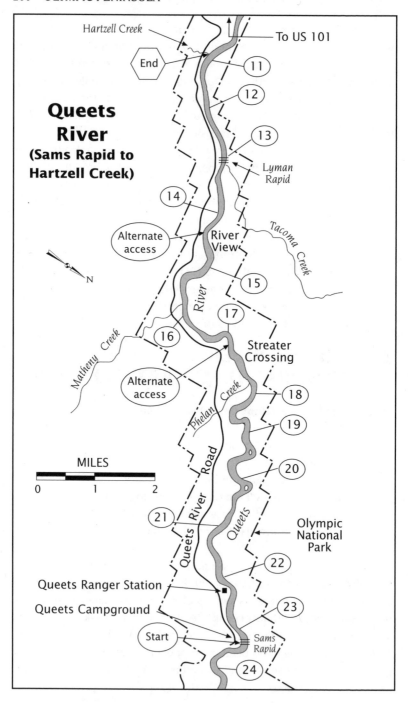

Hartzell Creek

To US 101

End

11

12

13

Lyman Rapid

Queets River
(Sams Rapid to
Hartzell Creek)

14

Tacoma Creek

Alternate access

River View

River

15

17

16

Matheny Creek

Streater Crossing

Alternate access

18

Phelan Creek

19

20

MILES

0   1   2

21

Queets River Road

Queets

Olympic National Park

22

Queets Ranger Station

Queets Campground

23

Start

Sams Rapid

24

N

Access. All of the launch sites and take-out points for this trip (with a single exception) are reached from the Queets River Road in Olympic National Park, which leaves US 101 in the northern part of the Quinault Indian Reservation. The single exception is an access at the confluence of the Clearwater and Queets Rivers on the Quinault Indian Reservation.

Driving Directions. Turn north off US 101 onto Queets River Road about 7 miles east of the bridge across the Queets River, near its mouth (17 miles west of Lake Quinault). Follow Queets River Road north, then east. The suggested take-out at Hartzell Creek (RM 11) is only 2 miles from the highway. Turn left and leave a shuttle vehicle here (a mountain bike will serve).

To reach any of the alternate accesses or the proposed put-in, continue east on the gravel road toward the Queets Campground at the end of the road. At the campground, scout out the river: launch can be made above or below Sams Rapid (RM 23.2), which lies on the bend of the river that wraps around the campground.

Alternate access points lie at Streater Crossing (RM 17.1), about halfway between Sams Rapid and the proposed take-out, and at River View (RM 14.4), about 3 miles southwest of Streater Crossing (4 miles northeast of Hartzell Creek).

To reach the access beneath the bridge across the Queets at the confluence of the Clearwater and the Queets, go back to US 101 and turn right (west) for about 2.5 miles; then turn right onto Clearwater Road. (See Map 41.) Technically, permission to use this access requires permission from the Quinault Indian Tribe.

Description. From Sams Rapid—a long, curving rock garden on the bend of the river at the campground put-in—the Queets flows southwest through a broad valley. Ancient trees that have survived the clear-cutting so devastating in this area appear along the bank: gigantic old Sitka spruce, huge cottonwoods, big-leaf maples covered with mosses, and massive Douglas fir.

The river meanders through braided channels from one side of its flood plain to the other: first hugging the north side (RM 22.3), then bending south past the Queets Ranger Station to approach the south side (RM 21.3), then heading west for a mile, splitting around small, low islands throughout these first few miles. Beware of logjams and sweepers, large rocks and confluence currents.

The Queets flows around a sizable island just above RM 20. Either side is normally passable, but paddlers must judge the flow for themselves in low water because annual winter floods rearrange the bars and islands (and logjams), determining where the current goes. The river bends southwest briefly, then northwest even more briefly, then southwest once more before starting a sharp horseshoe bend left, then back to the right. At the end of the horseshoe turns, the river again hugs the ridge on the right (north) at RM 18.

The straight stretch from RM 18 to RM 17 flows southwest through excellent elk habitat. A favorite spot for elk is the meadowland near the mouth of Phelan Creek, which enters the Queets from the left (south) at RM 17.8. Streater Crossing (RM 17.1) on the right (south) bank is a logical halfway point roughly 2 hours (6 river miles) from Sams Rapid. To find this spot from the river, scout it out from the access road on the drive up and establish a marker that will identify it from the river when it is reached.

Below Streater Crossing the river makes an abrupt left turn, with a nasty little rock and sweeper on the far left. At low water it may be difficult to avoid, but it can be lined on the right. Several small rapids (rock gardens) interrupt the flow of the Queets in this vicinity; they require

Large trees dominate the Queets River shoreline.

some skill in maneuvering to negotiate successfully. The road roughly parallels the river from RM 16.8 to the take-out; but it is rarely visible, never obtrusive. Mount Olympus is visible to the east from several points along this stretch of river.

Matheny Creek flows into the Queets from the left (RM 15.8) just before the river enters a shallow S bend that ends at River View, a possible access (RM 14.4) on the left bank. The river corridor is well vegetated throughout this stretch, though massive clear-cuts can be seen on the surrounding hillsides outside the gerrymandered national park boundaries. Tacoma Creek enters from the right (RM 13.1), and the road (always on the left bank) parallels the river closely for the final 2 miles.

The toughest rapid on this stretch of river, Lyman Rapid, lies immediately below Tacoma Creek's mouth. (No doubt the rocks that make the rapid were brought down the tributary stream during a heavy rain.) There is a ledge system of bedrock on the left from which to scout the lower part of this long rapid. Below the rapid the river continues in a southwestern direction, with a steep bank on the left and open meadows on the right where elk may be seen. A small rapid (more of a rock garden) leads to a deep pool at a slight right bend of the river just above the take-out. (From the rocky left bank, Mount Olympus is visible.)

41 CLEARWATER RIVER

Location	southwest of Olympic National Park
Distance	11.5 miles
River Time	3 to 4 hours
Map	Destruction Island (15')
Best Season	all year, but best at high water, November to May
Hazards	sweepers, logjams, moderate rapids
Shuttle	8 miles on paved road
Rating	Class II-

True to its name (and despite massive clear-cut logging in the drainage), the Clearwater is as healthy a stream as paddlers can canoe in western Washington. It abounds in aquatic invertebrates that provide good fish food. It is an intimate river: small and winding in its upper reaches, broader but nonetheless charming in its lower miles. Although logging operations scar the surrounding hills, little evidence of timber cutting exists on the river itself. Its shoreline vegetation is dense and natural—excellent wildlife habitat.

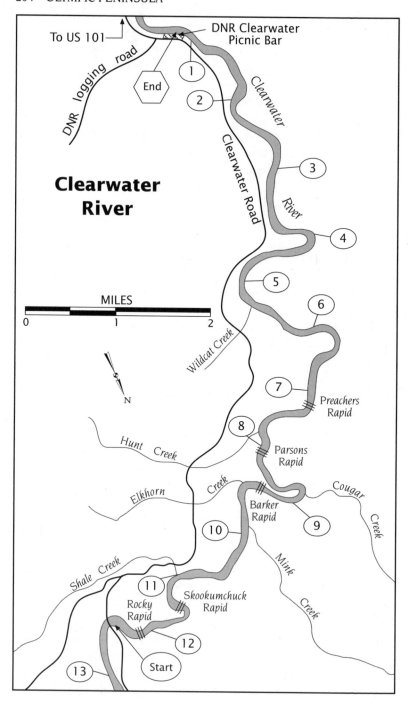

To US 101

DNR logging road

DNR Clearwater
Picnic Bar

End

**Clearwater
River**

Clearwater
Road

Clearwater

River

MILES
0   1   2

N

Wildcat Creek

Hunt Creek

Elkhorn Creek

Cougar Creek

Preachers
Rapid

Parsons
Rapid

Barker
Rapid

Mink Creek

Shale Creek

Rocky
Rapid

Skookumchuck
Rapid

Start

Access. Access to the Clearwater is by way of Clearwater Road, a paved second-grade highway (narrow, with plenty of turns). Clearwater Road heads north from US 101, a few miles east of the US 101 bridge over the Queets, a few miles west of Queets River Road.

Driving Directions. To reach the Clearwater, turn north off US 101 about 2.5 miles west of Queets Road onto Clearwater Road, about 4.5 miles east of the US 101 bridge over the Queets (19.5 miles west of Lake Quinault). In about 2 miles Clearwater Road crosses the Queets River near the mouth of the Clearwater. In less than a mile beyond the bridge (just after a DNR logging road turns right), turn left into the DNR Clearwater Picnic Bar on the left bank of the river, 0.8 mile from its mouth.

To reach the put-in, return to Clearwater Road and turn left (north), following it 8 miles to where it crosses the Clearwater River on a high bridge (stay left at all branch roads). The put-in is immediately beneath the bridge— but it is a steep, rough carry down the north side of the road, west of the river.

Description. At low water levels, the first 100 yards of this run require paddlers to lie flat in the bottom of the canoe to avoid overhanging trees. No doubt at higher water levels there is more current in midriver, away from the sweepers. In short, the first few hundred yards suggest the intimate character of this clear-water river: lots of shallows, riffles, sweepers, and minor logjams that can be gingerly negotiated.

At the put-in bridge (RM 12.3) there are deep, deep pools that serve as reflection ponds for everything in sight. But the huge pools narrow and shallow to barely negotiable chutes and to riffles so shallow it may be necessary to walk the craft through in late summer. The river flows due west after it breaks out of its initial bend at Rocky Rapid (so named on the USGS maps, but not all that severe). Then it makes a short, sharp horseshoe (Skookumchuck Rapid lies at the apex of the horseshoe, but is no big deal) and bends right into a sweeping curve that ends flowing westward again just as Shale Creek enters from the left (RM 11). This area is engulfed in dense rain-forest vegetation.

Mink Creek enters from the right (RM 10) on a mile-long nearly straight stretch flowing southwest. Wide gravel bars force the current against the bank and into the trees in many places. A named rapid (Barker) lies halfway between the mouth of Elkhorn Creek, on river left, and Cougar Creek, which enters on the right. The Clearwater bends northwest, then southeast in a sharp horseshoe; Cougar Creek enters at the apex of the bend (RM 8.8). The bend opens toward the south for half a mile, and Parsons Rapid (another insignificant riffle) shows up on the map at RM 8.

Sweepers and gravel bars mark the Clearwater at low water. Notice the flotation bags and the pole in the canoe.

Then the river makes a quick right and left in rapid succession, as Hunt Creek enters from the left (RM 7.8) to mark another westward run for half a mile. As the river swings south again, there is Preachers Rapid at RM 7.1. (Why did the mapmaker name all these insignificant rapids? None of them is worthy of the name.) Below Preachers Rapid (the last named rapid on the river), there is a half-circle loop to the west, with the river flowing southeast for nearly a mile after it breaks out of the bend (RM 6 to RM 5.2) and heads for the access road.

Wildcat Creek enters from the left (RM 5.3) just before the river bends sharply south. The river continues to the southwest, hugging the left side of its flood plain, with the road just above. Another horseshoe bend to the west and back subtracts a mile as the river reaches for its confluence with the Queets and once more edges the road (RM 3.7). The river valley has widened during the past few miles; in its final three, it flows through a broad valley where a few farms suggest civilization but logging is still king.

Informal, private, and pirate (not officially designated) campsites appear along the last 2 or 3 miles of the Clearwater, but a broad gravel bar on the left (opposite a low cut bank on the right) marks the take-out at a DNR picnic area that is used all summer for family camping. Paddlers will see the new Queets River bridge if they go too far, but the road is so near during the last 0.75 mile that they could take out along the road (it is a bit steep) or at the boat ramp beneath the new Queets River bridge at the confluence (but only with tribal permission).

42 HOH RIVER: OXBOW TO DNR COTTONWOOD CAMP

Location	west of Olympic National Park, south of Forks
Distance	5 miles; 14 miles with permission
River Time	1 hour; 2 hours with permission
Maps	Forks, Destruction Island (15')
Best Season	all year, but best at high water, November to May
Hazards	logjams, sweepers, fast, cold water
Shuttle	4.5 miles on gravel and paved roads, mountain bike ideal
Rating	Class II

The Hoh is the famous rain-forest river that serves as the centerpiece of the developed portion of Olympic National Park, but the segment described here lies below the park. A big, cold, fast river even in its lower portions, the Hoh offers excellent fishing and challenging boating, though this segment has no real rapids. It flows between parallel roads (US 101 on the south side and the Lower Hoh Road to Oil City on the north side) but meanders and braids its way through a mile-wide flood plain to offer picturesque vistas and interesting wildlife habitat.

Access. Access is from two Department of Natural Resources (DNR) facilities: a boat ramp just off US 101 near its Hoh River crossing and a campground off the Lower Hoh Road. It can be run all the way to its mouth if permission can be obtained from either the private property owner on the north bank of RM 1 or the Hoh Indian Tribe on the south bank near the river's mouth.

Driving Directions. To reach the take-out for this short, fast trip, about 15 miles south of Forks turn off US 101 onto Oil City Road (Lower Hoh Road), which roughly parallels the river on its north side. About 2.5 miles

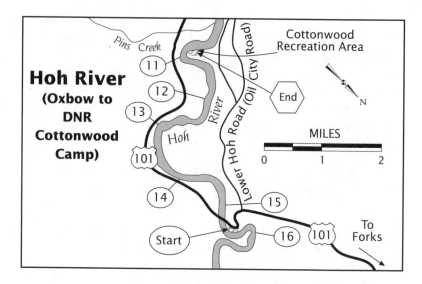

down that road, turn left toward DNR's Cottonwood Recreation Area, a primitive camping area that also serves as a boat launch. The shuttle is so short that a mountain bike makes an ideal shuttle vehicle.

To reach the launch site, return to Oil City Road and turn right (east) toward US 101. Turn right onto US 101 and go about a third of a mile to a spur road turning off to the left (east) into a DNR campground and fishing access area. Simply follow the signs to the boat launch area. Don't cross the bridge; the turnoff is north of the bridge over the Hoh.

Description. The Hoh is deep, swift, and cold at the launch site (RM 15.5), which is heavily used by fishermen with powerboats. It's a busy place for a paddle craft, but within a quarter mile the river takes the craft beyond the bend, beneath the bridge and west for a mile. RVs may be camped on the left bank as the river bends south. Paddlers may want to stop at RM 14 and visit the largest known spruce tree, the Helen Clapp Spruce. It stands (without its top) less than a quarter mile from the river. It was once 248 feet high, but it lost its top in a storm; it is 17 feet 9 inches in diameter and was once calculated to contain 50,500 board feet of lumber.

As the river continues its course south, it flows over a riffle (mild rapid) just as it touches the roadbed of US 101 (RM 13.6). Below the riffle

The Hoh River glides through a landscape of mountains and forests in Olympic National Park.

it begins a westward curve, flows around an island (RM 13.4), passes a favorite fishing hole known as Allens Bar (RM 13), and swings north. The river braids and meanders through massive gravel bars, swinging back and forth between the boundaries of its flood plain. At RM 12 (where it reaches the northern edge of the flood plain in one of its curves) is a DNR fishing access with limited parking, accessible from the Oil City Road. The river swings in a big bend around a promontory gravel bank that serves as Cottonwood Campground (DNR) at RM 10.7, the take-out.

If permission has been obtained to take out at the mouth of the river, another 8 miles downstream (not on accompanying map), paddlers will see the river broaden slightly and continue its meandering, braided course to tidewater, then fluctuate with the tide in its lower few miles. It splits around a few sizable islands, forms a few sloughs at high tide, and offers an interesting paddle that few people experience.

43 QUILLAYUTE RIVER/ LOWER DICKEY RIVER

Location	west of Forks, Olympic Peninsula
Distance	5.7 miles/5 miles
River Time	between 1 and 2 hours each
Map	La Push (15')
Best Season	all year, but best at high water, November to May
Hazards	sweepers, logjams, contrary tides
Shuttle	4 miles on paved road
Rating	Class I, Tidal

The Quillayute, one of the shortest rivers in Washington at less than 6 miles, is totally tidal—as is the section of its tributary, the Dickey River, covered here. True rain-forest rivers, they both provide delightful paddling through corridors of gigantic trees covered with mosses and ferns. There are log-jams, to be sure, and sweepers—but the flow is so mild in these rela-tively flat-terrain rivers that they present no real problem unless the whole river is blocked (as has been true on the lower Dickey in recent years) or the low tide causes strong currents.

Access. Both the put-in and the take-out for the Quillayute are from boat ramps directly accessible from La Push (Mora–Ocean Beach) Road (S.R. 110), northwest of Forks, off US 101. The upper Dickey is accessible

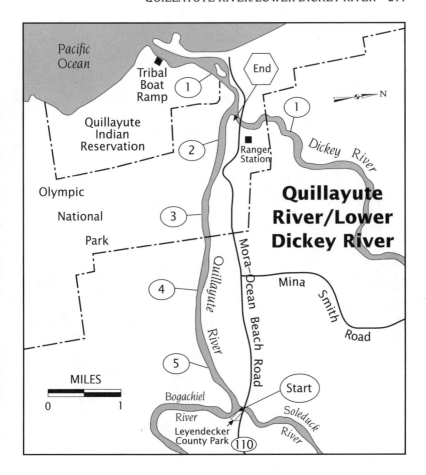

from Mina Smith Road, but such access may be meaningless if the recent massive logjam still exists on the lower Dickey. The best access to the Dickey (which involves traveling upstream) is from the boat ramp on the Dickey a mile west of the ranger station in this portion of Olympic National Park. With tribal permission, the Quillayute boat ramp on the left bank near the river's mouth at La Push may be used as a take-out.

Driving Directions. To reach the Quillayute (and the put-in for an upstream exploration of the Dickey), drive west from the La Push turnoff from US 101 about a mile northwest of Forks on S.R. 110. Follow this road all the way into Olympic National Park, about 14 miles from US 101.

Heading west, note Leyendecker County Park. Its boat ramp will serve

The Quillayute River Mouth at La Push is dominated by sea stacks.

as a launch site for the trip down the Quillayute, which begins at the confluence of the Soleduck and the Bogachiel Rivers. (This is also the take-out for Trip 44.)

The Quillayute begins at the confluence of the Bogachiel (left) and the Soleduck (right) and flows westward to the Pacific. A mile west of the park entrance station, turn left to a boat ramp on the left bank of the lower 0.1 mile of the Dickey. This boat ramp will serve as a take-out for a 4-mile trip down the Quillayute from its point of origin or a put-in for a paddle (or pole) up the Dickey River. Spot a shuttle vehicle here; a bicycle is ideal for this short shuttle.

To reach the launch site at Leyendecker County Park, retrace the route 4 miles to the boat ramp between the rocky Soleduck and the Bogachiel.

Description. The Bogachiel drops over a ledge into one of the deepest pools on a Northwest river; this is where the Quillayute is born. From the confluence of the Soleduck and the Bogachiel (RM 5.7), the Quillayute narrows briefly as it flows out of this deep pool. The road to its mouth crosses the Soleduck on the right as the Quillayute makes a long, straight, slow run toward the Pacific between borders of tall trees. There are massive gravel bars along the river.

At RM 4.3 an ancient oxbow formed years ago, but floods in the mid-1980s cut through to shorten the river by nearly a mile. Much of the land enclosed by the loop is open and developed, but there are always massive trees in view, relics of earlier times or second and third growth, evidence that this is great tree-growing country.

As the river heads west again below the shortcut (RM 3.3), it enters Olympic National Park and flows slightly north of west for nearly 2 miles. It makes its final left turn to the ocean just below the mouth of the Dickey, which enters from the right (RM 1.6). The take-out lies on the lower Dickey, only 0.1 mile from the Dickey's entry into the Quillayute. Simply paddle upstream on the Dickey, and the boat ramp is on the right (river left on the Dickey). With tribal permission, you can run all the way to the Quillayute boat ramp at the river's mouth.

The Dickey is a smaller, more intimate river. Its navigability varies from season to season as logjams come and go with local flooding. Paddling or poling up the Dickey from the Quillayute offers a special experience as the river meanders through lush rain-forest vegetation.

44 BOGACHIEL RIVER: BOGACHIEL STATE PARK TO CONFLUENCE

Location	south and west of Forks, western Olympic Peninsula
Distance	15.4 miles
River Time	4 to 5 hours
Maps	La Push, Forks (15')
Best Season	all year, but best at higher water, November to May
Hazards	logjams, sweepers, modest rapids
Shuttle	14 miles
Rating	Class II-

The Bogachiel River (whose name means "muddy waters") is a frequently flooding river of the Olympic Peninsula, one that has occasionally washed out US 101. It is also a prime steelhead stream and receives much fishing

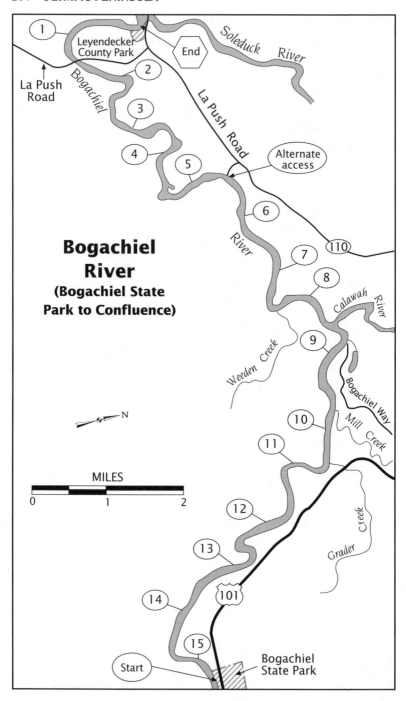

1
Leyendecker
County Park
End
Soleduck River
La Push Road
Bogachiel
2
3
4
5
La Push Road
Alternate access
6
110
Bogachiel River
(Bogachiel State Park to Confluence)
River
7
8
Calawah River
Weeden Creek
9
Bogachiel Way
Mill Creek
N
10
11
MILES
0   1   2
12
13
Grader Creek
101
14
15
Start
Bogachiel State Park

pressure. Most of its course flows through private lands, but there are a few public access points. Much of it is forested, though there is also agricultural land along the way, largely unobtrusive. Its waters clear whenever the rains stop long enough to let the river drop its suspended load of rock debris.

Access. Access to the put-in is provided at Bogachiel State Park on US 101, a few miles south of Forks. Access to either of two suggested take-out points is from La Push (Mora–Ocean Beach) Road, which turns off US 101 a mile northwest of Forks.

Driving Directions. The ultimate take-out for this segment of the Bogachiel is its end—its confluence with the Soleduck to create the Quillayute. To reach this point, drive northwest from Forks on US 101 and turn left (west) onto La Push Road (S.R. 110); it will become the Mora or Ocean Beach Road as you stay right at the Y. Drive to Leyendecker County Park (only 0.3 mile from the Y), where a boat ramp lies between the Bogachiel (which flows from the left) and the Soleduck (which flows from the right).

An alternate access (a possible put-in for a shorter run downstream or a take-out for a shorter run from the state park) lies off La Push (Mora) Road about 3.4 miles east of Leyendecker County Park. Return to Mora Road and turn right (east); it joins La Push Road at the Y. Continue another 3 miles eastward and turn right to a public fishing access about a mile south.

To reach the launch site at Bogachiel State Park, return to Mora (La Push) Road, and turn right (east); turn right on US 101; go through Forks and south to the state park on the right (about 7 miles after returning to US 101). Turn into the state park and seek a logical launch site (perhaps near the picnic shelter at the upper end of the park, near the Russell H. Barker Memorial Bridge).

Description. From the park launch area (RM 15.6), the Bogachiel flows west for half a mile, turns gradually south, then abruptly northwest (RM 14.7) through DNR lands. Then it heads northward in a series of loops, one of which kisses US 101 (RM 12.8). The river is clear most of the year and flanked by gravel bars backed by tall trees. The banks are well wooded.

Grader Creek enters from the right (RM 10.4) shortly after the river turns west and leaves US 101 for the last time. Mill Creek enters from the right (RM 9.7) as the river continues to flow slightly north of west. At RM 8.7 a state steelhead pond lies just off the river on the right bank,

A boat ramp at River Mile 5.5 on the Bogachiel offers an alternate launch site or take-out.

accessible from Bogachiel Way southwest of Forks. In another few hundred yards (RM 8.4) the Calawah River joins the Bogachiel from the right.

Moving southwest now, the river turns gradually south (RM 8). Weeden Creek enters from the left, and the river makes an abrupt bend to the northwest, then back to the southwest. The alternate access appears as a boat ramp on the right.

Below this intermediate access point the river continues to bend back and forth, making a southward swing for a mile, then turning abruptly west at a big pool (RM 4.6) on the bend. A slough comes in from the right just beyond the bend (RM 4.4). In half a mile the river heads north again, then begins a broad double U as it continues its meandering course to its confluence with the Soleduck. The final mile it flows almost due north.

45 WILLAPA RIVER: LOWER MAIN STEM AND FORKS

Location	south of Aberdeen; South Bend, Raymond, and east
Distance	10 miles plus sloughs
River Time	3 to 4 hours
Maps	Raymond (15'), South Bend (7.5'); NOAA Chart: 18405
Best Season	all year
Hazards	contrary tides, powerboats
Shuttle	10 miles, paved road
Rating	Class I, Tidal

The lower Willapa River and its convoluting sloughs offer an interesting look at a small West Coast timber and fishing town as well as an opportunity to paddle some quiet rural waters and explore a protected saltwater bay. The fishing is good in Willapa at certain seasons, and the boating is dependable year round because of the tidal influence on this entire segment. Oyster fishing still thrives in the bay, but timber is king in Raymond, a town bisected by the river.

Access. Excellent take-out access exists off US 101 northwest of South Bend, about 2 miles from the river's mouth as it flows into Willapa Bay. An excellent put-in access lies at the mouth of Wilson Creek (RM 12), a 10-mile shuttle for a 10-mile run.

Driving Directions. To reach the take-out, drive west on US 101 out of Raymond and through South Bend. At the northwest edge of South Bend, to the right of the highway, is a small turnout with a boat ramp on the left bank of the lower Willapa River as it broadens to become Willapa Bay. Leave a shuttle vehicle here.

To reach the put-in, return to Raymond on US 101 and cross the bridge over the Willapa River. Almost immediately beyond the bridge, turn right onto Willapa–Monohan Landing Road and follow it about 4 miles to the public fishing access to the right of the road at the mouth of Wilson Creek. There is a boat ramp here (on the right bank of the river) and ample parking.

Description. The Willapa River is placid at the launch site, unless the wind is up. The river, tidal all the way, hugs the road for the first 0.5

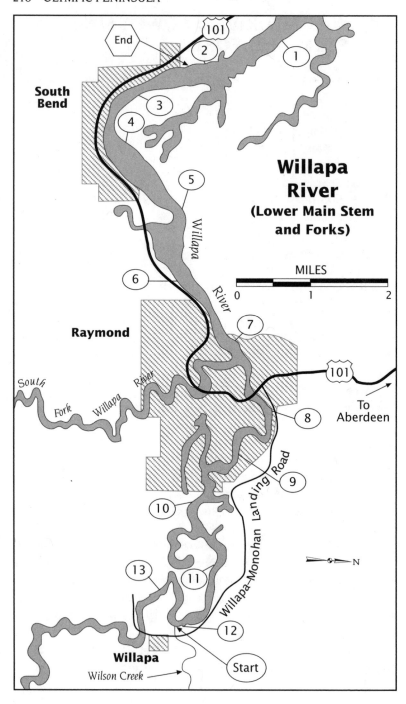

Willapa River
(Lower Main Stem and Forks)

A fisherman tries his luck at the mouth of Wilson Creek, a launch site for the Willapa River.

mile, past tall, scattered conifers and ancient pilings. It bends left to flow west and run straight for about a mile through low-lying marshlands, then bends left again to head southwest. At RM 10.4 a major slough branches off to the left (south) to double back to a point very near a loop of the river a mile above the launch site.

The river broadens and becomes almost sluggish unless the tide is flowing out. Two other minor sloughs branch off to the right in this vicinity, and another branches off to the left just as the river reaches the east edge of Raymond (a town totally dominated by the timber industry).

From here for the next 3 miles the river loops through town, bordered by timber-related activities (including a massive Weyerhaeuser sawmill). The small homes of a typical company town dot the slopes beyond the timber-processing facilities and huge piles of sawdust awaiting export. Sizable ships enter the harbor to carry away what used to be a waste product but is now a valuable resource.

The South Fork of the Willapa meets the main stem near the west edge of town and can be explored as a side trip. From the junction of the two forks, the river flows southwest, broad and busy with boating traffic (commercial fishermen, oyster gatherers, timber-related vessels). It's an interesting experience to dodge the power crafts in a paddle-powered boat, but most of the power-boat pilots are courteous drivers.

Another small slough heads south as the river narrows at RM 5, and South Bend begins on the left bank. The Willapa swings past South Bend in a broad U as a slough that branches off to the right at RM 2 sends its tentacles almost to the base of the open end of the U. The boat ramp that serves as take-out is hard to miss; it lies just beyond the last buildings at the western edge of South Bend at this writing.

COLUMBIA
RIVER

46 GRAYS RIVER/SEAL SLOUGH

Location	northeast of Astoria, OR; northeast of Grays Bay, Columbia River; south of Aberdeen/Hoquiam
Distance	up to 10 miles, Grays River; 2 miles on Seal Slough; 7 more miles on nearby Deep River
River Time	3 miles per hour, slack tide
Map	Grays River, WA/OR (7.5'); NOAA Charts: 18521, 18523
Best Season	all year, but best in rainy season, September through May
Hazards	contrary tides, wind on the Bay
Shuttle	3 to 10 miles, but no shuttle necessary
Rating	Tidal, Class I below the covered bridge, Class II above it

Grays River is a small tributary of the Columbia River named for Captain Robert Gray, who discovered the Columbia (the river was named for his ship). Seal Slough is a tributary of Grays River that enters it about 2 miles from its mouth. Nearby Deep River feeds into Grays Bay about 2 miles west of the mouth of Grays River. All these segments are tidal. Washington's only extant covered bridge lies on Grays River at RM 9.6, a mile above the upper extent of tidal influence. While this region is rainy, it offers excellent birding and unique paddling opportunities through a historical landscape.

Access. The only real public access is available at a boat ramp less than 0.5 mile south of the Rosburg Store, near the Rosburg Community Hall. There are also informal launch sites at a private campground less than a mile from the mouth of Deep River; at a private boat dock at Devils Elbow, the last bend of Grays River before it enters the Bay; at a gravel bar at RM 8; and near the confluence of the East and West Forks of Grays River north of S.R. 4. There is a public fishing access stile at the covered bridge that might also be used for launching a canoe under the covered bridge.

Driving Directions. The best launch site may also be the best take-out if the tides are played right: the boat ramp one third of a mile south of Rosburg at RM 4.2. To reach it, turn south off S.R. 4 at the Rosburg Store (between Naselle and Cathlamet) onto S.R. 403 (Altoona Road; the sign says "Dead End—7 miles"). Turn right onto a parallel road west of the

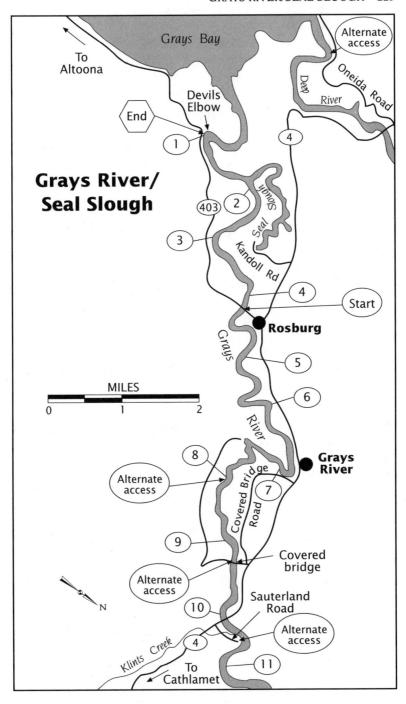

highway heading south just as the highway rises to cross Grays River on an elevated bridge. The unmarked road leads to the Rosburg Community Hall. The boat ramp is a few dozen yards southwest of the building.

To paddle downstream to the Bay (and perhaps explore Seal Slough on the way), paddlers may want to leave a shuttle vehicle (a bicycle is ideal) at Devils Elbow (RM 1), about 3 miles by road from the launch site. To reach it, return to S.R. 403 and turn right; cross the bridge; head south for less than 3 miles to Mattson Road; and turn right. Park alongside the road, preferably on the left-hand (southwest) side. It is best to ask permission to use the private dock to the right of the road for launching or taking out.

To reach two other accesses, return to S.R. 4 and turn right, heading northeast. Take Covered Bridge Road south (right) off S.R. 4 at the village of Grays River, and follow the road to the covered bridge. On the south side of the river are the public access stiles that offer rough access. The gravel-bar access at RM 8 (above the covered bridge) can be reached by crossing the bridge and following Covered Bridge Road upstream to a point about 2 miles above the bridge. A rough road offers access to a big gravel bar left of the road, on the left bank of the river.

For a longer run of Grays River above tidewater, launch at the rough access near the confluence of the river's main forks. Return to S.R. 4 and head east toward Cathlamet. Two miles from Grays River village, the highway crosses Grays River. Turn left onto Sauterland Road; follow it to where it peters out at a school bus turnaround; then follow the track to the riverbank (RM 10.6). A standard vehicle will make it in most road conditions.

To reach the launch site on Deep River, return to S.R. 4 and head west. Just after crossing Deep River, turn left onto Oneida Road. There is rough access from the road 4.7 miles from the highway and a commercial campground access 5.2 miles from the highway. (The paving ends 3.7 miles from S.R. 4.)

Description. From the boat ramp near the Rosburg Community Hall, paddlers can head upstream toward the covered bridge (if the tide is coming in) or downstream on the outgoing tide. Either route offers a unique experience.

Heading upstream between blackberry-festooned banks, paddlers weave northeast through agricultural lands about 3 miles to the village of Grays River. (A new boat ramp is scheduled to be located here at a tiny park at the south edge of town.) From the village the river swings abruptly

A *covered bridge over the Grays River lies less than 10 miles from Grays Bay on the Columbia River.*

south and then east through pasturelands, to flow beneath the covered bridge (RM 9.6). Going upstream beyond this point is likely to be difficult for two reasons: (1) the tidal influence subsides a mile below the bridge; and (2) in summer the water can become shallow.

Heading downstream, paddlers also encounter the blackberry banks and thick bank vegetation of red osier dogwood and viburnum as the river loops widely through dairy farms and pasturelands, bordered by dark, brooding Sitka spruce trees that in places overhang the shore. It turns left to flow south for a mile, then swings right to flow westward, past occasional rural homes and backyard logging operations where second- and third-growth forests survive and wildflowers (lotus, jewelweed, tall orchids) abound in summer.

Just below RM 2, Seal Slough enters from the right and can be followed all the way to the old Finnish Church just off S.R. 4, a full 2 miles north by water. Taking a right turn at the fork 1.3 miles upstream, the paddler can go almost another mile up the branch of the slough that leads to Kandoll Road a few hundred yards west of Rosburg.

The lower 2 miles of Grays River are totally tidal, lined with tall trees and houses, boat docks, and moored boats. If the tide is right, boaters can paddle down to the Bay, explore its northern reaches, even enter Deep River 2 miles to the west. If a shuttle vehicle has been left at the lower end of Deep River, paddlers can take out there along a stretch of river again lined by small houses, fishing shacks, and moored boats.

To run the upper stretch of Grays River, launch at the forks access (RM 10.6) off Sauterland Road. From here the river is small, winding, and shallow in summer, with splits around brushy gravel islands and tight corners, a moderate Class II river unless it is flooding (which may be much of the year, given the heavy rains of the area). The river flows south as it begins a sharp S curve which ends beneath the Grays River (S.R. 4) bridge. Then it moderates as it enters agricultural lands, still lined by trees and shrubbery as it meanders through the valley to flow beneath the covered bridge.

47 COWLITZ RIVER: MASSEY BAR TO I-5 BRIDGE

Location	near Toledo
Distance	7 miles
River Time	about 1.5 hours
Map	Castle Rock (15')
Best Season	all year, fine in summer, fall
Hazards	minor rapids, sweepers, logjams
Shuttle	8 miles
Rating	Class I+/II-

The Cowlitz, one of the premier steelhead fishing rivers of the Northwest, is a big, deep, lovely river where it flows beneath and alongside I-5, north of Longview and Kelso. It is more of a mountain stream—a big one to be sure, but a mountain stream nonetheless—east of I-5 in the vicinity of Toledo. This river offers views of both Mount Rainier and Mount St. Helens, as well as excellent fishing, birding, and boating on a big open river that moves with good speed. It is rural but with little evidence of the adjacent farms, except for the launch site in a cow pasture.

Access. The take-out, a public fishing access, lies just downstream

The Cowlitz River is framed by streamside vegetation in some reaches.

from the Cowlitz River (I-5) Bridges. It is reached from a local access road southwest of Toledo. The best launch site, another public fishing access, lies off a local access road northeast of Toledo.

Driving Directions. Although the take-out is almost immediately beneath the Cowlitz River Bridges on I-5, it is complicated to reach. Take Exit 60 off I-5 onto S.R. 505 and head east toward Toledo. After 2 miles, turn right at the Jackson Highway in Toledo; follow it through town, crossing the Cowlitz and turning right onto South Jackson Highway, 0.3 mile from the bridge. Follow this highway southwest to Mandy Road; turn right, then left onto River Road; and follow it under the I-5 bridges to the public fishing access just west of the freeway.

To reach the launch site, return to Toledo and head north out of town on Winlock-Toledo Road. Veer right at the north end of town and follow signs toward Lewis and Clark State Park (North Jackson Highway). At the Cowlitz Mission Historic Site, turn right; in 0.3 mile, turn left onto Spencer Road; turn right onto Buckley Road, which leads to what looks like a dead end. Turn right onto a gravel road that winds down a hill into a cow pasture. On an open flat by the river, the launch site is on the right bank of the river at Massey Bar. It's a boat ramp heavily used by steelhead fishermen for drift boats or dories.

Description. From the launch site at Massey Bar, the river is broad and fast, clear and shallow, its banks riprapped with basalt blocks. In low water there is a riffle just below the put-in. The river flows through open country with a fringe of vegetation along the banks, swinging gradually to the left to pass Toledo (which lies on the right bank in about 3 miles). Bill Creek enters from the right just before Toledo.

The river passes beneath the S.R. 505 bridge and swings right—still broad and shallow for the most part, though a few deep stretches alternate with riffles. Walking access used by fishermen in steelhead season lies along the inside (right bank) curve at the bend below town. The river gradually deepens, flows around an island or two, and swings left at a point where the river is less than a mile from I-5 and the sound of highway traffic may intrude.

The river parallels I-5 about a mile from the freeway as it flows south, then curves right to flow westward in a long, straight stretch for more than a mile. The take-out lies on the left bank 100 yards below the double span of the I-5 bridges. There are a few good river access points along River Road, which is the extension southwest of the road along the Cowlitz.

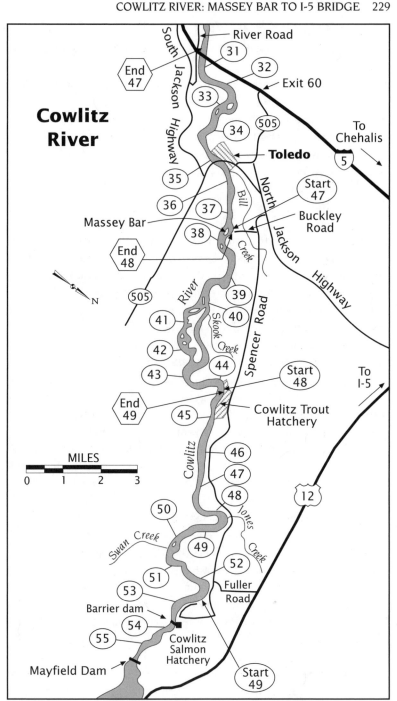

48 COWLITZ RIVER: TROUT HATCHERY TO MASSEY BAR

Location	northeast of Toledo, southeast of Chehalis
Distance	7 miles
River Time	1.25 hours
Maps	Castle Rock and Toutle (15')
Best Season	all year, especially summer, fall
Hazards	minor rapids, sweepers, logjams
Shuttle	7 miles
Rating	Class II-

One boater has called this stretch "the best river this side of the mountains for new boaters." That's a personal opinion, but it does suggest the quality of experience available on the upper Cowlitz. Mount Rainier can be seen from the put-in and from several points along the river. And there is plenty of wildlife to see: bald eagles and ospreys, deer and beavers. The river is broad, tree-lined, and rural—almost wild in nature—its forested banks giving it a more pristine appearance that its surroundings suggest. This is a good run for sea kayaks.

Access. Both the take-out at a public fishing access at Massey Bar and the launch site at the state trout hatchery are reached from Spencer Road, which roughly parallels the river on its north side. The shuttle drive offers views of both Mount St. Helens and Mount Rainier.

Driving Directions. To reach this segment take Exit 60 off I-5 and head east to Toledo, turning left as S.R. 505 T's into the main north-south street in Toledo, which becomes the Winlock-Toledo Road. In less than a mile (just past Toledo High School), veer right at the Y toward Lewis and Clark State Park, and head northeast on North Jackson Highway. At 1.3 miles from the Y, turn right at the Cowlitz Mission Historic Site; after a third of a mile turn left onto Spencer Road; and head east toward the Cowlitz Trout Hatchery and the Cowlitz Salmon Hatchery.

At Buckley Road, less than a mile from the Mission, turn right and follow it to the end of the pavement; turn right on the gravel road toward the public fishing access (Massey Bar) that has a boat ramp and ample parking. Leave a shuttle vehicle here. (This is also the launch site for Trip 47.)

Return to Spencer Road and turn right (east). In 4.8 miles turn right into the state trout hatchery; 0.7 mile from the turnoff is a boat ramp at

A powerboat is loaded onto its trailer at a Cowlitz River boat ramp that is also a popular launch for canoes and sea kayaks.

the far (downstream) end of the public fishing access area and considerable parking. Many people camp here as well.

Description. From the double boat ramp at the western end of the public fishing access area at the Cowlitz Trout Hatchery, the river is broad and shallow, its banks well forested. The river bends to the left (there is private access on the left bank, just below the bend), and there may be ospreys and eagles, kingfishers, and great blue herons fishing the clear waters in this vicinity.

As the river bends to the right again, it becomes braided, but the main channel is obvious. Pasturelands lie on the left, a slight bluff on the right. There are many islands for lunch stops and excellent birding in summer. Skook Creek enters on the right a mile before the river gathers itself together—still broad, clear, and fast. It makes one more swing to the north against the bluffs before it reaches the take-out boat ramp on the right bank of a shallow bend to the south.

49 COWLITZ RIVER: SALMON HATCHERY TO TROUT HATCHERY

Location	northeast of Toledo, southeast of Chehalis
Distance	8 miles
River Time	1.5 hours
Maps	Toutle and Onalaska (15')
Best Season	all year, best in summer
Hazards	Class II rapids, sweepers, logjams
Shuttle	7 miles
Rating	Class II

This uppermost segment of the Cowlitz, just below Mayfield Dam, gets heavy fishing use, but it is a more challenging stretch of river for paddlers (in fact, the Cowlitz gets progressively more challenging with each segment, moving upstream). This is the most scenic and pristine of the Cowlitz segments as well, a mountain stream that yields salmon and steelhead as well as trout. Its rapids are easy—except for one, and that one can be lined or portaged on the right (though it is not that difficult a rapid).

Access. Both the take-out (the put-in for Trip 48) and the launch site are reached from Spencer Road, which parallels the river on the north side. The whole Cowlitz complex lies just a few miles south of US 12.

Driving Directions. To reach this segment take Exit 60 off I-5 and head east to Toledo, turning left as S.R. 505 T's into the main north-south street in Toledo, which becomes the Winlock-Toledo Road. In less than a mile (just past Toledo High School), veer right at the Y toward Lewis and Clark State Park, and head northeast on North Jackson Highway. At 1.3 miles from the Y, turn right at the Cowlitz Mission Historic Site; after a third of a mile, turn left onto Spencer Road and head east toward the Cowlitz Trout Hatchery and the Cowlitz Salmon Hatchery.

After following Spencer Road for 5.3 miles, turn right at the sign to the Cowlitz Trout Hatchery, and follow the road to the public fishing access (a double boat ramp 0.7 mile from the turnoff). Leave a shuttle vehicle here. (This is also the launch site for Trip 48.)

To reach the launch site, return to Spencer Road and turn right (east). After about 5 miles, there is a stop sign at Fuller Road. Go straight ahead 0.2 mile to a yield sign, which offers a free right turn; stay right (essentially straight ahead) into the Cowlitz Salmon Hatchery, and follow the road to the public fishing access several hundred yards below the barrier dam below Mayfield Dam. The launch site is on the right bank of the river.

Description. Immediately below the boat ramp the river bends sharply to the left. Within a quarter mile you are out of sight of civilization, heading south along a pristine corridor between tall trees where migrant eagles and ospreys fish, along with the resident kingfishers and great blue herons. The river is shallow except at flood stage (and its level is controlled to some extent by the upstream dams) and amazingly intimate for so large a river.

The river bends sharply to the right 1.5 miles below the launch site, as two small streams enter from the left and an island appears in midriver. Either side of the island will normally be negotiable, and in low water the flow will be obvious. From this bend, the river flows northwest for another 1.5 miles between tall cottonwoods and conifers with an understory of alders and numerous native shrubs.

The upper Cowlitz run offers some lively water.

The river bends sharply once more to the left near Spencer Road. A small creek enters from the right after the river flows beneath the adjacent road, creating one of the most serious rapids on the run, a modest Class II. (It can be scouted from the road while you are driving to the launch site.) The river flows south briefly, then bends back to the west as a steep bluff on the left bank gives the river relief.

Once the river takes its westward course, it flows relatively straight for 3 miles, the last 0.5 mile along the Cowlitz Trout Hatchery grounds. You will find the take-out at the lower (downstream) end of the hatchery property.

Note: The three Cowlitz segments (Trips 47–49) can easily be run in a day. The entire 22-mile stretch from the salmon hatchery to the I-5 take-out has been poled in 4 hours and 15 minutes of river time in midsummer, when the river was relatively low. Any one of the stretches can easily be done after work on a late-spring day when daylight hours are long, and all three can easily be done on any weekend of the year.

50 LOWER KALAMA RIVER

Location	40 miles north of Portland
Distance	8 to 10 miles
River Time	2 to 3 hours
Map	Kalama (7.5'); NOAA Chart: 18524
Best Season	all year; may be too low in late summer, too high in winter (flood stage)
Hazards	sweepers, logjams, modest rapids
Shuttle	6.4 miles on paved roads (take-out unpaved)
Rating	Class II-

One of the best steelhead tributaries of the Columbia, the Kalama has some fine whitewater stretches above this segment. At the lower reaches, this clear, swift stream provides a few challenging miles of modest rapids before it breaks out of its confining canyon a few miles from the Columbia (into which it flows). The paddler is suddenly thrust into a modern world of freeways, nuclear power plants, and grain elevators feeding ships carrying food for a hungry world. Despite logging trucks on adjacent roads, as well as rural homes and vacation cabins along its shoreline, the Kalama is a pleasant run less than an hour from Portland.

Access. One take-out on the lower 0.5 mile of the river and another

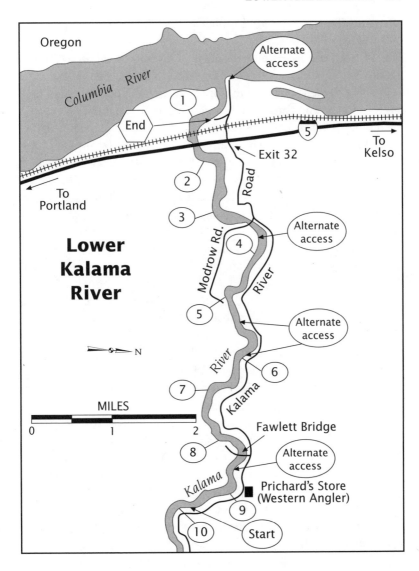

on the right bank of the Columbia River (a few dozen yards downstream from the Kalama mouth) offer excellent access at the end of this trip. Since Kalama River Road hugs the river for much of this segment, there are a number of possible launch sites right from the road.

Driving Directions. The take-out for this segment can be reached from I-5 by taking Exit 32 (Kalama River Road) 2 miles north of Kalama. It is also 7 miles south of the S.R. 4 Exit 39 south of Kelso. Head west over the railroad tracks to a public fishing access left of the road, on the last bend of the river.

To reach the access on the Columbia River itself, follow the county road past the public fishing access to where it officially ends. Then turn left, following signs that lead to a Sportsman's Club; but instead of turning left into the Sportsman's Club, go straight to the Columbia River beach on the right bank, a few dozen yards below the mouth of the Kalama.

To get to the launch areas, return to the county road that crosses over the railroad tracks and I-5 to become Kalama River Road, and follow it east (upstream). There are several roadside accesses, but the farthest upstream that is still sáfe Class II water is opposite a red barn on the left, 6 miles from the I-5 exit. The rough launch site is right (south) of the road, on the right bank of the river.

Other possible launch sites include the one at Prichard's Store (Western Angler), 0.6 mile downstream from the red barn put-in (RM 8.6); public fishing access areas at RM 6 and RM 5.4; and on the left bank just above the Modrow Road bridge (RM 3.5). Modrow Road crosses the Kalama River at this point as it heads south, then east to access the residents living south of the river.

Description. At the red barn put-in there is only roadside parking, and there is no boat ramp (just a rough carry to the right riverbank). The river gets busy quickly. An island forces a choice of routes; right is usually better. A big rock in mid-river offers another challenge, then Prichard's Store (known as Western Angler) appears on the right bank across the road.

Below Prichard's Store is a solid Class II rapid that can be cheated, but its tail waves offer some nice haystacks (standing waves). Kingfishers and ouzels make their presence known. Beaver cuts line the bank, and peeled sticks cover the sandy bottom in the eddies. Fern-festooned cliffs steer the river through the forested gorge, and a kinky cable crosses the river not far above Fawlett Bridge, where a Class II swing rapid lies on a sharp left-hand bend.

This rapid can be tricky. The current flows strongly along the left bank (which is essentially a cliff), and the right side of the river is a rock garden. Strong eddies mark the confluence of counter currents, but experienced paddlers should have few problems here. (If this rapid, which can be scouted from the road, seems too challenging, launch just downstream at the public fishing access a mile below.)

The tidal reaches of many western Washington rivers exhibit muddy banks at low tide. Even the Kalama, a Columbia tributary, is influenced by the tides.

A waterfall on the left adds to the scenery, as does the presence of birds (Steller's jays, chickadees, more kingfishers). The river widens to shallow riffles. A series of waterfalls appears on the left and houses on the right, along with some domestic mallards. The public fishing access lies on the right (well used by steelhead fishermen), and a large rock splits the river. (The right channel is normally the way to go.)

Licorice fern grows here in the shade of Douglas fir, western red cedar, hemlock, grand fir, maple, and alder. Old houses appear on the left bank, and the river glides past a fish hatchery near a problem rapid. A gravel bar on the right pinches the river into a narrow, turbulent channel on the left. Watch for logjams and sweepers. Another access lies at a riffle on a big bend where cabins appear on the left, and there is a pipeline on the right at a green bridge with a logjam.

The green gas pipeline and a gauging station mark the entry into civilization. A trio of yurts appears along the river, and soon Modrow Bridge comes into view with the fishing access on the left bank under the bridge. The river is out of the canyon now, and it widens and slows. Oak trees and planted orchards appear. Red osier dogwood lines the banks, and tall cottonwoods replace the conifers of the canyon.

There are a few sweepers, but the current is now so slow that they seem not to matter. The Trojan Nuclear Power Plant appears to the west (it lies just opposite the mouth of the river), and gulls join the ravens and robins that now occupy the shoreline. Livestock appears, and the sound of the freeway intrudes even as more beaver cuttings suggest wilder times and places. The final mile is almost sluggish; on windy days you will probably want to take out at the public fishing access 0.5 mile above the mouth rather than fight the wind and experience the waves on the Columbia.

APPENDIX A: FURTHER READING

No magazine or book will turn a novice into a proficient paddler, but there are a number of publications well worth reading to whet the appetite for the sport, to aid in understanding some of the basic concepts, and to gain the feel of river travel. Reading about river running will provide prospective paddlers with the background to lead them in appropriate and safe directions.

MAGAZINES

Canoe & Kayak
P. O. Box 3146
Kirkland, WA 98083
Phone: 800-829-3340
www.canoekayak.com

Paddler
P. O. Box 775450
Steamboat Springs, CO 80477
Phone (editorial): 970-879-1450
Phone (distribution and business office): 703-455-3419
www.paddlermagazine.com

American Whitewater
P. O. Box 636
Margretville, NY 12455
Phone: 914-586-2355
www.awa.org

These three magazines offer good technique articles; how-to and where-to pieces; and just plain fun, interesting, and educational articles. They also review books, offering insight into the literature of the sport.

HOW-TO BOOKS

American National Red Cross. *Canoeing*. Garden City, NY:
Doubleday, 1977 (updated regularly). A good, basic book.

Bechtel, Les, and Slim Ray. *River Rescue*. Boston: Appalachian Mountain Club Books, 1997.

Bennett, Jeff. *Rafting*. Portland, OR: Swiftwater Publishing Company, 1993.

———.*The Essential Whitewater Kayaker*. Camden, ME: Ragged Mountain Press, 1999.

Conover, Garrett. *Beyond the Paddle*. Gardiner, ME: Tilbury House, 1991.

Davidson, James, and John Rugge. *The Complete Wilderness Paddler*. New York: Vintage Books/Random House, 1983. Practical lessons for paddlers. The authors plan and execute a major expedition.

Dowd, John. *Sea Kayaking: A Manual for Long-Distance Touring*. Seattle: University of Washington Press, 1997. Another useful book about saltwater paddling.

Evans, Jay, and Robert R. Anderson. *Kayaking: The New Whitewater Sport for Everyone*. Battleboro, VT: Stephen Greene Press, 1975.

Gullion, Laurie. *Canoeing and Kayaking*. Newington, VA: American Canoe Association, 1987. This American Canoe Association Instructors Manual is one of the best basic books on both canoeing and kayaking.

Harrison, David. *Sports Illustrated Canoeing*. New York: Harper & Row, 1981. A good, basic book.

Hutchinson, Derek C. *The Complete Book of Sea Kayaking*. Guilford, CT: Globe Pequod Press, 1995. For those interested in saltwater paddling.

Keizer, Milt. *Western Steelhead Fishing Guide*. Seattle: Frank Amato Publications, 1989.

———. *Complete Handbook on Washington Steelheading*. Seattle: Hunting and Fishing News, 1988.

Kuhne, Cecil. *River Rafting*. Mountain View, CA: World Publishing, 1979.

Mason, Bill. *Path of the Paddle*. Minocqua, WI: NorthWard Press, 1995. A classic book on canoeing that belongs in every paddler's library.

————. *Song of the Paddle*. Minocqua, WI: NorthWard Press, 1988.

McGinnis, William. *Whitewater Rafting*. New York: Quadrangle/New York Times Book Company, 1975.

Nealy, William. *Kayak: An Animated Guide to Intermediate and Advanced Kayak Technique*. Birmingham, AL: Menasha Ridge Press, 1997. This book may seem a bit advanced for beginning and flatwater paddlers, but it offers good technique.

Rock, Harry. *The Basic Essentials of Canoe Poling*. Merrillville, IN: ICS Books, 1992. Out of print.

Washburne, Randel. *Kayaking Puget Sound, the San Juans, and Gulf Islands*, second edition. Seattle: The Mountaineers, 1999.

WHERE-TO BOOKS

At least five books about Washington rivers have appeared during the past two decades. Some of them include lakes and saltwater segments; most of them deal largely in whitewater. There are river segments in this book that duplicate a few found in these other books, but those segments are simply good, popular runs and belong in any book that claims to be representative.

Furrer, Werner. *Water Trails of Washington*. Everett, WA: Signpost, 1979. The earliest of the five books.

Jones, Phil N. *Canoe and Kayak Routes of Northwest Oregon*. Seattle: The Mountaineers, 1997. Includes several trips in Washington.

Korb, Gary. A *Paddler's Guide to the Olympic Peninsula*. Self-published, 1997. A comprehensive treatment of forty Olympic Peninsula rivers, this book deals largely in whitewater (20 of the 40 river segments are Class III or above, and four more are Class II+ segments).

La Roux, Dave, and Martha Rudersdorf. *Paddle Washington*. Sequim, WA: Neah Bay Books, 1984. Covers five or six rivers in each of several parts of the state.

Landers, Rich, and Dan Hansen. *Paddle Routes of the Inland Northwest*. Seattle: The Mountaineers, 1998. Covers 50 flatwater and whitewater trips for canoe and kayak.

North, Douglass A. *Washington Whitewater: The 34 Best Whitewater Rivers*. Seattle: The Mountaineers, 1992. Both of North's previous books, *Washington Whitewater* I and *Washington Whitewater* II concerned whitewater, though some of the runs described were relatively modest ones. The two books were recently combined into one updated volume.

GENERAL BACKGROUND

Felt, Margaret Elley. *Rivers to Reckon With*. Forks, WA: Department of Natural Resources, 1985.

Haig-Brown, Roderick. *A River Never Sleeps*. New York: William Morrow, 1946. Includes descriptions of fishing trips on several rivers covered in this book. Now out of print, the anthology is scheduled to appear in a new edition from the University of New Mexico Press early in the new century.

Huser, Verne. *River Running*. Chicago: Henry Regnery Company, first edition 1975. Revised edition to be published by The Mountaineers in spring of 2001.

————. *River Reflections: An Anthology*. Albuquerque, NM: University of New Mexico Press, 2001. A collection of excerpts from 43 writers who dealt with rivers in some way.

Kellogg, Zip, ed. *The Whole Paddler's Catalog*. Camden, ME: Ragged Mountain Press, 1997. One of the best overall books on the paddling experience.

McManus, Patrick. *They Shoot Canoes, Don't They?* New York: Holt, Rinehart, & Winston, 1981. For outdoor humor, it is difficult to beat this book and McManus's other books about hunting and fishing, camping and boating. McManus lives in eastern Washington.

Murray, John A., ed. *The River Reader.* New York: Lyons Press (The Nature Conservancy Readers), 1998. Murray's anthology offers an interesting array of river literature.

NATURAL HISTORY BOOKS

All the books in the Peterson Field Guides series (published by Chapters Publishing Ltd of Shelburne, VT) are good to have along on a river trip. A few of the titles are *A Field Guide to Pacific States Wildflowers*, *A Field Guide to Western Trees*, and *A Field Guide to the Stars and Planets*; other field guides in the series will help you identify birds, mammals, amphibians and reptiles, butterflies, animal tracks, even rocks and minerals.

Arno, Stephen F. *Northwest Trees.* Seattle: The Mountaineers, 1977. This book will help identify the numerous trees and some of the shrubs found along the rivers.

Drucker, Philip. *Indians of the Northwest Coast.* Garden City, NY: American Museum of Natural History, 1963.

Pandell, Karen, and Chris Stall. *Animal Tracks of the Pacific Northwest: Washington, Oregon, B.C. and Southeast Alaska.* Seattle: The Mountaineers: 1981. A good reference to bird and animal tracks.

Robbins, Chandler S., et al. *Birds of North America.* New York: Western Publishers, 1983. A particularly good guide to identifying birds.

Watts, Tom. *Pacific Coast Tree Finder: A Manual for Identifying Pacific Coast Trees.* Nature Study Guild, 1973.

RIVER PROTECTION BOOKS

McNulty, Tim, and Pat O'Hara. *Washington's Wild Rivers: The Unfinished Work*. Seattle: The Mountaineers, 1990. Includes a list of Washington state rivers deserving protective legislation.

All five books by Tim Palmer rank high on the subject of river conservation:

Palmer, Tim. *America by Rivers*. Washington, D.C.: Island Press, 1996.

————. *Endangered Rivers and the Conservation Movement*. Berkeley, CA: University of California Press, 1988.

————. *Lifelines: The Case for River Conservation*. Washington, D.C.: Island Press, 1994.

————. *The Columbia: Sustaining a Modern Resource*. Seattle: The Mountaineers, 1998.

————. *The Wild and Scenic Rivers of America*. Washington, D.C.: Island Press, 1993.

APPENDIX B: RECOMMENDED RESOURCES

PADDLE CLUBS IN WESTERN WASHINGTON

Paddle Trails Canoe Club
P.O. Box 24932
Seattle, WA 98124

Puget Sound Paddle Club
P.O. Box 111892
Tacoma, WA 98411-1892

The Seattle Canoe and Kayak Club
5900 W. Greenlake Way N
Seattle, WA 98103
Phone the Greenlake Small Craft Center: 206-684-4074

Washington Kayak Club
P.O. Box 24264
Seattle, WA 98124
Phone: 206-433-1983

Washington Recreational River Runners
P.O. Box 25048
Seattle, WA 98125

Washington Water Trails Association
4649 Sunnyside Avenue N
Room 305
Seattle, WA 98103-6900
Phone: 206-545-9161
www.eskimo.com/~wwta/
Email: wwta@eskimo.com

OUTDOOR RECREATION ORGANIZATIONS

American Whitewater Affiliation
P.O. Box 636
Margaretville, NY 12455
www.awa.org

Northwest Rafters Association
10117 SE Sunnyside Road, F1234
Clackamas, OR 47015

The Mountaineers
300 3rd Avenue W
Seattle, WA 98119
Phone: 206-284-6310
www.mountaineers.org

CONSERVATION ORGANIZATIONS

American Rivers, National Office
1025 Vermont Avenue NW, Suite 720
Washington, DC 20005
Phone: 202-347-7550
www.amrivers.org

American Rivers, Northwest Office
150 Nickerson Street, Suite 311
Seattle, WA 98109
Phone: 206-213-0330
Email: arnw@amrivers.org

Friends of the Earth
4512 University Way NE
Seattle, WA 98105
www.foe.org

National Audubon Society
700 Broadway
New York, NY 10211-0660
www.audubon.org

National Wildlife Federation
8925 Leesburg Pike
Vienna, VA 22182
Phone: 703-790-4000
www.nwf.org

Rivers Council of Washington
1731 Westlake Avenue N, Suite 202
Seattle, WA 98109-3043

River Network
P.O. Box 8787
Portland, OR 97207-8787
Phone: 503-241-3506 or 800-423-6747
www.rivernetwork.org/index.htm
Email: rivernet@igc.apc.org

Sierra Club, National Office
85 Second Street, Second Floor
San Francisco CA, 94105-3441
Phone: 415-977-5500
www.sierraclub.org

Sierra Club, Cascade Chapter
8511 15th Ave NE
Suite 201
Seattle, WA 98115
Phone: 206-523-2147
www.cascadechapter.org
Email: cascade.chapter@sierraclub.org

The Izaak Walton League of America
707 Conservation Lane
Gaithersburg, MD 20878-2983
Phone: 301-548-0150 or 800-453-5463
www.iwla.org

The Nature Conservancy of Washington
217 Pine Street, #1100
Seattle, WA 98101
www.tnc-washington.org

The Wilderness Society
900 Seventeenth Street, NW
Washington, DC 20006-2596
www.wilderness.org

Washington Environmental Council
Seattle (main office)
615 Second Ave, Suite 380
Seattle, WA 98104
Phone: 206-622-8103
www.greenwec.org

Washington Wildlife Federation
P.O. Box 1966
Olympia, WA 98507-1966
Phone: 360-705-1903

MAP SOURCES

Captain's Nautical
1914 4th Avenue
Seattle, WA 98101
Phone: 206-448-2278

Metsker Maps
702 1st Avenue
Seattle, WA 98104
Phone: 206-623-8747

U.S. Geological Survey
Box 25286 Federal Center
Denver, CO 80225

Washington Department of Transportation
Public Transportation and Planning
Highway Administration Building
Olympia, WA 98504

WEATHER INFORMATION

National Oceanic and Atmospheric Administration (NOAA)
River Information Hotline: 206-526-8530

NOAA/National Weather Service
Northwest River Forecast Center
5241 NE 122nd Avenue
Portland, Oregon 97230-1089
www.nwrfc.noaa.gov/

U.S. Geological Survey (USGS)
Real-Time Water Data website:
http://water.usgs.gov/realtime.html

Leopard frogs frequent western Washington riparian zones.

INDEX

Tubers float the Nooksack's South Fork beneath the Twin Sisters.

ABOUT THE AUTHOR

Verne Huser, a professional river guide for over 40 years, has run more than 100 different rivers in 22 states and two Canadian provinces; he has run 45 rivers in western Washington. Called "the dean of river writers," Huser has written hundreds of articles and six books about running rivers (both "how-to" and "where-to") and edited an anthology of river literature. A former National Park Service ranger/naturalist and an environmental mediator, he now serves as archivist at Albuquerque Academy in New Mexico.

THE MOUNTAINEERS, founded in 1906, is a nonprofit outdoor activity and conservation club, whose mission is "to explore, study, preserve, and enjoy the natural beauty of the outdoors . . . . " Based in Seattle, Washington, the club is now the third-largest such organization in the United States, with 15,000 members and five branches throughout Washington State.

The Mountaineers sponsors both classes and year-round outdoor activities in the Pacific Northwest, which include hiking, mountain climbing, ski-touring, snowshoeing, bicycling, camping, kayaking and canoeing, nature study, sailing, and adventure travel. The club's conservation division supports environmental causes through educational activities, sponsoring legislation, and presenting informational programs. All club activities are led by skilled, experienced volunteers, who are dedicated to promoting safe and responsible enjoyment and preservation of the outdoors.

If you would like to participate in these organized outdoor activities or the club's programs, consider a membership in The Mountaineers. For information and an application, write or call The Mountaineers, Club Headquarters, 300 Third Avenue West, Seattle, Washington 98119; (206) 284-6310.

The Mountaineers Books, an active, nonprofit publishing program of the club, produces guidebooks, instructional texts, historical works, natural history guides, and works on environmental conservation. All books produced by The Mountaineers are aimed at fulfilling the club's mission.

Send or call for our catalog of more than 450 outdoor titles:

The Mountaineers Books
1001 SW Klickitat Way, Suite 201
Seattle, WA 98134
800-553-4453
mbooks@mountaineers.org
www.mountaineersbooks.org